HIDDEN®
PUERTO
VALLARTA

Richard Harris

SECOND EDITION

Ulysses Press

THE MANY FACES
OF PARADISE

Although visitors may think they know what Puerto Vallarta is all about—high-rise all-inclusive resorts where you can sunbathe, splash in the gentle surf, sip margaritas and be towed into the sky on a parafoil—resorts are just one facet of what has evolved into the most varied and fascinating vacation destination on Mexico's Pacific Coast. It's a one-of-a-kind place where you can plan your day to include a morning of ziplining through the rainforest canopy, an afternoon of gallery-hopping, a gourmet dinner in a first-class French restaurant and an evening of people-watching on the waterfront promenade. *Hidden Puerto Vallarta* will show you how.

More than that, the book describes a rich array of authentically Mexican places, little touched by tourism, that you can reach within a half-day's rental-car trip from the city—remote fishing villages and surfing beaches, sacred sites of the mysterious Huichol people, 400-year-old colonial towns seemingly frozen in time—for a holiday adventure you're sure to always remember.

MEXICAN CRAFTS

Beautiful handicrafts have long been a tradition in rural Mexican villages, where they provide a vital source of income. In recent years, many low-priced curios have been pushed out of the market by look-alike knockoffs from Central America and even China; but in Puerto Vallarta, new shops have proliferated that specialize in unique native arts and crafts that were all but unknown a few years ago.

The Huichol Collection Galería Museo boasts traditional beaded artwork.

Most conspicuous are the works of Huichol Indians, who live in remote areas of the neighboring state of Nayarit and make brightly colored yarn paintings and woodcarvings that are coated with beeswax and covered with beads in shamanic patterns inspired by peyote visions. Look for them at such galleries as **Huichol Collection Galería Museo** *(p. 115)* in the surfing village of Sayulita, where you may have a chance to watch a Huichol artist at work. High-quality handicrafts from all over Jalisco are sold at the government-run **Instituto de Arte Jalisciense** *(p. 114)*. You'll find traditional crafts brought from Spain by early colonists, such as the fine Talavera ceramics at **Mundo de Azulejos** *(p. 135)*, as well as emerging new craft forms like the museum-quality Mata Ortiz pottery on display at **Galería de Ollas** *(p. 115)*.

Artists at Mundo de Azulejos hand paint each distinctive Talavera tile.

SECRET BEACHES

You might not think it would be possible in one of Mexico's top beach resorts to find a secluded stretch of sand where the only footprints are your own, especially if you've seen the main public beach with bathers shoulder-to-shoulder or endless rows of people sunning themselves along the Hotel Zone shoreline in peak season. But the fact is that enterprising sun, sand and sea worshippers can find idyllic spots within easy reach of Puerto Vallarta.

While they don't quite qualify as "undiscovered," beachfront villages like **Playa Quimixto** *(p. 151)* and **Playa Yelapa** *(p. 152)* certainly feel like your own private tropical paradise, especially if you can arrange to be there when the tourist booze cruises are not around. For truly hidden beaches, try hiking along the shore beyond **Boca de Tomatlán** *(p. 150)* to Playa Los Caballos and **Playa Las Animas** *(p. 150)*. Another option is to search out the small local beaches such as **Playa Las Islitas** *(p. 197)* in San Blas or stroll along the wide, long, hard-to-access public beach that extends from Sayulita to San Pancho and goes by various names—**Playa Questos, Playa Litibu** and **Playa Malpasos** *(p. 191)*. Heading northward along the Riviera Nayarit, you'll find boundless beaches, like **Playa Chacala** *(p. 191)*, that nobody has heard about—yet.

The sands at locally loved Playa Las Islitas are perfect for sunbathin

autiful, secluded Playa Quimixto has the only surf break on the bay.

COLONIAL HERITAGE

Puerto Vallarta is a young city, having grown in less than 50 years from a ramshackle fishing village at the end of a long, dusty dirt road into one of the country's busiest resort areas, with a population nearing half a million. Even its stately church, patterned after Old World cathedrals, was only completed in 1941. But experiencing a taste of Mexico's Spanish colonial heritage is easier than you might think. All you have to do is rent a car and explore beyond the city and the bay to discover some of the centuries-old historic places that lie within a half-day's drive.

For instance, you might head north along the Riviera Nayarit to **Parque Hidalgo** *(p. 108)* in San Blas, a forgotten town that, in the 18th century, was the most important seaport on Mexico's west coast. Or journey into the mountains of the Sierra Madre Occidental, protected until recently by the lack of paved roads, where you can visit **Casa Museo de Doña Conchita** *(p. 205)* in San Sebastián del Oeste, a silver mining ghost town that was once Jalisco's second-largest city. Trek to **Templo de la Virgen de Dolores** *(p. 209)* in Mascota, home of Mexico's finest horses and a colorful local saint, then move on to **Arco Monumental** *(p. 215)* within Talpa de Allende, one of the holiest towns in western Mexico, where four million faithfuls a year make pilgrimages in search of miracles.

Dating back to 1780, the Templo de la Virgen de Dolores is an elaborate Catholic sanctuary.

IGUANA ARTIFACTS

In Gringo Gulch a "love bridge" connects the former homes of stars Elizabeth Taylor and Richard Burton.

Puerto Vallarta first garnered international attention in the early 1960s when filmmaker John Huston chose the beach and jungle south of the tiny fishing village as the shooting location for the movie version of Tennessee Willliams's play *The Night of the Iguana.* The parade of American movie stars Huston brought with him included Richard Burton and his paramour, Elizabeth Taylor, whose illicit affair became the most notorious scandal in the annals of Hollywood. The film received a lukewarm reception from critics at the time, though it has since come to be acknowledged as a classic, but the publicity surrounding it made Puerto Vallarta famous.

Today, the legends surrounding the movie live on in and around Puerto Vallarta. You can see the **John Huston Statue** *(p. 121)* on Isla Río Cuale, then climb the steep stairway to **Gringo Gulch** *(p. 107)* to see the mansion that Elizabeth Taylor called home for 25 years, which connected to Richard Burton's old home across the street by a "love bridge." You might venture a few miles south to **Mismaloya** *(p. 139)*, where the movie was filmed, only to find that some of the sets have been replaced by high-rise condominiums. Catch a boat to **Playa Quimixto** *(p. 151)*, once John Huston's secret hideaway, then return to town for dinner at **Archie's Wok** *(p. 131)*, the restaurant founded by Huston's personal chef.

BOUTIQUE HOTELS

Casa Obelisco features ocean views and Mediterranean charm.

More than 90 percent of visitors to Puerto Vallarta stay in the large resorts of the hotel zones, where they find a vacation that is easy and convenient, though expensive and impersonal. But there is an alternative for those seeking a more intimate lodging experience. To the bewilderment of many people who work on staff at the big resorts, both gringos and Mexicans have begun to open bed and breakfasts and small boutique hotels, and, amazingly, they have succeeded to the point where they are booked up well in advance during the high season, often by returning guests.

Small European-style boutique hotels like the 42-room **Casa Doña Susana** *(p. 126)* may be found tucked away on little side streets just a short walk from the beach in Puerto Vallarta's Zona Romántica. Or they may be in historic haciendas in remote towns, like the 12-room **Mesón de Santa Elena** *(p. 212)* in Mascota or the 21-room **Hacienda Flamingos** *(p. 195)* in San Blas. Small bed and breakfasts with only a handful of rooms can also be found both in the city, like the elegant **Hacienda San Angel** *(p. 109)*, as well as in more out-of-the-way places, like the wonderful **Villa Bella Bed & Breakfast Inn** *(p. 177)* in La Cruz de Huanacaxtle or the **Casa Obelisco** *(p. 187)* in San Pancho.

Spanish-themed elegance is unparalled at the luxurious Hacienda San Angel.

INTERNATIONAL CUISINE

Puerto Vallarta may seem an unlikely place to find Austrian *zweibelrostbraten*, Singapore-style satay or Japanese sashimi on a restaurant menu. But the fact is, driven in part by the annual Puerto Vallarta Gourmet Festival as well as the growing sophistication of visitors both Mexican and international, the city has developed an impressive array of restaurants featuring cuisines from around the world. Culinary Puerto Vallarta is one of the best reasons to avoid the all-inclusive resort scene, where you take all your

Chic Frascati Ristorante serves exquisite authentic Italian cuisine.

meals at restaurants within the same hotel, and instead explore the city's world of tantalizing tastes.

To illustrate the range of possibilities, a few international restaurant possibilities you may want to consider are **Kamakura** *(p. 99)*, Puerto Vallarta's oldest and best Japanese restaurant; **Suzie Wong's** *(p. 87)*, a favorite for Chinese fare; **Kaiser Maximilian** *(p. 129)*, with its Austrian chef and white-tablecloth ambience and **Los Pibes** *(p. 131)*, where everything is authentically Argentinean. Near Banderas Bay, **Frascati Ristorante** *(p. 180)* puts an Italian twist on superfresh seafood. And, of course, no listing of international fine dining restaurants would be complete without Bucerías's renowned **École de Cuisine Le Fort** *(p. 179)*, a combined cooking school and French restaurant where the chef prepares a three-course classic French dinner with wine pairings for limited seatings of six patrons each night.

EATING LOCAL

It's no surprise, of course, that Puerto Vallarta offers plenty of possibilities for enjoying great Mexican cooking, but the rich variety of dishes available is a real eye-opener to first-time visitors whose idea of south-of-the-border food has been defined by so-called Mexican restaurants in the United States. Like all towns along Mexico's 5800 miles of coastline, Puerto Vallarta's local cuisine emphasizes fresh seafood, often prepared in traditional styles like fish *sarandeado* or shrimp *al diablo*. Yet fast-growing Puerto Vallarta has also attracted people from every part of Mexico, so you'll also encounter regional dishes such as Oaxacan-style chicken *en mole amarillo* and gourmet dishes like roast duck marinated in dark beer and served in a tomatillo sauce with agave.

The ubiquitous grilled huachinango (snapper) is a regional specialty.

Dining Mexican can be as simple as a stand-up repast of fish tacos or *birria* (goat stew) at a little open-air stand like **El Moreno** *(p. 134)* or a *comedor* at the **Mercado Artesanía** *(p. 114)*, or it can be as elaborate as a romantic dinner at **Murales** *(p. 101)* or **Los Xitomates** *(p. 111)*. For an extra special evening, dine on *arachera* (skirt steak) or *huachinango* (red snapper) at **Las Carmelitas** *(p. 114)*, high on a hillside with the best sunset view in town.

Barbecued lobster is found on the menus of many Puerto Vallarta eateries.

El Moreno, a streetside taco stand, prepares delicious local fare at wallet-friendly prices.

Elote (roasted corn on the cob) is a popular street treat that's served dusted with chile powder and a squeeze of lime.

TEQUILA

Ah, tequila! It's one of the proudest products of the state of Jalisco, which includes Puerto Vallarta. It should come as no surprise that tequilas in all price ranges, from inexpensive mass-produced brand names to lovingly handcrafted, aged, pricier varieties, can be found all over town, and even at stands by the side of the highway. Some places include a small tasting patio where you can sip the Mexican beverage before deciding on your bottle of choice. Raicilla, a potent wild-agave moonshine, is also widely available here, and aside from just tasting it, you can head to an authentic distillery and watch it be transformed from slow-roasted plant to crystal-clear liquor.

Reposado is a smooth, barrel-aged tequila.

At **La Casa de Tequila** *(p. 118)* in Downtown Puerto Vallarta, you will discover selections of tequila little-known to the average palate; some are infused with sweet vanilla, some with juicy tamarind, others with a hint of almond. Or witness the production of this coveted liquor at the little distillery **Parador San Sebastián** *(p. 204)*, perched on the rim of a gorge high in the mountains. To simply enjoy the signature flavor of tequila, head to the aptly named **Tequilas** *(p. 119)*, where a strolling mariachi band will serenade you as you peruse the long cocktail menu. In the Riviera Nayarit area, you can pair a festive Mexican meal with tequila poured from a wooden keg at **Si Hay Olitas** *(p. 188)* or chase a shot with salt and lime at the seafront **Le Kliff** *(p. 148)* in Yelapa. Whatever your choice, you're bound to return home with a new appreciation of Mexico's national spirit.

Yelapa's seaside Le Kliff is an ideal spot for sipping tequila.

To be authentic, tequila must be harvested from blue agave grown in the state of Jalisco.

Fermented agave syrup drips from a wooden still into a clay pot during production.

WILDLIFE WATCHING

The best time to glimpse Puerto Vallarta's underwater giants is between mid-December and March.

For nature lovers, Banderas Bay and its surroundings offer a multitude of opportunities to view the rich tapestry of tropical wildlife underwater, in the air and deep in the rainforest. In the winter, humpback whales take center stage as local guides and sportfishing operators offer trips to the outer reaches of the bay to watch these gentle leviathans in their calving waters. Summer presents the chance to search for wild bottlenose dolphins and giant manta rays and to attend "turtle camps" that help hatchling sea turtles survive.

Experienced local guides include **The Whale Watching Center** *(p. 158)*, **Vallarta Adventures** *(p. 158)* and **Wildlife Connection** *(p. 159)*, among others. Birding opportunities range from sea expeditions in the Islas Marieta National Park to out-of-town trips to boat excursions through the labyrinthine mangrove channels of the **Río Tovara** *(p. 194)*. And while visiting San Blas, don't miss the **Cocodrilario** *(p. 193)*, where river crocodiles are rescued and their offspring are set free. Of course, you don't have to venture far into the wilderness to view the fauna of the Puerto Vallarta region. In a valley secluded in the forest just a few miles south of the city, you'll find **Zoologico de Vallarta** *(p. 140)*, an ambitious family-run operation where you can get a close look at animals of the region, such as

Puerto Vallarta is a prime region for birdwatching.

jaguars, pumas, coyotes, tepezcuintles, scarlet macaws and iguanas.

Iguanas thrive in the tropical climate of Banderas Bay.

Many animals, such as this spider monkey, live in natural
habitats at Zoologico de Vallarta.

ART GALLERIES

Unique among Mexican resorts, Puerto Vallarta has emerged as one of the major fine-arts markets in Latin America. About two dozen downtown galleries form the nucleus of the art scene. While most of the work exhibited is by Mexican artists, there are also pieces by hundreds of Americans and Canadians who have made their homes in the Puerto Vallarta area, as well as top Mexican artists who have trained in Mexico City, New York and the capitals of Europe.

Galleries throughout Puerto Vallarta showcase original handmade Mata Ortiz pottery.

Puerto Vallarta's art scene got its start in the late 1980s when American expatriates like Texan Barbara Peters of **Galería Vallarta** *(p. 116)* and painter Judith Ewing Morlan of **PV Art Gallery** *(p. 117)* opened up shop in what was then the city's low-rent district. Exploring Puerto Vallarta's galleries will take you to the chic **Galerie des Artistes** *(p. 117)*, the ultramodern **Galería Uno** *(p. 116)* and a score of others. But art doesn't stop with downtown Puerto Vallarta.

Today you'll find first-class galleries everywhere, from the painter-owned **Estudio Café** *(p. 87)* in Marina Vallarta to **La Hamaca Gallery** *(p. 189)* in the village of Sayulita and even the **Bistro Selvático** *(p. 149)* in remote Yelapa.

The downtown galleries serve as the cornerstone of the local art scene.

HIDDEN® PUERTO VALLARTA

Including Banderas Bay and Sierra Madre Mountains

Richard Harris

SECOND EDITION

Ulysses Press

BERKELEY, CALIFORNIA

Published by: ULYSSES PRESS
P.O. Box 3440
Berkeley, CA 94703
www.ulyssespress.com

ISSN 1559-6184
ISBN 978-1-56975-571-6

Printed in Canada by Transcontinental Printing

10 9 8 7 6 5 4 3 2

MANAGING EDITOR: Claire Chun
EDITORIAL ASSOCIATES: Emma Silvers, Elyce Petker, Lauren Harrison,
    Abigail Reser, Kate Kellogg
PRODUCTION: Judith Metzener
CARTOGRAPHY: Pease Press
HIDDEN BOOKS DESIGN: what!design @ whatweb.com
INDEXER: Sayre Van Young
COVER PHOTOGRAPHY: front © Joel Rogers; back © 2007 Nicole C. Bratt
COLOR INSERT: *page i* © Anne Forte; *page ii* © Victoria Brenner; *page iii*
    top © Wonderlane, bottom © 2007 Nicole C. Bratt; *page iv* ©
    Hugo H. Rodriguez; *page v* © Claudia Arenas; *page vi* © Richard
    Harris; *page vii* © Jon Arnold/DanitaDelimont.com; *page viii*
    top © Casa Obelisco, bottom © Hacienda San Angel; *page ix* ©
    Frascati Ristorante; *page x* top © Amanda McCreary, bottom
    © Kevin Key; *page xi* top © Marin Moran, bottom © Amanda
    McCreary; *page xii* top © Jim Rees, bottom © Le Kliff/Alfonso
    Lepe; *page xiii* top © shutterstock.com/Carlos Sanchez Pereyra,
    bottom © Richard Harris; *page xiv* top © Vallarta Adventures,
    middle © Pat Gaines, bottom © Danel W. Bachman; *page xv* ©
    Jay Ailworth; *page xvi* top © Jorge Medrano, bottom © Ursula
    Haigh

Distributed by Publishers Group West

HIDDEN is a federally registered trademark
of BookPack, Inc.

In memory of Carol Delattre

CONTENTS

MAPS

OUTDOOR ADVENTURE SYMBOLS

The following symbols accompany national, state and regional park listings, as well as beach descriptions throughout the text.

▲	Camping	🤿	Snorkeling or Scuba Diving
🚶	Hiking	🏄	Surfing
🚲	Biking	🛶	Canoeing or Kayaking
🐎	Horseback Riding	🚤	Boating
🏊	Swimming	🐟	Fishing

HIDDEN LISTINGS

Throughout the book, listings that reveal the hidden realm—spots that are away from tourists or reflect authentic Puerto Vallarta—are marked by this icon:

There are also special maps at the start of each section that guide you to some of these hidden listings. Each place is identified with this symbol:

EXPLORING PARADISE

Greater Puerto Vallarta

Imagine a tropical village on the shore of a vast, pristine bay. Gentle waves lap an endless beach of pale sand the consistency of sugar. Palm trees whisper softly in the sea breeze as young couples watch the magenta sun sink into the Pacific. Fishermen, their *pangas* gliding smoothly across the water, fill their nets with *huachinango, dorado* and *camarones*. Lush jungle seems to drip down the steep mountainsides behind the village. Boys emerge from the rainforest carrying iguanas, giant lizards destined to become taco filling for food stands on the plaza. Laughing children chase stray chickens through the cobblestone streets. The church bell tolls, summoning the faithful to mass. *Borrachos* cluster on a rock jetty, passing a bottle of tequila around and eying women as they pass by. A lone painter attempts to capture it all on canvas. The weather is perfect. Time means nothing. . . .

This secret paradise was Puerto Vallarta around 1960, before the first narrow road into town was paved. Then something unforeseen happened. In 1963, movie stars arrived. There was Deborah Kerr, the ladylike Scottish actress who had received more Academy Award nominations than anyone else in the history of film but never won an Oscar. And Sue Lyon, whose portrayal of a 15-year-old seductress a year earlier in *Lolita* had catapulted her to brief, wild stardom. And sex goddess Ava Gardner, notorious for her affairs with the likes of Frank Sinatra and Howard Hughes. And above all, there were Richard Burton and Elizabeth Taylor, whose affair, kindled the year before on the set of the astonishingly expensive epic *Cleopatra*, ranked as the biggest scandal in Hollywood history. Chasing after them came all the top gossipmongers and paparazzi of the international press, and suddenly, sleepy little Puerto Vallarta found itself famous around the world.

Since then, the town's population has skyrocketed from 1200 to about 450,000 full- and part-time residents—an astonishing increase of some 37,500 percent in just two generations. The economy depends exclusively on tourism, real estate and construction. With three million international visitors per year (70 percent from the United States, 25 percent from Canada and only 5 percent from Europe and Asia), Puerto Vallarta has been transformed from a tiny fishing village into one of Mexico's top tourist destinations (second only to Cancún) and one of its wealthiest communities.

Big, beautiful Banderas Bay is still there. True, parts of its picture-perfect blonde beaches are lined with sprawling resort hotels and towering condominium developments, and in some places the surf is full of jet skiers, parasailers, windsurfers and boogieboarders. Nearby, cruise ships make landfall, dwarfing everything around them. Beyond the touristy tumult, though, the vastness of the tranquil, empty ocean still beckons the thoughtful visitor to contemplate the infinite. And the sunsets are still as spectacular as ever.

Wetlands and farmers' fields of old have been turned into some of the finest golf courses in Mexico, but nature endures. Wildlife still asserts its claim to the habitat. Iguanas sun themselves on the greens. Crocodiles give a whole new meaning to the term "water hazard."

As you move on to the downtown area, many of the picturesque red-roofed houses that line the old cobblestone streets have been transformed into trendy galleries, gourmet restaurants, chic boutiques and jewelry stores, but they—along with the stately old church that is the city's trademark—still stand against a spectacular, verdant backdrop of jungle-clad mountains.

Paradise has not been lost. It's certainly gotten a lot more crowded, though.

My purpose in *Hidden Puerto Vallarta* is to share with you the discoveries I've made during more than two dozen extended visits to the region since 1984, as well as observations from conversations with many wonderful expatriate friends who live in Puerto Vallarta and nearby towns. In these pages I provide the most comprehensive information possible for planning your visit, whatever your preferred travel style, including a survey of the big beach resorts in the hotel zones as well as small lodgings and restaurants in all price ranges in the old part of the city—and, of course, plenty of "hidden" places that other guidebooks don't mention. I also provide the most up-to-date internet information possible to help you negotiate the maze of literally thousands of web pages about Puerto Vallarta, get an up-to-date full-color preview of your itinerary possibilities and make your own travel arrangements.

I offer a complete rundown on fun things to see and do, plus everything you need to know to take road trips outside the city and discover for yourself idyllic beaches and secluded fishing villages that are still much like Puerto Vallarta was once upon a time, before the world discovered it. I'll also show you where to find the magic of old colonial Mexico, whether in little-known towns high in the Sierra Madre or in the heart of Guadalajara, the country's second-largest city.

I hope you will find in this book not just another directory of places to stay, eat and sightsee but also a practical resource on *how* to visit—how to experience the pleasures of a region that is renowned for its friendliness, and how to understand and respect the natural environment as well as the cultural diversity of the people who live here.

The key to responsible tourism lies in knowledge, in understanding consequences, in knowing when enough is enough—and what to do instead. In this book I have made every effort to present a balanced overview of tourism in the Puerto Vallarta region, examining not only established tourist zones but also what the future may hold—the good, the bad and the ugly. I believe that we can work together to make sure it's the good that prevails for visitors, local residents, the local economy and the natural surroundings.

Read this book ahead of time. Bring it along when you board that jetliner to Puerto Vallarta. Browse through it while you soak up that glorious tropical sunshine. Feel the pull of other wonderful places that lie just down the street or over the horizon. Armed with the information these pages contain, you may well find yourself without an excuse for remaining long in the confines of $200 hotel rooms, high-decibel dance clubs and prepackaged group activities. This is your invitation to rent a car or buy a bus ticket and set out on your own in search of paradise.

If you would like to share your own discoveries with me—and, of course, with the readers of this book's next edition—please drop me an e-mail in care of Ulysses Press.

WHERE TO GO

The majority of international visitors to **Puerto Vallarta** go directly from the airport to their choice of modern beach resorts in the Hotel Zone, Marina Vallarta or Nuevo Vallarta, where they can relax on the beach to their heart's content and, in many cases, not leave the hotel grounds during the entire duration of their stay. Some people find this is the ultimate strategy for a relaxing vacation—nothing to think about and plenty to do. It can be the most hassle-free solution for family vacations, since many resorts have special play facilities and activity schedules for children and teens that free the parents up to pursue their own interests. Other travelers, though, start to go stir-crazy within the first 24 hours at an all-inclusive beach resort. If you're one of them, I hope this book will make you curious to explore what lies beyond the resort districts.

The old part of Puerto Vallarta, with its red roofs and cobblestone streets, absolutely throbs with ambience. This lively, walkable area is divided in two by the shallow Río Cuale and the island in its center, where you'll find a museum, a cultural center and several trendy bistros, not to mention burros, iguanas and lots of curio vendors. On the north side of this river, downtown Puerto Vallarta is all about shopping. Here you'll find most of the city's world-class art galleries, as well as an abundance of fine jewelry stores and shops that showcase the region's magnificent native folk-art traditions. The *malecón*, or promenade, along the waterfront, offers free concerts, street performers and spectacular sunsets over the bay, while the other side of the street bursts after dark with boisterous nightlife.

South of the river, the area dubbed the Zona Romántica surpasses even downtown when it comes to nightlife and fine dining. It boasts the most popular public beach in the city, as well as comfortable small hotels in all price ranges. While part of the Zona Romántica has recently come out as the most popular gay destination in Mexico, heterosexual singles and couples will find it equally romantic and welcoming.

Banderas Bay has a long coastline, and the city takes up only a fraction of it. If you travel south of Puerto Vallarta, you'll almost immediately find yourself on a narrow scenic highway that winds along steep, rainforest-covered mountain slopes, occasionally descending to secluded beachfront resort areas such as Mismaloya (famed as the location for the movie that made Puerto Vallarta famous), the idyllic hideaway of Boca de Tomitlán and the remote fishing village of Yelapa, which is only accessible by boat.

If you choose instead to journey north of Puerto Vallarta, you can follow the **Riviera Nayarit** coastline—and the inevitable path of future real estate development—around Banderas Bay to the still-charming little towns of Bucerías and Cruz de Huanacaxtle on the way out to Punta Mita, the northern lip of the bay, where an entire town was moved out to make room for a single gated luxury resort. If you continue north along the main highway, you'll pass other towns that are still outside the touristic mainstream and known (so far) only to a few insiders. There's Sayulita, a surfers' paradise brimming with young Americans in baggy bathing suits and dreadlocks, and San Pancho, a town designed and built from scratch by a Mexican president who planned to retire to his lavish mansion there—but was forced into exile instead.

Finally, if you head east from Puerto Vallarta, you can visit old mining towns deep in the **Sierra Madre** highlands, where they have remained isolated for centuries until new paved roads were built to them in the past few years. You can be among the first international visitors to explore San Sebastián del Oeste, Mascota or Talpa de Allende, mountain towns suspended in time.

WHEN TO GO

SEASONS

Peak season in Puerto Vallarta, when you'll want to make reservations well in advance, runs from Christmas to Easter. During this time, as well as the October-November and April-May shoulder seasons, it hardly ever rains, and the temperature—as long as you avoid the siesta-time sun—is perfect, with highs in the mid-80s and lows in the mid-70s.

The monsoon season is from June through September—the same time of year that Americans and Canadians have no cold weather to escape from. A growing number of Americans and Canadians are discovering what people who live in hot parts of the Mexican interior have always known: summer weather in Puerto Vallarta is usually quite nice. Even in July and August, the rainiest months, the climate is quite pleasant. The temperature rarely rises much above 90°F, and the cooling breeze off the bay is delightful. Most rain falls as brief, pleasantly warm afternoon downpours or spectacular nighttime thunderstorms, while the mornings are clear and sunny. Humidity is high in summer, but mosquitoes and other biting insects are rarely a problem. While some shops and small restaurants close for a month or so in summer, hotel room rates are bargain-priced. While most tourists are Mexican, these days jetliners from the United States to Puerto Vallarta, even in summer, run full to capacity with travelers escaping the Midwestern heat.

People in Puerto Vallarta will assure you that there is no hurricane season, and it's true that hurricanes and tropical storms are much rarer along Mexico's Pacific coast than in the Atlantic and Gulf of Mexico. In fact, when Hurricane Wilma hit Cancún and the Yucatán Peninsula in 2005, most early-season tourists transferred their trip plans to Puerto Vallarta or Manzanillo, both of which experienced their highest resort occupancy rates in history—more than 90 percent—even before the peak season started.

Of course, anything is possible. The most devastating storm in recent memory, class 5 Hurricane Kenna, ripped through the region on October 25, 2002, destroying 85 percent of the historic port town of San Blas to the north. But in Puerto Vallarta, thanks to the protection of the Bahía de Banderas, it washed away only 5 percent of the beaches and caused no deaths. Most businesses were open again within two days. Before Hurricane Kenna, no hurricane had struck Puerto Vallarta since at least 1949, when the U.S. government began keeping records of storm activity on Mexico's Pacific coast.

CALENDAR OF EVENTS

JANUARY
Countrywide   Año Nuevo (New Year's Day) is a national holiday. Banks, government offices and many businesses are closed. **Día de los**

Reyes Magos (Three Kings Day, or Epiphany), January 6, is when holiday gifts are traditionally exchanged. The **Fiesta de San Antonio**, January 17, is observed throughout Mexico by priests blessing domestic animals; in Puerto Vallarta, the Blessing of the Animals is sponsored by the local Society for the Prevention of Cruelty to Animals.

Sierra Madre The **Fiesta de San Sebastián**, January 20, is a major religious festival in San Sebastián del Oeste.

FEBRUARY

Countrywide **Día de la Candelaria** (Candlemas), February 2, is celebrated in Puerto Vallarta and most Mexican communities with dance, music, feasts and candlelight processions, though it is not a legal holiday. **Día de la Constitución** (Constitution Day), February 5, celebrates the signing of the Mexican Constitution of 1857, on which the country's present constitution is based, with parades; banks and government offices are closed. **Día de Amistad** (Friendship Day), February 14, is roughly the equivalent of Valentine's Day in the United States. **Día de la Bandera Nacional** (Flag Day), February 24, is another legal Mexican holiday.

Puerto Vallarta The **Becas Ball**, a traditional fundraising dinner-dance held in late February or early March to provide scholarships for needy students, is one of the biggest social events of the winter season in Puerto Vallarta.

MARCH

Countrywide **Carnaval**, celebrated in Puerto Vallarta with costumes and a children's parade, fills the three days preceding Ash Wednesday (the beginning of Lent, the 40-day period leading up to Easter Sunday). **Natalicio de Benito Juárez** (Benito Juárez Day), March 21, is a national holiday marking the birth of the president known as the "Abraham Lincoln of Mexico."

Sierra Madre The **Fiesta de San Jose** (March 10–19) is the biggest pilgrimage time in Talpa de Allende.

APRIL

Countrywide **Semana Santa**, the week leading up to Pascua (Easter Sunday), is observed in most parts of Mexico with religious processions; banks, government offices and many businesses are closed from Wednesday through Easter Sunday. On **Día de los Niños** (Children's Day), April 30, communities throw parties for the local children on the town plaza, and relatives and godparents give children gifts and candy; this is the only day of the year when schoolchildren aren't required to wear uniforms, and many choose to wear costumes.

Puerto Vallarta Since **Semana Santa** is the spring break for all Mexican colleges and universities, it is the busiest week of the year in Puerto Vallarta, with packed beaches and round-the-clock partying throughout the city. In years when Semana Santa coincides with spring break in the United States, look out!

MAY

Countrywide **Día del Trabajo**, May 1, is a national holiday honoring Mexico's workers, equivalent to Labor Day in the United States and

Canada. **Cinco de Mayo**, May 5, also a national holiday, commemorates the Mexican victory against the French at the Battle of Puebla in 1862, but it is observed much more within Hispanic communities in the United States than in Jalisco or most other parts of Mexico. As in the United States and Canada, **Día de las Madres** (Mothers' Day), the second Sunday in May, is celebrated throughout Mexico, where it is an especially important holiday. Yet another official national holiday, **Día de la Expropriación Petrolera** (Oil Nationalization Day) commemorates the seizure of foreign oil holdings by the Mexican government in 1938.

Puerto Vallarta   The two-week **Festival Cultural**, the biggest arts event in Puerto Vallarta and one of the biggest in Mexico, features musical concerts, art exhibitions, theater and dance performances, and literary readings—all free—in venues throughout the city. The festival ends on May 31 with the **Aniversario de Puerto Vallarta**, marking the incorporation of the municipality in 1918 with a parade, a free concert, fireworks and a birthday cake large enough to feed 2000 people. Meanwhile, El Pitillal, a large working-class Puerto Vallarta suburb, hosts the **Fiestas de Mayo**, a month-long fair with carnival rides, contests, livestock exhibits, food and music.

Riviera Nayarit   La Cruz de Huanacaxtle celebrates with a carnival and fireworks for nine days leading up to **El Día de la Santa Cruz**, May 3.

Sierra Madre   The annual three-day **Fiesta de Plata**, held in San Sebastián in late May, features mine tours, dance performances and food and crafts booths.

JUNE
Countrywide   **Día de los Padres** (Fathers' Day), the third Sunday in June, is celebrated in Mexico as it is in the United States and Canada.

Puerto Vallarta   Musicians and music lovers flock to Puerto Vallarta for the month-long **World Jazz Festival** (formerly the Cancún Jazz Festival).

JULY
Countrywide   Mexico's one-month school vacation begins at the end of July.

Riviera Nayarit   The Marina Riviera Nayarit in La Cruz de Huanacaxtle hosts the **International Marlin and Tuna Fishing Tournament** in mid-July.

AUGUST
Countrywide   Most middle-class Mexicans take summer vacations during this month and head for Puerto Vallarta and other beach resorts to beat the stultifying summer heat of the country's interior.

SEPTEMBER
Countrywide   The **Grito de Dolores** (Cry of Pain) kicks off Mexico's Independence Day celebration on the evening of September 15; after a parade, revelers gather in town plazas across the country to echo the legendary shout for independence from Spanish colonialism, followed by spectacular fireworks displays. September 16, **Día de la Independencia**, is an important national holiday with more fireworks and parades.

Sierra Madre   Talpa de Allende celebrates the anniversary of the miraculous **Restoration of the Virgin of Talpa** on September 10. About a week later, the **Fiestas Patrias** in Mascota is known for performances by many of Jalisco's top mariachi bands.

OCTOBER

Countrywide   **Día de la Raza** (Columbus Day), October 12, celebrating the Spanish discovery of the New World, is given more significance in Mexico than in the United States.

Puerto Vallarta   Though not a traditional holiday in Mexico, many children in Puerto Vallarta and Guadalajara now celebrate **Hallowe'en** in North American fashion as a lead-in to **Todos Santos** and the **Day of the Dead**.

NOVEMBER

Countrywide   Most Mexicans do not work from **Día de Todos Santos** (All Saints' Day), November 1, when Mexicans pay homage to children who have died, through **Día de los Muertos** (Day of the Dead), November 2, which is among the most important Mexican holidays. **Día de la Revolución Mexicana** (Revolution Day), November 20, celebrates the start of the Mexican Revolution of 1910 with fireworks and parades and is a national holiday. **Día de Santa Cecilia**, November 22, honors the patron saint of musicians.

Puerto Vallarta   The municipal government stages an elaborate altar exhibition on the main plaza in front of City Hall for **Día de Todos Santos** and **Día de los Muertos**, as does the cultural center on Isla Cuale. After that, November is the most event-packed month of the year. Local chefs strut their stuff for ten days in mid-November in the **Puerto Vallarta Gourmet Festival**. Also in mid-month, Marina Vallarta hosts the **Mexican Boat Show**, the largest such event in Mexico. Through the rest of the month, the city holds its annual **Festival de las Artes**, showcasing local and national performers and visual artists in events all over the city. In late November, **SeaFest** includes jetski races and the **International Sailfish and Marlin Fishing Tournament**. Other November events include the **International Puerto Vallarta Half Marathon**, the **Puerto Vallarta Cup Golf Tournament** and the **Puerto Vallarta Cattle Expo**.

DECEMBER

Countrywide   The **Fiesta de La Virgen de Guadalupe**, December 12, starts the Christmas holiday season with solemn observances honoring Our Lady of Guadalupe, the patron saint of Mexico. **Las Posadas**, processions re-enacting Joseph and Mary's search for lodging before the birth of Jesus, are held during **Semana Navidad** (Christmas Week), December 15 through 25. **Noche Buena** (Christmas Eve) is a time for family dinners and midnight mass. **Navidad** (Christmas), a mainly religious holiday, is observed in Mexico much as it is in the United States and Canada, except that gifts are not exchanged until 12 days later.

Puerto Vallarta   The annual **Tequila Festival** is held the first week of December. Moviemakers and celebrities from all over North and

South America congregate for the **Puerto Vallarta Film Festival** in early December. The **Fiesta de La Virgen de Guadalupe** is celebrated with special fervor in Puerto Vallarta, where Our Lady of Guadalupe is the city's patron saint; most businesses, neighborhoods and civic groups make Guadalupe processions to the main cathedral during the period from December 1 through 12, with masses followed by folk dancing, singing and fireworks. **Año Viejo** (New Year's Eve) is especially festive in Puerto Vallarta, where most hotels and restaurants sponsor lavish galas and partiers fill Los Muertos Beach and the main streets of the Zona Romántica.

South Shore In the village of Quimixto, by tradition baptisms, first communions and weddings are held the morning of the **Fiesta de La Virgen de Guadalupe**, culminating with a procession of decorated fishing boats.

BEFORE YOU GO

VISITORS CENTERS

MEXICO TOURISM BOARD ☎800-446-3942 (in the United States or Canada) ⌨www.visitmexico.com, contact@visitmexico.com To order an information packet about travel in Mexico, contact the Mexico Tourism Board. For additional information, tourists cards and maps, contact one of the following offices in the United States and Canada:

✉400 Madison Avenue, Suite 11C, New York, NY 10017 ☎212-308-2110
☎212-308-9060 ⌨milmgto@interport.net
✉1010 Fomdren Street, Houston, TX 77096 ☎713-772-2581 ☎713-772-6058
⌨mgtotx@ix.netcom.com
✉300 North Michigan Avenue, Fourth Floor, Chicago, IL 60601 ☎312-228-0517
☎312-606-9012 ⌨mgtochi@compuserve.com
✉1 Place Ville Marie, Suite 1931, Montreal, Quebec H3B 2C3 ☎514-871-1052
☎514-871-3825 ⌨turimex@cam.org
✉2 Bloor Street West, Suite 1502, Toronto, Ontario M4W 3E2 ☎416-925-0704
☎416-925-6061 ⌨mexto3@inforamp.net
✉999 West Hastings Street, Suite 1610, Vancouver, British Columbia V6C 2W2
☎604-669-2845 ☎604-669-3498 ⌨mgto@bc.sympatico.ca

Many major cities in the United States and Canada also have Mexican consulates. They can provide general travel information as well as specifics about legal aid and lawyers in Mexico.

ONLINE RESOURCES

Internet surfers will find literally hundreds of websites about the Puerto Vallarta region. Use the web information throughout this book to find out more about individual lodgings, including current room rates and availability, and to make reservations. For general travel and sightseeing information, here are the most informative websites.

Those that cover the greater Puerto Vallarta metropolitan area include:

www.allaboutpuertovallarta.com
www.em-vallarta.com
www.go2vallarta.com
www.puertovallarta.net
www.pvmirror.com
www.vallarta-info.com
www.vallartaonline.com
www.virtualvallarta.com.

Information about the smaller communities north of Puerto Vallarta can be found at:

www.yelapa.info
www.bucerias.com
www.buceriasmexico.com
www.lacruzdehuanacaxtle.com
www.puntamita.com
www.sayulita.com
www.sanpancho.com
www.visitsanblas.com

State tourism agencies offer information about Jalisco, including areas south of Puerto Vallarta as well as the Sierra Madre and the Guadalajara area, at www.visita.jalisco.gob.mx. Points north of Puerto Vallarta, from Bucerías to San Blas and beyond, are the focus of:

www.rivieranayarit.com and
www.nayarit.gob.mx (Spanish only)

Finally, a good source of maps of the region and the rest of Mexico is www.maps-of-mexico.com.

PACKING

Pack light! A camera plus whatever else you can pack into your day-pack or weekender would be perfect for most situations. A couple of freedom-loving Californians I met on a recent trip went even further and started their month-long Mexican odyssey carrying nothing but belt packs. The less stuff you bring with you, the more stuff you can buy and bring back. There is nothing like lugging 75 pounds of suitcases around on cobblestone streets to make one feel absurdly materialistic.

Bring along a minimum of sporty, summery clothing. T-shirts, shorts, swimsuit, sunglasses, a good pair of hiking boots and a bandana (soak it in water and wear it as a neckerchief or headband for hours of relief from the heat).

If you plan to visit fishing villages or remote mountain towns—or Catholic churches even in Puerto Vallarta itself—you will want to have some modest clothing on hand so as not to offend local sensibilities. Men should always wear a shirt and long pants in churches, and women should wear a modest skirt and blouse. No shorts, two-piece bathing suits, tight tops or other suggestive outfits, though in most other situations all of these are perfectly acceptable attire in Puerto Vallarta, Manzanillo and nearby towns. Nudity is against the law in Mexico. If you want to sunbathe in the buff, find a very private place to do so or seek out one of the Puerto Vallarta hotels that has a clothing-optional rooftop sundeck.

Bear in mind that just about anything you neglect to bring along, you can buy in Puerto Vallarta, where shopping ranges from chic fashion boutiques to big department stores, including a huge Wal-Mart super-store. When it comes to toiletries, larger towns carry almost everything you'll find in the United States: toothpaste, deodorant, shampoo, soap, insect repellant, shaving cream and batteries. Items like tampons and sunscreen are also widely available. These days, most brand names in Mexican pharmacies and supermarkets look hauntingly familiar. In the days before the North American Free Trade Agreement (NAFTA), many foreign manufacturers built factories in Mexico to avoid stiff import tariffs, so Mexican-made Colgate toothpaste, for instance, looks and tastes just like in the United States except for the words *Hecho in Mexico* on the package. Today, with NAFTA in effect, many American-made goods can be imported to Mexico with minimal tariffs, but most goods sold in Mexico are still made in Mexican plants because the cost of labor is much lower.

If you're planning to go far from the city, you should definitely pack a first-aid kit. Include a painkiller such as aspirin, bandages, cold med-ication, vitamins, motion-sickness tablets, an anti-diarrheal, calamine lotion or a small bottle of white vinegar (for insect bites), prescription drugs you use, iodine or alcohol for disinfecting wounds, antibiotic ointment, water purification tablets, sunscreen and lip balm.

MEDIC ALERT FOUNDATION INTERNATIONAL ✉*2323 Colorado Avenue, Turlock, CA 95382* ✆*209-668-3333, 888-633-4298* 📠*209-669-2450* 🖱*www.medicalert.org* Anyone with a medical condition should consider wear-ing a medic-alert tag that identifies the problem and gives a phone number to call for more information. Contact Medic Alert Foundation International.

LODGING

This book's hotel listings range from budget to ultra-deluxe. While it contains a comprehensive survey of mainstream resorts in the Puerto Vallarta area, its emphasis is on smaller, unique establishments. Hotels are rated as follows: *budget* ($), less than US$60 a night in season for two people; *moderate* ($$), from $60 to $120; *deluxe* ($$$), from $120 to $180; and *ultra-deluxe* ($$$$), above $180. Some of the major all-inclusive re-sorts in Puerto Vallarta cost *much* more than this, and on remote private beaches and deep in the Sierra Madre there are a few "hidden" lodges I'll tell you about where the rates are simply beyond belief. If, like me, you can't afford to actually stay there, it doesn't hurt to fantasize.

In a competitive resort zone like Puerto Vallarta, it's often possible to stay at upscale resorts for a fraction of their standard rates by visiting outside of peak season or taking advantage of airline promotional packages or internet specials. Special low rates are offered for seniors during the spring, and rates for everybody often drop by as much as 60 percent from late April through October.

What is more surprising is that even trendy Puerto Vallarta offers plenty of lower-cost alternatives. In fact, most of the budget and moderate lodging options have the best locations—downtown and in the Zona Romántica, within walking distance of all the best restaurants, art galleries and sights that big-resort guests must take guided tours to visit for a mere few hours. You can get a decent room with private bath, a ceiling fan, sometimes air conditioning and always plenty of character for under $100 or less at any time of year. In other words, lodging in Puerto Vallarta costs roughly the same as in United States vacation destinations. Away from the city, it often costs much less.

Many of the big resorts in Puerto Vallarta operate on an *all-inclusive* basis. This means all meals, alcoholic beverages and nonmotorized water sports equipment such as kayaks, sailboards and snorkeling gear, as well as organized activities, are included in the basic room rate. Sometimes "all meals" includes fine dining at the hotel's "specialty restaurants"; at other places, you can eat at the buffet for free or pay extra to eat at the classier restaurants. At some places, free liquor is limited to "domestic" or house-brand drinks, while you pay for imported name brands; other hotels make a selling point of offering both domestic and imported liquor for free. Some resorts in Puerto Vallarta's Hotel Zone and Marina Vallarta districts offer guests a choice between all-inclusive plans and European plans (no meals or free drinks). A European plan is worth considering since it leaves you free to try some of the many outstanding restaurants in downtown Puerto Vallarta and the Zona Romántica, which few resort restaurants can compete with in terms of quality. A small minority of resorts offer only a European plan. Farther north in Nuevo Vallarta, a long trip from the downtown restaurants, virtually all resorts operate only on an all-inclusive basis.

Bed and breakfasts and small luxury hotels are abundant in the downtown neighborhood known as "Gringo Gulch" and in the Zona Romántica. They are also springing up in several small beach towns north of the city and even in good residential areas of Puerto Vallarta where few tourists ever go. These places tend to be small—sometimes no more than four or five guest rooms—and often cost about the same as staying at a big resort, though the experience couldn't be more different. Rooms typically are individually decorated, with many small luxury touches that make you feel like you're staying in a mansion instead of an institutionlike resort. Personal contact with the owner/innkeepers, who are usually North Americans and usually live on the premises, is a big plus for many B&B buffs; if you value your privacy, though, a B&B may not be for you.

Moderate hotels tend to be comfortable but not lavish, with plain, functional furnishings and private bathrooms with showers. Many have TVs, but not necessarily satellite TV with English-speaking channels. Some have patios, balconies or rooftop sundecks, and a few have rooftop or courtyard swimming pools. (A swimming pool is well worth paying a little more for.) Some have older window-fit air conditioners, though most guests find air conditioning unnecessary as long as their room has a ceiling fan.

There are still a few typically Mexican budget hotels ("one-star," according to the government's rating system) in Puerto Vallarta today, mostly located on the fringes of the Zona Romántica. You'll also find quite a few in outlying towns north and south of the Banderas Bay area. These tend to be dark and spartan, with beds consisting of concrete block pedestals with foam rubber mattresses on top, and very little else in the way of furnishings or decor. Some have televisions, though no English-language channels, and most, though not all, have private baths with showers. Expect to pay no more than $25 a night at these places.

The other option for budget lodging is an older, run-down tourist motel, of which there are virtually none left in Puerto Vallarta itself but quite a few in the smaller towns along the north shore of the bay. These tend to command lower prices because they are poorly maintained, falling deeper into disrepair as they languish in wait for some buyer to come along with enough capital to refurbish them. An all-too-typical such place I "discovered" (to my chagrin) outside Cruz de Huanacaxtle a while back had a kitchen with a stove that didn't light, a sink that didn't turn off and no pots, pans or dishes; a bathrooms with a bare lightbulb dangling by exposed wires in the shower stall; a full dining room with ancient, heavy dark wood furnishings carved with the initials of previous guests and with lights that didn't work; and a television stuck on one channel that seemed to show soccer games whenever it was plugged in. Still, it was right on the beach, cost under $50 a night, and might have been ideal for four to six backpacking students.

In all price ranges, reservations are essential during the high season (Thanksgiving through Easter), when the scramble for rooms can be fierce. Confirm your reservation, preferably in writing, before you go. If the hotel reneges (many resorts overbook during holidays to make sure they are filled if any parties fail to show), make a complaint to the local tourist office and swift action is likely to be taken. Many hotels demand a two-day (but sometimes up to 30-day) cancellation notice before refunding your deposit. Check on cancellation policies at the outset, and remember that cancellation by mail can be fiendishly slow. Use e-mail, keeping a copy of your message and their response. Or better yet, use a knowledgeable, Spanish-speaking travel agent. During the April–May and September–October "shoulder seasons," my favorite time to travel in Mexico, finding nice rooms without reservations should be no problem, though classy bed and breakfasts almost always tend to be full or closed. The hotel information included in this guide should be enough to help you find the kind of lodging you want on short notice.

The Mexican government regulates room rates at all hotels. A notice stating the maximum authorized rate per night is required to be posted beside the front desk and often is also placed inside the room's door. Outside of peak season, you'll often find that the rate you are paying is lower than the authorized rate. If it is higher, you can complain to the national tourism authority (or at least threaten to do so when you discuss the rate with the hotel manager).

At the bottom of the lodging chain there's camping. In Puerto Vallarta and elsewhere around Banderas Bay, there really isn't anyplace where camping is allowed these days, but if you rent a car and drive a few hours out of town, you can still find secluded bays and empty beaches where you can pitch your tent, sometimes for free and other times by paying a local caretaker a few dollars.

ABOUT TIME-SHARES The sale of time-shares—fractional interests in condominiums amounting to subscriptions to future two-week vacations—is a huge industry in Puerto Vallarta. Real estate promoters employ literally thousands of commissioned salespeople to find promising sales leads among the waves of tourists arriving in the city every day. You'll meet them on downtown sidewalks, in supermarkets, restaurants and shops, in the airport arrival area, on the beach and in the lobbies of resort hotels. They'll offer inducements ranging from free tours, meals, bottles of tequila, discounts on store purchases and jeep rentals to cash—sometimes several hundred dollars—if you'll just come and sit through a "one-hour" (i.e., all-day) sales pitch. To qualify, you must be a married couple with a major credit card. If you do go to a time-share presentation, do it at a place in Nuevo Vallarta or Bucerias. The state of Nayarit has a law limiting such sales pitches to 90 minutes, whereas Jalisco, including Puerto Vallarta, has no such law.

Time-share front men often urge you to "Play the game—what, you don't like money?" And indeed, some bargain-minded visitors who don't mind exercising superhuman sales resistance actually turn a profit on succumbing to these freebie offers, which are negotiable and can sometimes be haggled up to US$300 cash. (What the touts don't tell you is that you have to actually sign on the dotted line to buy a time-share before you'll get cash or other big rewards, though by law you can rescind the contract within three days, cancel your credit card downpayment, and still keep the reward.) But for most of us, sitting through high-pressure sales presentations is no way to spend a day in paradise. Here are some proven ploys for repelling time-share touts:

When a friendly stranger asks you where you're from, respond "Australia" (only U.S. and Canadian citizens are targeted for time-share sales). Or say "Right here—I just bought a beautiful home in San Pancho."

Claim you don't have a credit card (which automatically disqualifies you).

Buy one of the widely sold T-shirts or baseball caps that declare "Leave me alone—I'm bankrupt!"

DINING

This book's restaurant listings range from budget to ultra-deluxe, with an emphasis on unique establishments. They are rated as follows: *budget* ($) restaurants usually cost US$8 or less for dinner entrées; *moderate* ($$) restaurants range between $8 and $16 at dinner and offer pleasant surroundings and usually a more varied menu than budget restaurants; *deluxe* ($$$) restaurants tab their entrées between $16 and $25 and feature sophisticated cuisines, decor and personalized service; and *ultra-deluxe* ($$$$) restaurants are generally priced above $25. Restaurants add a 15-percent IVA (*Impuesto de Valor Agregado*, or value-added tax) to the menu price, and some resorts add a 15-percent tip service charge on top of that; check before paying an additional tip. These ratings are necessarily very approximate because of fluctuating currency exchange rates and different demand for tourist services on various parts of the coast. Restaurants listed in this book offer lunch and dinner unless otherwise noted.

Seafood—*mariscos* in Spanish—is the traditional local cuisine of Puerto Vallarta. It's everywhere. You'll find it at inexpensive stands on the beach in the form of ceviche (raw, shredded fish or other seafood marinated in lime juice), lobster or shrimp on a skewer, fish tacos or steamed mussels. You'll find it in boisterous all-the-shrimp-you-can-eat tourist restaurants and swanky gourmet establishments. You'll even find it on pizzas. As a rule, the price of a seafood meal in most restaurants is about the same as you'd expect to pay in the United States, but the serving sizes tend to be enormous. For example, I recently ordered a *caldo de mariscos* at a palapa restaurant on a North Bay beach, even though US$8 sounded like a lot to pay for a bowl of soup. When it arrived, I stared in amazement at the huge bowl with half a lobster tail, four hefty prawns and a whole grilled fish sticking out of a broth thick with clams in the shell and chunks of calamari—enough to feed a whole hungry family!

Most international cuisines are well represented in Puerto Vallarta. For some reason, there is an abundance of Italian restaurants, even though very few European tourists visit this part of Mexico's Pacific coast. You will also find world-class Chinese, Japanese, Thai, French, Austrian, German, Argentinian and Brazilian restaurants, among other nationalities. And of course, if pangs of homesickness should set in, a McDonald's, Subway or Domino's Pizza is never far away.

But the real stars of the Puerto Vallarta dining scene are fusion restaurants. Creative cookery has become enormously competitive here. If you're the kind of food enthusiast who often finds yourself craving, for instance, to begin your dinner with an appetizer of fresh bluefin tuna tartare with pear and honey confit, corn-mushroom-olive bread, or perhaps a salad of mixed greens, endives, grilled figs and marinated goat cheese, and a curried mussel soup accompanied by seared Bernal foie gras in Aztec wild apple sauce, then (after cleansing your palate with an appropriate wine such as a Monte Xanic Cosecha Tardía 2002 chenin blanc) a mahimahi filet stuffed with crab meat, with *hoja santa* and anchovy sauce, or perhaps a guanabana-mustard-seed-glazed venison loin with apple chutney and paradise-pepper Malbec essence, and finish off your meal with an apple and ranch cheese dessert burrito topped with fresh fruit coulis and homemade lavender ice cream . . . well, you've come to the right place. Puerto Vallarta haute cuisine makes San Francisco's California nouveau fare seem downright bland by comparison. (By the way, I didn't make any of these dishes up; all have appeared recently on Puerto Vallarta menus—at ultra-deluxe restaurants, needless to say.)

Favorite dishes that locals cook at home include tacos (usually stuffed with shredded fish, served flat on soft tortillas and rolled before eating), tostadas (hard-baked tortillas usually topped with shrimp or fish ceviche) and quesadillas (flat tortillas topped with grilled cheese, often garnished with chorizo sausage or guacamole). To try these for yourself, visit one of the many open-air food stands around town or a *comedor* (food stall) on the upper level of the Río Cuale arts-and-crafts market. Eating at these places is usually quite safe. To make sure, watch before you order and make sure that the person doing the cooking washes his or her hands often and is not the same person who washes the dishes or handles the money.

HEALTH

There are modern hospitals in Puerto Vallarta, as well as in Manzanillo and Guadalajara. Private hospitals are generally better funded, better equipped and less crowded than public hospital emergency rooms. English-speaking hospitals are also much more expensive than public hospitals, though not as high as equivalent medical services in the United States. Both public and private facilities require payment in advance.

U.S. medical insurance plans seldom take care of health care costs outside the United States unless you purchase supplemental coverage. While some health insurance covers emergency treatment, you will usually be required to pay first and apply to the insurer for reimbursement later. U.S. Medicare and Medicaid programs do not provide payment for medical services outside the United States. Many travel agents and private companies offer short-term health insurance plans that will cover health care expenses incurred overseas, including emergency services such as medical evacuations. Check with your insurer or HMO, and if your policy doesn't cover you in Mexico, consider purchasing a policy that does.

Visits to local doctors are relatively inexpensive—expatriates report that the entire cost of treatment in Mexico is less than their health insurance copayment would be for the same treatment in the United States, supposedly because Mexican doctors face less malpractice liability, thus practice medicine less defensively and invest less in state-of-the-art diagnostic equipment. Hotels can usually recommend English-speaking physicians.

For truly serious medical emergencies, **Critical Air Medicine** (858-300-0224 [collect], 95-800-010-0268 [toll-free from Mexico]), a San Diego–based service, provides air ambulance service to Guadalajara or Mexico City 24 hours a day, every day of the year. There are also air ambulance services that will take you all the way to the United States—for a cost of about $50,000.

One little-known option is **SkyMed International Insurance** (13840 North Northsight Boulevard, Scottsdale, AZ 85260; 480-946-5188, 800-475-9633 [from the U.S.], 001-866-805-9624 [from Mexico]; www.sky

med.com, info@skymed.com), a membership program that guarantees "flying emergency room" evacuation to the United States, as well as assistance in returning family members, vehicles and pets, for a very reasonable annual payment.

No special vaccinations are needed to visit Puerto Vallarta or other areas covered in this book. For routine vaccination recommendations and a health update on areas you're visiting, contact the **Centers for Disease Control** (800-232-4636; wwwn.cdc.gov/travel/regionCentral America.aspx).

Canadian Provincial Health Insurance Plans provide limited coverage for medical expenses incurred during short-term stays outside the country. In the event of a serious medical emergency, the **Consulate of Canada** (Edificio Obelisco Local 108, Avenida Francisco Medina Ascencio No. 1951, Zona Hotelera Las Glorias, Puerto Vallarta; 322-293-0098, fax 322-293-2894; vallarta@canada.org.mx) can assist in arranging for evacuation to Canada, including a medical escort, if it is deemed medically necessary.

DIARRHEA   The illness most people fear when visiting Mexico is diarrhea, euphemized as *turista* or "Montezuma's revenge." This unpleasant condition may possibly become part of your vacation experience, but it's relatively easy to avoid if you follow some simple precautions.

First, heed the old adage "Don't drink the water." For more than a decade, Puerto Vallarta's water purification system has been certified annually as producing the highest-quality drinkable water, exceeding U.S. clean-water standards—one of the few places in Mexico to receive the honor. However, this doesn't mean you should drink tap water, especially in older parts of the city. While the water is safe when it leaves the purification plant, it may not be after it has run through century-old water pipes in the older parts of the city. Avoid using tap water to brush your teeth, though there's little risk in using it to shower or wash your hands with soap.

All hotels that cater to tourists have purified water *(agua purificada)* available, either in individual-sized bottles in the room, where it is sometimes charged to your bill if you use it, or in large water coolers called *tambas* in the hallways. Chilled, inexpensive bottled drinking water is also available in the small grocery stores found throughout Puerto Vallarta and just about every other town and village mentioned in this book.

If you're feeling super-cautious about preventing gastrointestinal distress, you may want to eat only thick-skinned fruits that you peel yourself, avoid salads and consume only vegetables that have been cooked thoroughly. Raw seafoods such as ceviche (and in Puerto Vallarta there's also sushi) have a reputation for being risky. In fact, there's probably a slight risk of *turista* any time you eat meat, seafood, ice cubes, candy or any foodstuffs on which flies may have taken their siestas. Generally, though, restaurant food is perfectly safe, and so is most food from market stalls and street vendors. Locals tend to shun unsanitary eateries, so if a place is doing a brisk business, the facilities look clean and the food is hot off the grill, it's probably okay. Use your own judgment, and for heaven's sake don't pass up anything that smells delicious for fear of germs.

By far the greatest risk of diarrhea, stomach upset or other mild infections comes from your hands. In particular, you're far more likely to come into contact with germs by handling money than by eating food. The best preventative is to wash your hands frequently with soap and water. This is a good health policy at home, but it's much more important in Mexico, where your body has not built up an immunity to local germs. At a minimum, wash before eating, smoking a cigarette or handling anything else that you might put in your mouth, such as a pen or pencil or a postage stamp. Many travelers carry a small bottle of alcohol-based hand disinfectant gel to use after washing their hands in tap water.

Many people believe in preventive medicine. Some take a slug of Pepto-Bismol before every meal (effective enough, though it has the peculiar side effect of turning your tongue and stool black). Others take a shot of tequila, believing it will extinguish any threatening organisms, while still others take Pepto-Bismol to overcome the gastric effects of too much tequila. Mexicans believe that powdered chile, lime juice, and/or coconut milk help stave off digestive problems.

If you do get sick, rest and relaxation will help your body recover faster than if you run around and wear yourself down. *Manzanilla* (chamomile) tea, popular in Mexico, soothes the stomach and often works wonders, especially when blended with *yerba buena* (peppermint). Papaya restores the digestive tract. Light, easy-to-digest foods like toast and soup keep up your strength. Lots of nonalcoholic liquids—any kind—prevent dehydration. Carbonated water with lime juice is another popular stomach soother.

The symptoms should pass within 24 hours or so. A case of *turista* seems to have an immunizing effect—any subsequent bouts you may have will be less severe, and eventually your body will adjust to the foreign water. If you spend a month or more in Mexico and Central America, you may find that you have similar problems with the water back home when you first return—just like Mexican tourists, who sometimes suffer from *turista* when they visit the United States.

In rare cases, diarrhea may be a symptom of a more serious illness like amebic dysentery or cholera—unlikely in the Puerto Vallarta area but possible in the Sierra Madre backcountry. See a doctor if the diarrhea persists beyond three days, if your stool is bloody or foamy, or if you have a high fever.

SHOTS AND PRESCRIPTIONS No inoculations are required to enter Mexico, and international visitors are unlikely to find themselves exposed to any of the tropical diseases that can occasionally occur in rural areas of the country. If you plan an extended stay in a remote area where public sanitation and health services are lacking, your doctor may recommend tetanus and hepatitis vaccinations and perhaps one for typhoid. For the ultracautious, there is also a vaccine for cholera, which rarely reaches as far north as Mexico's central Pacific coast;

many doctors are loath to recommend it because of its possible side effects. If you are planning to venture into wilderness areas or wetlands, especially during the summer rainy season, you may want to ask your doctor about pills to prevent malaria. The pills are taken one per week, beginning a week before your trip and continuing four weeks after your return. By long-standing custom, travelers in tropical areas around the world take their malaria pills on Friday, making it easy to remember and remind one another.

Many pharmaceuticals that are available in the United States and Canada only by prescription are sold over the counter in Mexican pharmacies. In fact, drug stores in Puerto Vallarta typically plaster their windows with sale prices for high-demand drugs like Viagra, Cialis, Paxil, Xanax and Prozac. These drugs cannot be taken back to the United States, though (unless they're in a vial with a prescription label from a pharmacy in the U.S., in which case U.S. Customs and Border Security agents can't prove that you didn't buy them before you left). The reason, the U.S. government claims, is that drugs made in Mexico aren't under the jurisdiction of the Food and Drug Administration and so may not be safe. In reality, drugs sold by Mexican pharmacies are usually made in the same factories as those sold in the U.S. As long as you buy them in an established pharmacy and check the bottle they're being dispensed from to make sure it's the real item, there's an overwhelming likelihood that the product is genuine and safe. In many cases, though, self-medication is *not* safe. This is especially true of antibiotics, the unnecessary use of which can destroy beneficial organisms in your digestive system and put your body at risk for antibiotic-resistant microbes. Never buy any pharmaceuticals outside of pharmacies. Some cab drivers and street hustlers do a brisk business selling counterfeit and sometimes dangerous "Viagra" and "Cialis" lookalikes.

SEXUALLY TRANSMITTED DISEASES   AIDS (*SIDA* in Spanish) is among the leading causes of death in Mexico's young adult population, according to the federal government. Reports suggest that the epidemiological pattern of AIDS in Mexico is unique: 95 percent of the cases to date among men and 45 percent among women are due to sexual transmission. Among men with sexually acquired AIDS, 60 percent were classified as homosexuals, 25 percent as bisexuals, and 15 percent were heterosexuals. HIV transmission due to injection drug use is less than 1 percent. In Mexico there are more than 180,000 HIV/AIDS cases, most of which have occurred in men (85 percent) and in Mexico City (56 percent). The state of Jalisco ranks fourth in the country, with 9000 people living with AIDS, about 80 percent of them in Guadalajara. The high prevalence of bisexual behavior among men is said to account for much of the risk of HIV infection among women and children.

There are no reliable statistics on the incidence of AIDS in Puerto Vallarta since much of the population, both Mexican and North American, is made up of seasonal residents. Health officials say there are just under 500 full-time Puerto Vallarta area residents living with AIDS. Whether Puerto Vallarta really has an extraordinarily high AIDS incidence or not remains uncertain, but members of the local gay community warn that it does. U.S. and Canadian citizens, who are not eligible for free diagnosis and treatment under the Mexican health care system's FONSIDA program, have often found it difficult to access testing and anti-retroviral drugs in Puerto Vallarta.

CAPSITS (Aldama #1013; 322-229-4715), which stands for Centro de atención Ambulatorio Para Infecciones de Transmision Sexual y el SIDA, opened in late 2006. It's a joint effort of state and local governments, the now-defunct Vallarta Contra el SIDA information clearinghouse and AIDS Healthcare Foundation, the largest United States–based HIV/AIDS nongovernment organization. CAPSITS provides comprehensive, sliding-scale clinical care.

Other sexually transmitted diseases such as gonorrhea, syphilis and herpes are also found in the Puerto Vallarta area. Comprehensive statistics are not available because of the extreme social stigma associated with these diseases in Mexico. However, a recent study in Puerto Vallarta revealed a very high incidence of all STDs among teenage male hotel workers—several times higher than among prostitutes, who are required by law to have weekly health examinations and to carry cards proving they have been certified disease-free within the past seven days.

SAFETY

BANDITOS   Travelers from the United States often have a mistaken notion of Mexico as a dangerous place peopled by highway bandits, leftist guerrillas, brutal or corrupt police, torturers and midnight death squads. The cliché of Mexican "banditos" is rooted in the *norteamericano* consciousness largely because of *The Treasure of the Sierra Madre*, a film by director and Puerto Vallarta legend John Huston. In it, American gold prospectors played by Humphrey Bogart and Huston's father, Walter, are attacked by bandits posing as rural police, who with evil grins deliver the famous line, "Badges? We don't have to show you no steenking badges!" What people forget is that the film was made in the 1940s, based on a book written by American expatriate author B. Traven in the 1920s, and was set in the 1880s—an era when bandits were also common north of the border. It has no more present-day substance than the idea of wild Indians on the warpath in the American West.

Yet the impression has been heightened in recent years by reports of corruption and skyrocketing crime rates in Mexico City, nearly 1000 kilometers away from Puerto Vallarta, and of organized crime fueled by drug trafficking. True, evil forces may exist, but as foreign tourists we almost never get a chance to find out. You may be surprised to find yourself feeling much more at ease in coastal Mexico than you do at home. The reason is simple: the crime rate is much lower here than north of the border.

The fact is, traveling anywhere in Jalisco, Nayarit or Colima—even in the huge city of Guadalajara—is probably at least as safe as strolling the streets of your own home town. Thanks to tough firearms prohibitions that have been in force ever since the Mexican Revolution nearly a century ago, the only people who own handguns in Mexico are gangsters and revolutionaries whom travelers will never meet.

Though you may not realize it, Latin Americans often have the same kind of anxiety about visiting the United States, believing it to be dominated by organized crime and filled with shootings, racial prejudice and promiscuity, a stereotype that comes from American movies and TV shows. But this notion was confirmed in 1994 when the leading candidate for the Mexican presidency was shot and killed during a speech in Tijuana on the U.S. border—with a gun the assassin had just bought over the counter in the United States. Fortunately, gun violence has not spread to the Puerto Vallarta area. Military checkpoints on the highway approaches to the city are on the lookout for guns, the possession of which is a much more serious offense in Mexico than drugs. Unlike in the U.S., Puerto Vallarta's Wal-Mart superstore does not sell firearms, ammunition or any other deadly weapons.

That said, it's also true that both drug cartel violence and kidnapping have spread away from the border and the capital recently. Serious incidents occurred in 2008 in the major tourist destinations of Acapulco and Mérida, and a drug cartel-related terrorist grenade attack rocked Morelia, the capital of Michoacán, on Mexican Independence Day, killing eight civilian bystanders and injuring 100. No such violence has reached the streets of Puerto Vallarta, but reasonable caution is in order.

As a general rule, downtown Puerto Vallarta, the Zona Romántica and the hotel zones, where there is a lot of activity after dark, are completely safe—safer than outlying neighborhoods of the city. Avoid dark back streets and areas around sleazy local bars and *clubes caballeros* (strip joints), where you're likely to run into drunks. Carjackings and roadside holdups occasionally happen at night north of the city, especially in unpopulated areas near Punta Mita, Sayulita and San Pancho, where road-building creates obstacles. Rocky detours around bridges that are under construction are the most hazardous spots. The best precaution is to avoid driving after dark in remote areas or, to be on the safe side, anywhere without street lights.

DRUGS AND THE LAW   Back in the day, Mexico was where people went to smoke pot without paranoia. But that was then; this is now. Although in Puerto Vallarta you'll see marijuana leaf T-shirts and baseball caps in curio shops all over town, if you're actually in possession of any weed it definitely pays not to advertise. (If you're looking for some, it may be a different story.) Shopkeepers, taxi drivers and beach vendors will sometimes inquire furtively if you want some *mota* (marijuana). You may also encounter people selling small amounts of cocaine, especially in nightclubs. (Although heroin is an increasing problem in Mexico, as a tourist you are unlikely to run across any.)

Just remember that Mexican law allows the authorities to stop and search you without cause, and it's not unheard of for local police officers to bust tourists in order to solicit bribes, sometimes on information from the person who sold the drug in the first place. Of course, the

U.S. government *does* bribe the Mexican government to the tune of many millions of dollars to interdict narcotics traffic, which is why there are army checkpoints—usually with drug-sniffing dogs—on all major highways, and they conduct random vehicle searches.

Possession of any quantity of marijuana or any other drug that's illegal in the United States is now a serious crime in Mexico. You do not enjoy such rights as the presumption of innocence, and you can be held in jail without bond for up to 13 months before trial.

Don't even think about bringing any amount of any illegal drug back home to the United States (or through the U.S. en route to Canada). Homeland Security is vigilant about drugs, and it's hard to get even a small amount of marijuana past a system of dogs, x-ray machines and chemical-sniffing devices designed to detect explosives and heroin.

TRAVELING WITH CHILDREN

Should you bring the kids on a Mexican adventure? That depends. Lots of Latin American women travel and sightsee with infants in arms, and tourist mothers I've met experienced no problems doing the same. In fact, thanks to the Mexican reverence for motherhood, a baby is likely to mean special treatment, attentive service and sometimes lower prices all along the route. Although for some people, traveling by public transportation with an infant could be one too many stressors, it is also true that many travelers find it fairly easy to enjoy the best of both worlds—parenting and adventuring. Remember to get a tourist card for each child. See "Passports and Visas" later in this chapter.

Older kids? Take them along, by all means. It's easy in resort areas like Puerto Vallarta. If you travel to more remote villages, beaches or mountain areas, it can be more challenging. (It's much easier to travel by car than public bus, but still nerve-wracking.) You'll be amazed at how fast your children become fluent in Spanish.

Vacationing with kids is one of the best reasons I can think of to consider an all-inclusive beach resort. Many of them are family-oriented (I've made a point in this book to mention which ones), with day-care facilities for infants, special play areas for younger kids, "clubs" with facilities ranging from video arcades to climbing walls for teens, and nonstop activity schedules for all age groups that can offer your kids a lot of vacation independence while freeing you to enjoy other activities—perhaps browsing art galleries or jewelry stores or just taking a romantic stroll on the *malecón*—without children in tow. Even if you rent a suite with a separate bedroom and TV for the kids, a week at an all-inclusive resort will cost no more than a Walt Disney World vacation.

TRAVELING WITH PETS

If you want to bring a pet with you to Mexico, whether by car or by air, no advance arrangements are needed, but you do have to have an International Health Certificate for Dogs and Cats (Form 77-043) signed by a U.S. or Canadian veterinarian who has examined your pet within ten days before you enter Mexico, certifying that the animal is in good health. There is a $20 fee to have the certificate stamped at the border or at a Mexican consulate where tourist cards are issued.

23

You will also need a separate certificate that the animal has been immunized against distemper and rabies in order to re-enter the United States. The certificate must have been issued within the six months before re-entry, though the rabies vaccination itself can have been any time within the past three years if you can show the vet documentation that newer, three-year vaccine was used.

Travelers should be aware that Mexican law prohibits dogs in hotel and motel rooms, though some proprietors are willing to ignore the law for a small *propina* (tip). Mexican dogs are usually fed table scraps, so commercial dog food is harder to find around Puerto Vallarta and other towns in the area than it is in the U.S. and Canada. Try Wal-Mart.

In Puerto Vallarta, *norteamericanos* have organized an active spay-and-neuter program as well as a chapter of the Society for the Prevention of Cruelty to Animals, and local officials enforce leash laws. In outlying and rural communities, however, dogs—and, for that matter, most domestic animals—are allowed to roam free, so there is some risk of your own dog getting into a fight, catching a disease or, if not spayed, getting *embarazada* (no, it doesn't mean "embarassed.") Also be aware that many Mexicans grow up with a fear of dogs.

WOMEN TRAVELING ALONE

Although sexual assaults and other crimes of violence by local residents against women tourists are rare in the Puerto Vallarta area, unwanted sexual advances can be a nuisance for some gringas. This is less of a problem in the tourist areas, which comprise most of the city, than in working-class neighborhoods such as Pitillal and in isolated fishing villages. There, torn between the rising tide of feminism in Latin America and the old code of machismo, Mexican men often behave unpredictably toward North American and European women. There is a widespread belief, born of countless Hollywood sex-and-violence flicks, that many gringa women are wildly promiscuous. Anything a gringa does that a Mexican woman would not do may be seen by some men as provocative. This includes hitchhiking, drinking alone in a bar, wearing skimpy clothing away from the beach and, to a certain extent, simply traveling alone. Mexican women often travel on buses without a male companion, but they bring their children. Perhaps as a consequence of this strange attitude, many Mexican men turn into strutting, drooling idiots in the presence of a woman with blonde hair.

I've made a point over the years of interviewing women who are seasoned Mexico travelers about this subject. One gringa in her early forties, who has dark hair and speaks fluent Spanish, says she finds Mexico a comfortable place for women traveling alone. "To avoid problems, dress modestly," she suggests. "Flirting—or forwardness that may be mistaken for flirting—can attract more attention than you expect. But Mexican people are very friendly and like to flirt in a joking way that's not intended to be taken seriously. A light attitude goes a long way. Women travelers in small towns and villages are in a better position to meet local women, who may not speak to foreign men at all but will often invite a gringa to meet their children or see their kitchens."

The best way to obviate harassment is to travel with companions. Two or more women, or a woman traveling with children, will almost never be harassed.

GAY & LESBIAN TRAVELERS

Although the city's mainstream English-language press makes a policy of never mentioning the gay community or accepting gay-friendly advertising, presumably to keep it out of the consciousness of straight resort guests, the reality is that since the mid-1990s Puerto Vallarta has become Mexico's most popular gay vacation destination. Thousands of gay men and women have also taken up permanent residence here. Olas Altas in the Zona Romántica and the south end of the beach at Playa Los Muertos form the center of activity.

GAYGUIDE VALLARTA ☎*322-222-7980* ✐*www.gayguidevallarta.com, editor@gayguidevallarta.com* There are many information resources about the gay scene. The widely available quarterly *Gayguide Vallarta* provides information on gay and lesbian activities and events, as well as gay-owned and gay-friendly businesses, and publishes a free gay map book distributed through gay-owned and gay-oriented businesses.

GAY WEBSITES The website **www.doinitright.com** includes extensive information on gay-friendly Puerto Vallarta, including tours, restaurant picks, hotel and bed-and-breakfast recommendations and no-nonsense information about AIDS and teenage gay hustlers. Another website dedicated to gay and lesbian Puerto Vallarta, with a busy chat room and comprehensive news of interest to gay Puerto Vallarta visitors, is **www.outinpuertovallarta.com**.

AMBIENTE PUERTO VALLARTA ✉*c/o Blue Chairs Resort, Malecón #4* ☎*322-109-7695* ✐*www.pvglba.org* This is an association of gay-friendly and gay- and lesbian-owned businesses.

DIANA DECOSTE ☎*322-222-1510* ✐*www.dianastours.com, dianatours@gmail.com* Although Puerto Vallarta's gay community started out mainly male, it has grown increasingly lesbian-friendly in recent years. DeCoste, who conducts mixed gay-lesbian bay cruises and nature tours, also offers a gay and lesbian airport greeting and shuttle service that will take you to your lodging for slightly more than the standard taxi rate and includes a short orientation tour and money exchange stop.

BOANA'S TOURS ☎*322-222-0999* ☎*322-222-6695* ✐*www.boana.net, boana@pvnet.com.mx* Boana's offers gay group horseback riding tours daily.

JUNGLE SECRET OASIS ☎*322-168-9377* ✐*secret-oasis.com, oasisva@hotmail.com* From November through early April, Jungle Secret offers day trips for gay men to a secluded forest area 15 minutes outside the city for hiking, swimming and nude sunbathing.

Puerto Vallarta's ever-enterprising tourism department has designated the period from the day after Easter through the end of May to be "Spring is for Seniors" season, when the hospitality industry extends a special welcome to visitors over age 60. Hotels offer special rates and value packages, the city offers an extensive calendar of activities, concerts, events and excursions geared toward seniors, and many shops and restaurants in town offer senior discounts.

CLUB INTERNACIONAL DE LA AMISTAD (INTERNATIONAL FRIENDSHIP CLUB) ✉*Edificio Parian del Puente #13, Libertad at Miramar* ✆*322-222-5466* ✎*pvifc@pvnet.com.mx* Although the city has no Elderhostel programs or senior centers, it's easy for visitors and newcomers to meet like-minded Anglo residents through a variety of local nonprofit organizations such as this one, which has get-togethers once or twice a month.

There are also beach cleanup groups, bridge groups, writers' and artists' groups and other gatherings that can be located in the English-language newspaper Vallarta Today.

DISABLED TRAVELERS

Mexican society has traditionally been insensitive to the needs of physically challenged people. They are sometimes viewed as burdens imposed on their families as divine punishment and may even be reduced to begging. So far, this attitude has shown few if any signs of changing. Mexico has no regulations equivalent to the Americans with Disabilities Act; however, newer resort hotels in Puerto Vallarta and elsewhere along the central coast are designed to accommodate disabled visitors. In lower-priced hotels, the physically challenged are likely to encounter more challenges than they might wish.

MEXICO ACCESIBLE ✉*Oceano Indico #399, Colonia Palmar de Aramara, C.P. 48302, Puerto Vallarta* ✆*322-225-0989, 866-519-6165 (U.S.), 877-839-3484 (Canada)* ✆*322-225-0989* ✎*www.accesiblemexico.com, info@accesiblemexico.com* To counter this regrettable attitude—at least where visitors are concerned—this unique Puerto Vallarta travelers' service was founded on the principle that "Every one should be able to travel equally with dignity, comfort and joy, receiving the kindness from the locals, and to be embraced by the breathtaking natural wonders provided for us all." This organization provides equipment such as wheelchairs and oxygen tanks or concentrators, airport pickup service and specially equipped condos with amenities such as roll-in showers, and makes airline bookings and medical assistance arrangements. It also offers special excursions designed for physically challenged individuals, including sightseeing tours, dolphin encounters, healing therapy at Terra Noble spa and dinners at gourmet restaurants.

PASSPORTS & VISAS

Since the beginning of 2007 (air and sea travelers) and 2008 (ground travelers), the U.S. Department of Homeland Security requires every U.S. and Canadian national, including minors, to hold an individual passport to enter the United States. When this law came into effect, it caused a serious, though short-lived, slump in Mexican resort tourism, and the Mexican government responded by requiring all foreign nationals to have passports to enter Mexico, too.

Anyone under age 18 must have his or her own passport *and* the following documents: if traveling unaccompanied or with persons other than their parents, a notarized letter of permission signed by both parents or a legal guardian *or* an individual passport; or, if traveling with only one parent, a notarized letter of permission from the other parent or legal guardian (or, if applicable, divorce papers, a guardianship document or a death certificate for the absent parent) *or* an individual passport. All of these documents need to be authenticated at a Mexican consulate. Foreign students in Mexico are required to have an acceptance letter from the school and a letter certifying that they are financially secure.

When you enter Mexico, you will receive a Mexican tourist permit (commonly called a *tarjeta turistica*, or tourist card), which you need to keep on your person at all times and surrender when you leave. If you are flying from the United States into Puerto Vallarta International Airport or another Mexican airport, the airline ticket agent will check to make sure you have a valid passport; tourist card forms and customs declarations will be handed out aboard the plane—you fill them out and hand them to the Mexican customs and immigration agents at the airport when you arrive. Tourist cards are free; bribery is no longer common border-crossing practice. Tourist cards can be issued for up to 180 days. Multiple-entry tourist cards are also available. They are convenient but not necessary if you are planning to go to another Central or South American country and return via Mexico. To apply for a multiple-entry tourist card, you need two copies of a photo that meets passport standards. The procedure takes longer at the *Migración* desk than simply applying for a new single-entry card when you re-enter Mexico.

Puerto Vallarta has a large population of American and Canadian seasonal "snowbirds" and part-time or full-time expatriate residents. The vast majority of them are over 50, the age at which foreigners can apply for special permanent-resident status. Some American expatriates who live in Mexico, instead of applying for extensions or resident status, keep their paperwork up to date by simply returning to the United States for at least 72 hours every six months and getting a new tourist card. However, due to tensions about immigration policy between the United States and Mexico, the Mexican government has begun cracking down on this practice, and long-term expatriate residents are now better off applying for residency.

When entering Mexico from the United States, you will be required to sign a form certifying that you are not importing contraband. Many travelers are surprised to learn that Mexico has a problem with smuggling from the United States. Smuggling of foreign-made goods without paying import tariffs, once a major concern of the Mexican government, has become less of an issue in the NAFTA era. But organized crime relating to drug cartels has resulted in a huge increase in the trafficking of illegal firearms and ammunition from the United States. For this reason, customs inspections are becoming tougher, not easier, on those who enter Mexico by car or bus. Don't even think of bringing a gun or bullets into Mexico. The volume of red tape involved in importing a weapon legally (for hunting) is simply not worth it.

When entering Mexico, you will be required to certify, among other things, that you are not bringing in more than one still camera, one movie or video camera and one laptop computer per person. When you deplane at the airport and go through customs, you will be asked to press a button on a stoplight device, which gives a random signal—usually green, but sometimes red. If green, you will be waved through without an inspection, but if red, your bags will be searched. In case of a search, items travelers would not normally use, such as kitchen appliances, will raise official eyebrows. So will more than one of the same item, especially consumer electronics from Asia.

The North American Free Trade Agreement has reduced or eliminated most Mexican tariffs on items manufactured entirely in the United States or Canada, and a similar free-trade agreement exists between Mexico and the European Union. However, the government still imposes extremely high tariffs—sometimes as much as the price of the item itself—on goods made in many other countries, even if you bought them in the U.S. or Canada.

U.S. CUSTOMS

Even if you are a resident, the United States can be harder to enter than Mexico. When returning home, United States residents may bring $800 per person worth of purchases duty-free (or $200 per person if you have been out of the U.S. for less than 48 hours or if you have left the U.S. more than once in the past 30 days). The next $1000 worth of items is subject to a three-percent tax. Because of NAFTA, goods made in Mexico with no foreign materials or parts are exempt from taxation. However, other items, including gift items from Guatemala and China, which now account for the majority of souvenirs sold by market vendors in Puerto Vallarta, are subject to U.S. Customs duties. If you are bringing back an item worth more than $2500, such as a high-end artwork, you must have a Certificate of Origin signed by the seller to claim the made-in-Mexico exemption. In case customs officials question the values you declare, save the purchase receipts for goods you buy in retail stores and record your marketplace and street vendor purchases neatly in a notebook.

Persons over 21 are allowed one liter (or quart) of liquor tax-free, as well as 200 cigarettes and 100 (non-Cuban) cigars, as part of their $800 exemption.

Sport fish, shrimp and any seafood that can be legally caught in Mexico can be brought across the border. Many other fresh foods and agricultural products are not allowed into the United States and will be confiscated.

Pirata (pirated copies of copyrighted books, CDs or tapes, videos or DVDs and computer software, as well as clones of trademarked goods such as designer jeans) are produced in Mexico. Bringing these items into the United States is strictly prohibited.

Smuggling illegal drugs into the United States is a separate and often more serious crime than possessing them within the U.S. The same goes for Cuban cigars, absinthe and other contraband. Remember, they search air travelers for drugs when they *leave* Mexico. You are subject to search again when you enter the United States, and the usual U.S. constitutional search and seizure protections do not apply to border crossings.

The U.S. government has also become much more vigilant about imported prescription drugs in recent years. While many senior citizens used to visit Mexico routinely to buy pharmaceuticals at much lower prices than in the U.S., today the policy is to seize such drugs upon entry into the United States. To avoid confiscation of prescribed drugs, make sure they are labeled, carry them in their proper containers with prescription labels *from a pharmacy in the United States*, and bring along a doctor's certificate of prescription. At the present time, the government is zealously enforcing a ban on pharmaceuticals bought in Mexico, even if you have a prescription, so if you *do* refill a prescription in Mexico, put the pills in your old prescription vial before returning to the U.S. If a Mexican physician prescribes pharmaceuticals, you can't legally bring them into the U.S.

U.S. CUSTOMS AND BORDER PROTECTION ✉*130 Pennsylvania Avenue Northwest, Washington, DC 20229* ✆*202-927-6724, 877-227-5511* ✑*www.cbp. gov* For more details, contact this major agency of the Department of Homeland Security.

MONEY MATTERS

CURRENCY In Puerto Vallarta, U.S. dollars are accepted almost as readily as pesos, and many prices are posted in dollars. Elsewhere in the region, most people who deal with tourists, from hotels and restaurants to small shops and street vendors, will accept U.S. dollars at an exchange rate about 10 percent less than what you'd get at a bank, though they may be reluctant to do so on weekends and holidays when banks are closed.

The official symbol for pesos is the same as for U.S. or Canadian dollars, except that the "S" has one stroke through it instead of two. In Puerto

Vallarta it is customary to indicate dollars as "USD" and pesos as "$____ pesos" to avoid confusion. (For example, at the time of this writing, USD10 equals about $110 pesos.) In this book, though, I indicate dollar prices as "US$" and pesos as "pesos"; prices are in U.S. dollars unless otherwise specified.

Mexican coins come in denominations of 5 centavos (.05 peso); 10, 20 and 50 centavos; and 1, 2, 5, 10 and 20 pesos. There is also a 20-peso bill, and other paper currency comes in denominations of 50, 100, 200, 500 and 1000 pesos. The 20- and 50-peso bills are smaller in size, while the larger bills are of equal size but different colors. When you first change your money to pesos, it's a good idea to study the different denominations and fix an idea of their value in your head. The exchange rate has hovered between 10 and 11 pesos to one U.S. dollar in recent years. For simplicity's sake, though, it's easiest to think in terms of 10 pesos equaling a dollar. For instance, a 1-peso coin is like a dime; a 20-peso coin or bill is worth about $2, and you can think of 1000 pesos as the same as a US$100 bill.

CHANGING MONEY   Be smart and protect your vacation fund by carrying at least part of it in traveler's checks. Even if you get a slightly lower exchange rate or pay a small transaction fee when cashing them, it's worth safeguarding your money. Well-known brands—especially American Express and Visa—are easiest to cash. You will need your passport to cash them. You can report lost or stolen American Express traveler's checks and have them reimbursed quickly, at the local **American Express office** (Morelos #660 at Abasolo; 322-223-2955) open Monday through Friday from 9 a.m. to 6 p.m. and Saturday from 9 a.m. to 1 p.m.

An alternative to traveler's checks, prepaid travel cards called Cash Passports are available through any retail office of the international foreign exchange and travel insurance company **Travelex** (877-394-2247; www.cashpassportcard.com, cardservices@travelex.com), found in more than 800 cities around the world. The cards work like regular Visa debit cards in ATM machines and deliver funds in local currency. You pay for them in advance like a prepaid phone card. They provide added security because they are not connected to any bank account, and spending is limited to the prepaid amount, providing additional security. If they are lost or stolen, report it like any other card and the nearest Travelex office will quickly replace your funds with emergency cash or traveler's checks or issue you a replacement card. Prepaid travel cards are particularly useful if you are traveling to more than one country and don't want to repeatedly exchange currency, or if you want to give a friend or relative travel funds as a gift, or if a group traveling together wants to pool group funds and pay expenses with a single card.

American Express (800-528-4800; www.americanexpress.com) offers a similar prepaid card known as the Travelers Cheque Card, available at most places that sell American Express traveler's checks.

Both cards can be purchased online. Both companies also let you exchange currency at their offices or purchase foreign currency online so

1

EXPLORING PARADISE MONEY MATTERS

you will have pesos available immediately for taxi fares, food and other incidental expenses when you land at the Puerto Vallarta airport.

ATM CARDS   It's also a good idea to have your ATM card and keep it with your passport or someplace where it's not with your cash or credit card. Not only does this let you replenish your funds from your home bank account, but in the event that your spending money is lost or stolen, the easiest and fastest way to get a friend to transfer money to you from home is to have them deposit money into your account so that you can withdraw it from an ATM the next day. You'll find ATMs in downtown banks and Hotel Zone shopping plazas. They dispense 100-peso bills, charging your bank account at the prevailing bank exchange rate. A small transaction fee is assessed—the same amount regardless of how much or little cash you withdraw at one time.

BANKS   Most banks open at 9 a.m., close between noon and 2 p.m., and reopen until 6 p.m., Monday through Friday. (Check the Calendar of Events in this chapter for national holidays, when banks are closed.) They often have specified hours, which vary from bank to bank and day to day, for exchanging foreign money. Despite computerization, Mexican banks are very slow. Cumbersome documentation requirements make every transaction a long, leisurely procedure involving waits in several lines. Tellers type up various papers for you to sign. Allow at least an hour for banking, more if the bank is crowded.

Casas de cambio (currency exchange kiosks) give quicker service and are open longer hours than banks, and their exchange rates are slightly lower (some *casas de cambio* offer more favorable-looking rates but charge additional transaction fees). Waiting in the long, slow lines at most banks, you'll probably decide that the small extra cost of cashing a traveler's check, using an ATM or exchanging money at a *casa de cambio* is well worth it in terms of time saved and aggravation avoided.

CREDIT CARDS   Credit cards are just about as widely accepted in Mexico as they are in the United States, though as in the U.S. some restaurants have a cash-only policy. Visa and MasterCard are the most popular ones; American Express cards are sometimes frowned upon because of their stiff fees charged to merchants. A national bank charge of 7 percent is assessed on credit card transactions, and some hotels assess additional charges. In smaller towns, credit cards are usually not accepted.

TIPPING (AND BRIBERY)   While *propinas* (tips) are completely personal, the 15-percent guideline applies in Puerto Vallarta restaurants as elsewhere. Tip bellhops, porters, housekeepers and anyone who renders extra service the equivalent of at least 75 cents to $1. Taxi drivers in Mexico do not expect a tip unless they help you with your luggage, in which case you should tip about $1 per bag. Gas station attendants deserve one (50 cents) if they wash your windows, check your oil or put air in your tires. In small towns, children may assault your car, madly cleaning your windows or begging to watch your car for a tip. Musicians often perform for tips on the town plaza. Even a few pesos is much appreciated.

Though officially frowned upon, the custom of the *mordida* persists in modern Mexico. Literally, the word means "little bite"; in actuality it means bribery of law enforcement officers or public officials. Mexico has been making serious efforts to eradicate the practice, at least where tourists are involved, because it horrifies many gringos, who are unaccustomed to the practice and fail to understand that public officials in developing nations are woefully underpaid. If you would tip a waiter for giving you the best possible service, then why not reward a traffic cop for wisely exercising the discretion of his office?

If you find yourself in the position of having to discuss a bribe, never use the word *mordida* or in any way suggest that you are asking the officer to do anything illegal. The very suggestion is highly offensive and could even land you in jail. Sometimes a small bribe is referred to as a *propina* (tip) or as an unofficial *honorario* (fee). More often, if you ask the officer whether there is another way the matter can be worked out, you will hear the following line of reasoning.

"For me to fail to enforce the law would be a serious dereliction of duty and honor. It is for the court, not me, to assess a fine in a case like this.... But since you are a visitor in my country, and I like you, if you tell no one, I might let the *delincuencia* pass just this once. Of course, you must understand that in this land it is customary to exchange a favor for a favor. Now that I am doing this favor for you, it would be the right thing for you to give me a *regalo*, a gift. For my wife. The amount is whatever you think is right ... well, a little more than *that*...."

If the idea of bribery bothers you, pay up anyway and complain to the government tourism office later. Anybody who is in a position to solicit a bribe can also cause interminable delay and hassle if you don't hand over the cash. Local expatriates in Puerto Vallarta say that reporting police corruption does no good and can actually increase the likelihood that you will be harassed again later.

BARGAINING   In traditional towns in Mexico, haggling over prices is a tradition that unites Old World and New World heritages. When the Spanish conquistadors arrived in the Aztec city of Tenochtitlán (now Mexico City), they found huge marketplaces where food and handmade products were bought and sold in a manner very similar to that used in European cities and towns at the time.

Today, Mexico holds on to the custom of bargaining in public markets, but not in most retail stores, though low-priced curio shops expect bargaining. If a store has price tags on its merchandise, this is an indication that bargaining is unwelcome. If you don't see price tags, take this as an indication that you're expected to haggle. If prices are fixed, the shopkeeper will quickly inform you so. You can still inquire about discounts when purchasing multiple items. For artworks, prices are always fixed in galleries but are negotiable with artists showing their work on the *malecón*. Bargain hard any time you're doing business with a souvenir vendor on the beach.

Price bargaining can be a lot of fun as long as you maintain a cheerful attitude. It's only natural for market vendors to double or triple their asking prices when they see you coming their way. Just keep things in perspective: your plane ticket to Puerto Vallarta probably cost about as much as most vendors earn in six months.

Some people enjoy bargaining. It's an extrovert's game that pays off in savings. Give it a try. Cut the quoted price in half and start bargaining from there. Drift away and watch the vendor call a lower bid. But if you reach a good ballpark figure, don't quibble over nickels and dimes. So the vendor makes an extra 50 cents. You undoubtedly got a great deal, too. Everybody wins.

If you feel uncomfortable haggling over prices, you'll probably reach almost the same result if you simply look at an item with longing and ask, "*¿No me da un descuento?*" (Won't you give me a discount?), then wait patiently. The vendor will do all the work, running through repeated calculations and hypothetical price reductions before naming the bottom-line price.

ELECTRIC VOLTAGE

Electric outlets are the same in Mexico as in the United States and Canada—110 volts, 60 cycles, compatible with all North American portable appliances. If you need to convert appliances from other countries, bring your own adapters.

BUSINESS HOURS & SIESTAS

One of the more famous Latin traditions is the siesta, generally from 1 to 4 p.m. or 2 to 5 p.m. This midday break lasts two or three hours, when establishments close while workers go home to eat the main meal of the day and rest. Later, stores reopen until at least 7 p.m. and, in Puerto Vallarta's downtown and Zona Romántica areas, often 9 or 10 p.m. Department stores, supermarkets and stores in shopping malls do not close for siesta.

TIME ZONES

Puerto Vallarta, along with the rest of Jalisco state, is on Central Time *(huso horario central)*. If you want to phone home, keep in mind that when it's 6:00 in Puerto Vallarta, it's 4:00 in Los Angeles, 5:00 in Denver, 6:00 in Chicago and 7:00 in New York.

But there's a catch. When it's 6:00 in Puerto Vallarta, it's only 5:00 in Nuevo Vallarta and points north. The state of Nayarit is on Mountain Time *(huso horario montaño)*. You cross the state line at the Río Ameca Bridge just north of the airport, so if you're staying in Nuevo Vallarta, Bucerías or Punta Mita, it's an hour earlier than at the airport; people who forget this fact can miss their flights home. The situation is further complicated by some Nuevo Vallarta resorts that set their clocks to Puerto Vallarta time. The reason, they explain, is "to avoid confusing the guests. . ." Be sure to ask.

Both states included in this book—Jalisco and Nayarit—change from Standard Time to Daylight-Savings Time (one hour later) from the first Sunday in April to the last Sunday in October. In the United States, Daylight-Savings Time starts several weeks earlier and ends slightly later.

WEIGHTS & MEASURES

Whether you're getting gas, checking the thermometer or ordering a beer, you'll notice the difference: everything is metric. Mexico, like Canada, measures temperature in degrees Celsius, distances in meters and kilometers, and most substances in liters, kilos and grams.

To convert from Celsius to Fahrenheit, multiply times 9, divide by 5 and add 32. For example, 25°C—the average high temperature in Puerto Vallarta during the winter—equals (25 x 9)/5 + 32, or (225/5) +32, or 77°F. If you don't have a pocket calculator along (though you probably should), just remember that 0°C is 32°F and that each Celsius degree is a tad more than two Fahrenheit degrees. Here are some other useful approximate conversion equations:

> 1 mile (*milla*) = 1.6 kilometers (*kilómetros*)
> 1 kilometer = $^3/_5$ mile
>
> 1 foot (*pie*) = .03 meter (*metro*)
> 1 meter = $3^1/_3$ feet
>
> 1 pound (*libra*) = 0.45 kilogram (*kilo*)
> 1 kilo = $2^1/_5$ pounds
>
> 1 gallon (*galón*) = 3.8 liters (*litros*)
> 1 liter = about 1 quart

COMMUNICATIONS

TELEPHONE   Calling into Mexico used to be a frustrating experience, but it has become easy since phone numbers were standardized to seven digits preceded by a three-digit "city code" (equivalent to an area code), the same as in the United States and Canada. To place an international call to Puerto Vallarta, simply dial 011 (international code)—52 (Mexico's country code)—322 (Puerto Vallarta's city code) and the local number. If you're calling from within Mexico, you dial only the city code and the local number. If you're calling from within the same city code area, just dial the seven-digit local number.

Although the seven-digit area code has been in effect since 2002, some resources still list the old phone numbers. Puerto Vallarta used to have five-digit numbers preceded by the single-digit city code "3." If you run across one of these numbers, all you have to do to convert it is add four "2"s in a row before the last five numbers: change the "3" city code to "322" and add "22" to the beginning of the local number. For example, the old phone number for the American Consulate was 32-00-69. Now it is 322-222-0069.

To place a call from Puerto Vallarta to either the United States or Canada, simply dial the country code "001" (in place of the prefix "1" you would dial if calling long-distance within the U.S.) and then dial the area code and phone number as you normally would.

There are many options, including some very expensive rip-offs, for phoning long-distance from Puerto Vallarta to the United States or Canada. If you phone home from your hotel using a phone card or credit card, you will usually be charged a "connection fee" that can be substantial—about US$8 per call at resorts. Even more expensive, beware of the tourist phones found all over the tourist zone that have no dial or number, just a big sign that reads "Call the USA—credit card or collect." Another variation looks like a regular long-distance phone, with a slot where you insert your credit card and stickers showing the kinds of cards that are acceptable. These phones are easy to find, easy to use, and cost an outrageous US$8 to $15 per minute!

AT&T and some other U.S.-based long-distance companies have special toll-free numbers you can dial in Mexico that will connect you with an English-speaking operator and let you charge international calls to your calling card, often at a lower cost than you would pay through the local phone company. Ask your long-distance provider, or check their website, for a directory of international numbers.

The easiest option is to buy a TelMex prepaid long-distance card that works in pay phones marked Ladatel (which stands for Larga Distancia Automática). Many pharmacies, grocery stores and other stores sell the cards; look for a Ladatel sign on the storefront. You just insert the card with the gold electrode up and the picture side down, then dial normally. The largest denomination the cards come in is 100 pesos. The cost of phoning to the U.S. or Canada with a TelMex card is about seven pesos a minute, so for long calls you may wish to purchase several cards. *Do not* call collect to the U.S. or another foreign country—TelMex has a minimum charge of about US$40 on international collect calls.

Many cell phone companies, including Verizon and Cingular, let you phone home to the United States or Canada at international roaming rates, which usually range between 50 cents and about $1.40 a minute. Coverage is good within metropolitan Puerto Vallarta and most outlying areas. Verizon also offers a "North America's Choice" plan where you pay an extra US$20 for each month it is activated and can use your free minutes and evening and weekend minutes throughout Mexico as well as the U.S. and Canada. Call your cell phone provider or visit their website for current information on international calling.

You can also use your own cell phone in Puerto Vallarta by contacting **USACell** (322-222-6633), which will replace the SIMM chip in your phone with one of theirs at no charge when you subscribe to a short-term plan. Remember, though, that you have to have your phone reprogrammed again when you return to the United States, and keep track of the tiny SIMM chip in the meantime, and your Mexican phone number won't be the same one you have back home. For short stays, an easier solution is simply to stop into any of the numerous Telcel stores around town and buy a prepaid cell phone. Rates for calling the United States on either USACell or Telcel are considerably higher than on a public Ladatel phone, but a lot cheaper than most hotels' phone charges.

Public Ladatel phones are hard to find in many outlying towns and villages. Phone service of any kind is a recent development in such places as Yelapa and the Sierra Madre towns, and many more residents use cell phone than land lines.

FAXES   Since their invention, faxes have been more widely used in Mexico than in the United States because international mail is slow. Fax use is on the decline for most businesses and individuals in Puerto Vallarta, replaced by e-mail for many purposes, though most hotels can send and receive faxes for you.

INTERNET ACCESS

In downtown Puerto Vallarta and the Zona Romántica, there's always a cybercafé close by. Cybercafés pop up temporarily in just about any retail spaces that become vacant. Rates usually are inexpensive, often around US$1 to $3 per half hour.

In the Hotel Zone, Marina Vallarta and Nuevo Vallarta, many resort hotels have cybercafés on the premises, and most of them offer wireless internet access. (If you want to access the internet from your laptop in your room, be sure to let the hotel know in advance. In some highrise hotels wireless access is limited to certain floors or is blocked by the elevators in some rooms.) The cost of internet access at hotels is typically around US$10 for 24 hours, making cybercafés a cheaper option if you're just checking your e-mail. Most smaller hotels and bed-and-breakfasts also offer wireless internet access, though sometimes only from the lobby, and usually for no charge, though guests need to get an access code from the front desk. There's open wireless internet access at the airport.

Outside of the city, you'll find high-speed internet access in many smaller towns, including Bucerías, Sayulita and Mascota. Even the remote fishing village of Yelapa, which didn't have electricity until a few years ago, has internet cafés. The atmosphere runs the gamut from real estate offices and cluttered Internet Service Provider headquarters to clubs where you can surf while sipping a *latte,* herb tea, beer or tequila. Some also offer food service.

To send and receive e-mail from a cybercafé in Mexico, or anywhere else, simply go to your regular Internet Service Provider's website (such as www.comcast.net or www.aol.com), click on the "Mail" option and enter your username (usually the same as your primary e-mail account name) and your password. Be sure you know your password before you leave home; you can't retrieve a reminder of a lost password over a cybercafé computer, though if worst comes to worst you can usually reset your password if you know the correct answer to a prearranged security question (such as your mother's maiden name or your pet's name). If you use a local ISP back home, the procedure for accessing your e-mail is usually the same, but make sure by asking them before you leave home.

Of course, computers in Puerto Vallarta usually have Spanish-language versions of web browsers (Microsoft Explorer, Safari, etc.), but they work the same way. Using a Spanish-language keyboard can be a little trickier, because some of the punctuation marks and special characters aren't in the same places. You can usually change the computer's language setting to English in the system preferences, which will make all the keys do the same thing you're used to, even though the markings on the keys are different. If you do this, be sure to change it back when you're finished. It can be disconcerting if you don't realize that another user before you changed the language setting and the characters printed on the keys don't match what happens on the screen. When using a Spanish-language keyboard for the first time, you may have to ask for help finding "@" because it's an option character that doesn't show on the keyboard.

MAIL

Mail from Mexico to the United States is quite reliable and generally takes less than two weeks to reach its destination. If you want to mail goods to the United States from Mexico, you may send items valued at less than $50 duty-free to a particular address (but not your own) as often as every 24 hours. Mark the parcel "Unsolicited Gift—Value under $50" and enclose a sales receipt.

POST OFFICE ✉Mina #188 📞322-222-1888 While in Mexico, you can receive mail at your hotel or have it sent to the main downtown Puerto Vallarta post office (Oficina de Correos) via "Lista de Correos," similar to general delivery in the United States. The post office holds Lista de Correos mail for only ten days, then returns it to the sender. The post office will charge you a small fee, and you will need identification—usually a passport—to pick up your mail. The local American Express office (Morelos #160; phone/fax 322-223-2927) also holds mail for cardholders and persons carrying American Express traveler's checks.

COURIER SERVICES Puerto Vallarta does not currently have a FedEx office. For courier and shipping service, use **DHL** (Boulevard Francisco Medina Ascencio #1046; 322-222-4720) or **UPS** (at Mail Boxes Etc., Francisco Medina Ascencio #2180, local 7 y 8, Hotel Zone; 322-224-9434). For outgoing shipments, both are about as prompt and reliable as in the United States. If you are expecting to receive a package via one of these services, be sure you have a tracking number so you can check on the internet whether it has arrived. You may not be notified when it arrives, in which case you'll need to know whether it has been delivered at your hotel or is being held for you at the company's office.

TRANSPORTATION

AIR

GUSTAVO DÍAZ ORDAZ INTERNATIONAL AIRPORT The fastest way to get to Puerto Vallarta from anywhere in the United States or Canada is to fly. Commercial airlines offer frequent flights to Puerto Vallarta's recently expanded Gustavo Díaz Ordaz International Airport. American Airlines, US Airways, Continental, Alaska Airways, Delta and United offer daily flights, usually hubbing through Los Angeles, Denver or Houston. Air Canada, Air Transat, WestJet and Sunwing provide service from Canadian cities, with the most popular flights leaving from Vancouver, Kelowna, Edmonton and Calgary. Canadian travelers may want to search for a nonstop flight, since a stopover in the United States involves the hassle of clearing U.S. Customs and Border Protection as well as airport security, even if you're just changing planes. Aeroméxico and Mexicana also fly from selected U.S. and Canadian cities as well as from other parts of Mexico.

It is also possible to fly in to Guadalajara, rent a car there and take the toll expressway (about five hours) over the Sierra to Puerto Vallarta. Today, however, it is slightly more expensive to fly to Guadalajara from most departure points, and there are more direct flights to Puerto Vallarta, even though Guadalajara is a much larger city.

Baggage allowances on international flights are generally the same as on domestic flights—one carry-on item small enough to fit under the seat or in an overhead rack, one smaller personal item such as a purse or laptop computer, plus two pieces of check-in luggage. Some airlines also have weight limitations, typically 88 pounds, on checked luggage. All airlines allow considerably more luggage than you'd want to lug around on your trip.

Puerto Vallarta, like all Mexican airports, has an airport departure tax of about 100 pesos, payable in local currency, including a charge for security and baggage searches to comply with U.S. Homeland Security requirements. This is usually included in the price of international airline tickets, but you'll want to check and make sure before exchanging all your pesos for dollars at the airport on your way home.

GETTING TO AND FROM THE AIRPORT

Taxis are the main mode of airport transportation. The nonnegotiable fares are regulated according to a zone system, and the fares are posted conspicuously on the taxi booth. Buy a ticket at a booth near the front entrance on the arrival side of the airport and take it to the person in charge of the cab stand, who assigns you a taxi. Taxis that serve the airport must buy a special federal license, so the airport rates are considerably higher than other cab fares around town. For up to three people, it costs about US$18 to go from the airport to Marina Vallarta, $20 to the Hotel Zone or downtown, $25 to the Zona Romántica, and $30 to Mismaloya or Bucerias. It's even pricier to more distant north bay destinations—up to about $80 for the hour-long drive to San Pancho. Unlike other local cabbies, airport taxi drivers expect a tip if they help you with luggage.

A cautionary note: Time-share hucksters throng the airport arrival area and will approach you as soon as you're through customs, presenting themselves as someone who will arrange a taxi for you. They are actually there to get you to commit to a sales presentation in exchange for a free ride to your hotel. Even if you might be interested in a time-share (and somebody must be), you can get much better reward offers while shopping around downtown. Always arrange transportation from the official booth by the front doors of the airport arrival area.

If you packed light, it's possible to walk from the airport out to the main thoroughfare, Boulevard Francisco Medina Ascencio, and flag down a city taxi, which costs less than an airport taxi. Or you can catch one of the municipal buses that run up and down the boulevard constantly and cost about 50 cents to any place in the city.

BUS

Whether to travel by car or take public transportation is one of the fundamental quandaries of ecotourism. It's an indisputable fact that motor vehicles are inherently bad for the environment, as travelers who visit Guadalajara—where the air can be brown and nearly poisonous—will immediately see for themselves. So environmental ethics dictate that public transportation is better. In Puerto Vallarta and other parts of the central Pacific coast, where many people don't own cars, public transportation—buses, minivan shuttles and taxis—can take you many more places, often in greater comfort, than in the United States, so why not use it? Buses run frequently all over the Puerto Vallarta area and up and down the coast. Taxis, too, are everywhere. Traveling without a car can mean no worries about flat tires, fender-benders or *patrulleros* (highway patrolmen).

If you're traveling on a tight budget, long-distance bus travel is by far the most economical way to get from the border to Puerto Vallarta and from Puerto Vallarta to other major towns. From Tijuana or Mexicali on the California border, or from Nogales on the Arizona border, **Elite** (322-290-1001) run frequent first-class buses up and down the West Coast. Elite's parent company, **Estrella Blanca**, and its affiliates (**Greyhound**, **Transportes Norte de Sonora** and **Transportes Chihuahenses**) operate first-class service from the border cities of Tijuana, Mexicali, Nogales and Ciudad Juárez to Puerto Vallarta, sometimes transferring in Guadalajara. There's no reservation system—you just go to the bus terminal, buy your ticket and get on board. If you're traveling at a busy holiday time such as Christmas week or Semana Santa, you may want to buy your ticket at the bus terminal a couple of days early to make sure you get a seat. Most first-class buses leave before noon.

You can save even more money by taking a second-class bus, but the very reasonable cost of a first-class ticket (around US$80 one way from the border to Puerto Vallarta) saves you from having to ride all day and night on a tightly packed, hard schoolbus-type seat and lets you cruise in comfort in a spacious, well-upholstered seat on a carpeted bus with TV screens that play American action movies dubbed in Spanish and old black-and-white Cantinflas comedies until you go insane. Be sure to bring earplugs.

Puerto Vallarta's **Camionera Central** (Route 200, Km. 9), or central bus station, is located a mile north of the airport.

SEA

Puerto Vallarta is a port of call on most cruises of the "Mexican Riviera," which also includes Cabo San Lucas, Mazatlán and sometimes other Mexican West Coast destinations such as La Paz, Loreto, Topolo-bampo, Manzanillo, Ixtapa/Zihuatanejo or Acapulco. Many cruise ships also stop in Puerto Vallarta on Panama Canal trips between the U.S. East Coast and West Coast. All cruise ships put in at Puerto Vallarta between 7 and 9 in the morning and depart between 5 and 11 p.m. the same day. Passengers arriving in Puerto Vallarta are presented with a wide array of transportation and tour options for spending their day here, so it pays to study the range of possibilities presented in this book. You may also want to consult with the cruise concierge. (Bear in mind, though, that some cruise ship companies mark up the shore excursions they arrange for passengers much higher than the same tours or activities will cost if you arrange them on your own.)

Puerto Vallarta Maritime Terminal is presently expanding the capacity of its Maritime Terminal, where the cruise ships dock. As of 2009, nine cruise ship companies visit Puerto Vallarta for a total of more than 200 days in port per year: Princess, Carnival, Holland America, Royal Caribbean, Silversea, Norwegian, Crystal, Cunard and Celebrity.

Cruise lines do not accept direct bookings. Make your cruise arrangements through a travel agent or an online travel broker such as **Expedia. com, Travelocity.com, Vacationstogo.com** or **Cruise411.com.**

CAR

DRIVING TO PUERTO VALLARTA   It's possible to drive the 1676 kilometers (1041 miles) from Nogales on the Arizona–Sonora border to Puerto Vallarta in a passenger car or motor home in about 24 hours of actual driving (allow three days), passing through Guaymas and Mazatlán along the way. Most of the trip is along Mexico's Route 15, turning off onto Route 200 at Tepic. You will pay about US$75 in tolls for an automobile, or three times that much for a motor home, and the ease of driving on the fast, modern four-lane *Cuota* (toll highway) instead of the tedious old *libre* (free highway) is well worth the price.

MOTOR VEHICLE REQUIREMENTS   For driving in Mexico, your current U.S., Canadian or international driver's license is valid. If you're bringing your own car, you'll need a Mexican vehicle permit and Mexican auto insurance. To obtain a vehicle permit (a special stamp on the owner's tourist card, issued for up to 180 days), you'll need proof of ownership—the original and a photocopy of a current registration certificate and title. If the title shows a lien against the vehicle or if it is registered in another person's name or a company name, you need a notarized letter from the lienholder or owner authorizing you to take the vehicle into Mexico for a specified time. The owner or driver who has the car permit stamp on his or her tourist card must be in the car whenever it is being driven.

There is a $16.50 (including IVA) vehicle permit fee, which you must pay with a valid credit card bearing the same name as the one on the vehicle title. If you don't have a credit card, you will be required to post a bond (available through Mexican auto insurance agents) or make a cash deposit in the amount of the vehicle's total value. You must return to the United States through the same port of entry and have your vehicle permit cancelled to prove that you didn't sell or otherwise leave the vehicle in Mexico. Otherwise your credit card will be charged with the value of the vehicle (or your bond or deposit will be forfeited). The purpose of these requirements is to stanch the flow of stolen cars from the U.S. into Mexico and also to enforce the law that all cars bought and sold in Mexico must be manufactured in Mexico.

INSURANCE

Auto insurance policies issued in the United States are not valid in Mexico. Purchase motor vehicle liability insurance (and, if you wish, collision/comprehensive coverage) before crossing into Mexico It is sold by agencies on the U.S. side at all border crossings. Causing an auto accident is a crime under Mexican law, which presumes defendants guilty until proven innocent. This means that if you are involved in an uninsured accident that causes property damage, your vehicle will be impounded until you pay the damage and a fine. If any person is injured in the accident, you will go to jail until all claims are settled or a judge decides you weren't at fault, which can take up to 13 months. *Warning:* Under Mexican law, car insurance is invalidated if you were under the influence of alcohol or drugs at the time of an accident, and you will go to jail until you can prove that you are financially able to pay for all damages and injuries.

GASOLINE

In Mexico, the petroleum industry—from oil wells to gas stations—is owned by the federal government and is called Pemex (for Petroleo Mexicano). The only gas stations in the country are Pemex stations, recognizable by their green-and-white signs. Virtually all cities and towns have them, but they are not as numerous as gas stations in the U.S. Don't let your gas tank get dangerously close to empty; you may have to drive around for a while to locate a Pemex station. Unleaded gasoline (called *Magna Sin)* is available at all Pemex stations. Gas is sold by the liter and costs a little less than in the United States.

CAR RENTALS

Having the use of a car provides much greater flexibility than relying on public transportation. You can go where you want, when you want, without being straightjacketed by limited rural bus schedules. Without a car, some of the places described in this book would be hard to reach.

Relying on public transportation to visit remote areas can sometimes leave you stranded overnight in places where there are no hotels or campgrounds. A car lets you search out remote beaches and off-the-beaten-path wildlife preserves where there is no bus stop for miles. One of the most pleasurable aspects of traveling up and down the coast is the relaxing, carefree feeling you get as you cruise along the traffic-free roads (an aspect, ironically, that will quickly be lost if more people take to the highways by car). Having traveled the region many times by both car and public transportation, I must admit that, for me, driving makes for a much richer and more enjoyable trip.

That said, relying on public transportation within Puerto Vallarta is much more hassle-free, and the daily cost of a rental car will pay for a lot of taxi travel. If you plan to get out of Puerto Vallarta and take a road trip north, south or east of the city, arrange for a rental car to be delivered to your Puerto Vallarta hotel around the time you plan to check out. Anyone 25 years or older, with a credit card, can order a rental car. When it's delivered, you'll need your tourist card or passport, a driver's license and a major credit card. Take the optional collision damage waiver insurance that powers your deductible for damage to the vehicle, but shop around between agencies ahead of time for the best insurance rates—they can vary widely. Hotel managers like it if you book your rental car through them. They get a commission from the rental agency, and it costs you no more than if you dealt directly with the agency, though managers of smaller hotels may sometimes steer you toward agencies that pay them more and charge you more. Larger hotels have travel-agent desks that will help you arrange car rentals as well as guided tours.

In Puerto Vallarta, more than in most other Mexican cities, car rental agencies—especially international brand-name franchises with booths at the airport—are notorious for nickel-and-diming customers with extra charges that raise the cost of rental cars sky-high. It is common practice to charge renters much higher rates for Mexican car insurance than you would pay if you arranged for it on your own through an insurance agency. Collision Damage Waiver insurance is also likely to be overpriced, and if you decline it you may be required to place a credit card deposit in the entire amount of the insurance policy's deductible. Watch for extra charges that are calculated as a percentage of the rental cost. For instance, it's common to assess 10 percent of the rental for shuttle service from the agency's garage to the airport when you return the car; so if you rent a car for a day, you'll pay a (sort of) reasonable US$5 for the shuttle service, but if you rent it for a week, you'll pay $30 for the same one-time, five-minute trip. Rip-offs like these are so widespread that a few independent rental agencies have built booming businesses by offering fair deals.

After much scouting around, I recommend **Gecko Rent-A-Car** (Héroe de Nacozari #15, Bucerías, Nayarit; 329-298-0339; www.geckorentcar.com, geckorentcar@hotmail.com). Although they're located in Bucerías, Canadian owner Denis Beauvais and his wife Kaisa offer drop-off and pick-up service at the airport or any hotel in the greater Puerto Vallarta area.

RULES OF THE ROAD Mexican traffic laws and driving customs differ from those in the U.S. and Canada in several ways. By far the most important difference to be aware of has to do with left turns. Simply stated, when you're going to turn left, signal by turning on your emergency flashers and pull over to the right side of the road to wait for traffic to clear before you turn. It sounds weirdly counterintuitive, but that's how it has been done ever since motor vehicles first appeared on Mexican roads.

On the main boulevards in the modern part of Puerto Vallarta, as well as in other large towns up and down the coast, there is a frontage street called a *lateral* on each side of the boulevard, separated from the main traffic lanes by a concrete curb. To make a left turn, you exit from the boulevard onto the lateral on your right (sometimes you have to do this several blocks in advance), then stop in the *lateral*'s turn lane, wait for the left turn arrow and proceed all the way across the boulevard.

The hazard comes when turning left from a two-lane highway or rural road. If you try to do it American-style—turning on your left-turn signal, slowing or stopping in the traffic lane to wait for oncoming vehicles to pass, then making your turn—you're taking your life in your hands. You see, in Mexico the left flasher indicates to drivers behind you that it's safe to pass. So just about the time you make your left turn, the vehicle behind you will try to go around you on the left, believing you've told him to do so, and crash right into you. For safety's sake, remind yourself: emergency flashers, pull off on the right shoulder, wait for traffic to clear in both directions, then make your left turn.

Road Signs en Espanol

Here are some common road signs you'll encounter around Puerto Vallarta.

Alto = Stop (rarely obeyed!)
Camino Resbaloso = Slippery Road
Curva Peligrosa = Dangerous Curve
Despacio = Slow
Desviacion = Detour
Estacionmiento = Parking
Ganado Proximo = Livestock Nearby
Maxima = Speed Limit (rarely obeyed!)
No Rebase = No Passing
No Hay Paso = Road Closed
No Maltrate las Enseñales = Don't Mistreat the Road Signs
Obedesce las Enseñales = Obey the Road Signs
Poblacion Proximo = People Nearby
Retorno = U-turn
Salida = Exit
Semafora = Traffic Light
Se Usa Grua = Tow Trucks Are Used
Topes = Speed Bumps
Zona de Derrumbes = Rockslide Area
Zona Escolar = School Zone

Assume that all traffic signs will be ignored. Stop signs look just like U.S. stop signs (red and white, with the word "Alto"). However, Mexicans treat them as "yield" signs and hardly ever stop. In fact, if *you* stop at a stop sign when there's no vehicle coming to yield the right of way to, you're likely to be rear-ended by any driver behind you. On the other hand, if you run a stop sign, there's always a possibility that a policeman will pull you over and "fine" you on the spot for it; use your own judgment under the circumstances.

The same is true of speed limits. Most stretches of two-lane coastal Route 200 north and south of Puerto Vallarta are posted 60 kilometers per hour (about 35 mph). Yet the prevailing traffic speed is more than twice that fast. This is no assurance that the police won't stop you if *you* exceed the speed limit. A very common experience driving on Route 200 is this: You're driving along at a more-or-less normal speed when you see a police car in your rear-view mirror. You slow down to exactly the posted speed of 60 kph. The policeman turns his flashing red lights on. You mutter a curse under your breath and pull over to the side of the road. The police car roars past you, and the officer, cursing *you* under *his* breath for being a stupid slow gringo and believing everything you read, turns off his flashing lights and leaves you in the dust. You sigh with relief and continue on your way. (Of course, the one time you decided not to slow down would be the time the officer decided to pull you over for real.)

When there actually is a good reason for driving slow, such as when the highway goes through a populated area where there are likely to be dogs, chickens, children or nuns collecting for charity in the middle of the road, speed limits are enforced by traffic-calming devices, which can range from *vibradores*—ridges in the pavement that make a loud warning rumble as you drive over them—to *topes*—killer speed bumps that will send you flying if you hit them at even a little over the posted speed limit. At the outskirts of every highwayside village, you'll find a *llantería* (tire repair shop) right next to the *tope*. This is no coincidence.

THE LAND
& OUTDOOR
ADVENTURES

Although Puerto Vallarta itself has recently exploded into a midsized city, the Banderas Bay area was a thinly populated, pristine environment until quite recent times, and you still don't have to go far out to sea or into the mountains to find nature at its best—reefs and sea caves teeming with colorful fish, rocky islands bustling with bird life, rivers and ponds where crocodiles bask, tropical forests that shelter animals ranging from deer and javelinas to boa constrictors. Guides and sometimes rented sporting equipment such as bikes, kayaks or diving gear will help you make the most of the magnificent landscapes and seascapes that await a surprisingly short distance outside your hotel lobby.

THE LAND

On the boundary between the Mexican states of Jalisco and Nayarit, Puerto Vallarta is located on the "corner" of Mexico's central Pacific coast, where the shoreline veers sharply from a north–south angle to a west–east angle. Puerto Vallarta lies at 20.7 degrees north latitude—the same latitude as Cozumel in the Yucatán, the Big Island of Hawaii and the city of Bombay, India—about 200 miles south of the Tropic of Cancer and 1420 miles north of the Equator. It is due south of Denver, Colorado. If you continue south from Puerto Vallarta, there is nothing but open ocean all the way to Antarctica.

The city is at the center of the eastern shoreline of Banderas Bay, the largest protected bay on the Pacific coast of the Americas and seventh-largest in the world. Twenty-five miles in diameter, with 40 miles of shore and 40 separate beaches, the bay is believed to be an extinct volcano caldera. Geologists disagree as to whether the eruptions occurred underwater or whether a coastal volcano formed and later fell into the ocean as earthquake activity changed the shoreline. Within a mile offshore, the floor of the bay drops off abruptly into twin pits as deep as 10,000 feet.

The west rim of the ancient volcano crater forms a range of undersea mountains, which protrude above the water's surface as the Marieta Islands, separating Banderas Bay from the open ocean.

Beyond the outer undersea rim of Banderas Bay lies an even more remarkable geological formation, the Middle American Trench. Here, two tectonic plates collide—the westward-moving North American Plate on which most of Mexico rests and the northeastward-moving Cocos Plate, which forms the floor of this part of the Pacific Ocean. The underwater trench forms where the Cocos Plate slides underneath the North American Plate and reaches depths of more than 20,000 feet, three times deeper than the ocean floor farther out in the Pacific. The trench runs right along the coastline from Puerto Vallarta south to Manzanillo and then continues in a straight line farther offshore for 1600 miles to the Pacific coast of Guatemala, Nicaragua and Costa Rica.

The continuing pressures generated as the Cocos Plate slides beneath the North American Plate cause volcanic and earthquake activity along Mexico's central Pacific coast. The huge, ancient volcano that formed Banderas Bay was just one result of this action. Another was the abrupt upthrust of the volcanic Sierra Madre Occidental east of Puerto Vallarta.

The largest seismic event in 60 years along the Middle American Trench took place off the Colima coast about 150 miles south of Puerto Vallarta in October 1995. An earthquake measuring 7.5 on the Richter scale caused 40 deaths and about 100 serious injuries in the city of Manzanillo, mostly due to the collapse of the concrete roof of the municipal market there. The earthquake was felt as far north as Puerto Vallarta, where it toppled the crown from the top of the Church of Our Lady of Guadalupe into the town's central plaza. Today, most Puerto Vallarta hotels have bilingual "In Case of Earthquake" instructions posted on the inside of guest room doors and earthquake evacuation route signs around the grounds.

To the east of Puerto Vallarta rise the forested slopes of the Sierra Madre Occidental, which runs almost the entire length of western Mexico. (All three of Mexico's major mountain ranges are named Sierra Madre, or "Mother Range." The other two are the Sierra Madre Oriental—where the novel and film *The Treasure of the Sierra Madre* was set—in the east and the Sierra Madre del Sur in the south.) The sierra above Puerto Vallarta is an ancient layer of volcanic rock uplifted by the Cocos tectonic plate sliding beneath the Continental Plate. The mountains rise abruptly in an almost sheer wall from the coast, then descend very gradually eastward into the highlands around Guadalajara. The sierra has a median elevation of about 7500 feet, with rounded peaks and a few volcanoes rising to about 10,000 feet. From the window of a plane approaching Puerto Vallarta over land, you can see that the sierra is cut by deep river gorges that make many areas all but inaccessible, so that much of the land east and north of Puerto Vallarta is roadless and inhabited only by small groups of Huichol Indians.

FLORA

The dominant vegetation zone of the land surrounding Puerto Vallarta is tropical deciduous forest. Though often called "rainforest," or *selva* in Spanish, it is denser but not as tall as the towering forests of equatorial Central and South America. In areas where the largest old-growth trees have not been cut for timber, the main forest canopy stands about

50 to 60 feet above the forest floor, while the tallest trees reach up about 100 feet.

In the rainy summer season, the forest forms a solid wall of greenery, as even the seasonal weeds in the undergrowth reach impressive size. Ferns and palmettos can loom higher than the roof of a house. Because the winter season is so dry in the Sierra Madre Occidental, the leaves of a number of species of trees turn red or gold in autumn and fall to the ground, leaving many tree branches bare through the winter. But even then, the impression given by the forest from a distance is one of lush greenery, as some trees keep their leaves and others grow new ones at the same time the old ones are falling. The most spectacular time to visit the forest is spring, when it bursts forth in brilliant red, pink, white and yellow flowers.

Foremost among the numerous tree species commonly found in the forest above Puerto Vallarta are 21 distinct species of neo tropical ficus, or American fig trees, including six that only grow only in the western Sierra Madre. Some ficuses are the same as familiar house plants, but in their native tropical habitat they grow into large trees with extensive root systems. Although humans commonly eat only one variety of figs, most ficuses bear edible fruit that is an important food source for forest mammals such as coatimundis. The most noticeable of the ficuses is the strangler fig, known in this region as *higuera malpalo* (evil fig tree). Its seeds lodge in the branches of other trees and send tendrils down to the ground; then the pale, twisted strangler fig grows around the trunk of the host tree, gradually restricting its growth until it dies, leaving the mature strangler fig its place.

Another distinctive species is the gumbo-limbo, known locally as the *arbol gringo* (tourist tree) because its copper-colored bark, which peels away in thin layers, looks like sunburned skin. Other common trees include kapok, jungleplum, torchwood and *palo de culebra* (snake tree), whose wood is used for construction timbers, fine furniture, cabinets, pool cues and archery bows. Several trees in the forest have healing properties, including the *leche de María*, traditionally used as an antibiotic to treat infections, and the *palo santo*, whose roots are used to bring down fever. The taller trees that rise above the main forest canopy include laurel and *vera blanca*, as well as *parota* (also known by its Indian name, *huanacaxtle*), a prized, termite-proof hardwood used to make doors and fine furniture, and *prima vera*, stunning in spring when it is covered with bright yellow blossoms, used to make guitars. The Pacific coast mahogany is also native to the forest, though loggers have cut most mature specimens.

Orchids and other bromeliads are relatively rare in the forests above Puerto Vallarta, though Spanish moss grows on the trees, along with other tillandsia air plants, many with colorful blooms.

At higher, cooler altitudes in the Sierra Madre Occidental, the vegetation changes to tropical pine-oak forest. Though strikingly different from the deciduous forest, it is equally diverse, with at least 26 species of pine, fir and juniper and more than 100 species of oak. Motorists will pass through one short, impressive stretch of this forest at the highest point on the drive south from Puerto Vallarta to the Costa Alegre.

In areas north of Banderas Bay, where the mountains level off into coastal plains at lower elevations, the vegetation zone is called thorn forest. It consists of prickly scrub trees with beanlike pods, such as mesquite and *guamachil* (manila tamarind), which form a canopy about 20 feet high. A thick undergrowth of vines makes the thorn forest impenetrable in many places. Also native to this lowland forest are palapa or cohune palms and several large species of cactus, including the *nopal* (prickly pear), *cardón* (similar to a saguaro but larger), *pitahaya* (organ pipe), candelabra and old man cactuses.

Mangrove forest lines lagoons and rivers in the region, especially at the mouth of the Río Tovara near San Blas and the Marisma Nacional ("National Swamp," so called because its islands are believed to be the ancestral home of the Aztecs) farther north in Nayarit. Mangroves reach about 20 feet in height and form dense thickets along muddy, salty shorelines and provide vital protective habitat for fish, shellfish and birds. In some areas, developers bulldoze mangrove jungles to create beaches.

The most common palm tree around Puerto Vallarta, the coconut palm is not native to the region but is widely grown in large plantations for its meat, milk and oil. It is also the most popular plant for landscaping at resort hotels because it's a romantic symbol of the tropics. Wild stands of coconut palms line many beaches because floating coconuts washed ashore there more than a hundred years ago.

Tropical flower gardens are easy to grow. Within Puerto Vallarta you'll find beautiful landscaping on the grounds of resorts, in the courtyards of smaller hotels and throughout residential areas. Among the most common garden plants is the hibiscus, which is native to the area, and comes in white, yellow, pink, lavender and orange hues as well as the familiar red. High in vitamin C, hibiscus flowers are edible and are commonly used in cooking and in making a colorful tea called *agua de jamaica*, as well as for medicinal purposes. Another showy garden flower, native to the region's thorn forests, is the *tabachín*, or Mexican bird of paradise.

Bougainvillea are native to Brazil but have grown wild in Mexico since they were first imported as ornamentals three centuries ago. Besides their common magenta color, they grow in bright purple, orange, yellow and white hues. Bougainvillea grow cyclically: every month or so they lose all their flowers and grow new leaves; then in another month they lose the leaves and grow new flowers. Another colorful imported flower that is an essential of every Puerto Vallarta garden is red ginger, native to Polynesia.

No tropical garden would be complete without avocados and mangos. The fruits of both trees were mainstays in the local diet long before the arrival of tourism. Avocados—*aguacate* in Spanish—are native to the region, while the Spanish imported mangos from South Asia in the

1600s. A major export crop, mangos are grown commercially in large orchards on the outskirts of Puerto Vallarta.

FAUNA

SEA CREATURES   Fish, shellfish and crustaceans were the main food of local people before the first tourists came to town, and today they also fill the menus at most Puerto Vallarta restaurants. The most common fish caught for food is the ideally meal-size *huachinango,* or red snapper. Also popular is the *dorado,* also called by its Hawaiian name, mahimahi, an iridescent green-gold fish that grows to about 30 pounds. Yellowfin (ahi) tuna, sought both for food and for sport, usually run 150 to 200 pounds; the largest tuna caught in Puerto Vallarta waters, in November 2005, was 382 pounds—just six pounds shy of the world record. Other good eating fish that local fishermen bring in for sale to restaurants include *sierra* (mackerel), *pargo manchado* (blackspot snapper), *cavilla* (amberjack), *aguaji* (grouper) and wahoo, which grow to prodigious size in Banderas Bay. While wahoo typically run 10 to 30 pounds, one specimen caught here in 2004 weighed in at 221 pounds.

Banderas Bay also has a great abundance of lobster and octopus, as well as large prawns and blue shrimp, crabs, squid, oysters, mussels and clams. All of these make their way to local restaurants.

Big-game billfish are abundant in the deep Middle American Trench, which starts west of Banderas Bay and runs south to Manzanillo and beyond. Striped marlin is found here from July through November, black marlin and blue marlin from August to November and March to April, and Pacific sailfish year-round. Blue marlin as large as 500 pounds have been caught in Puerto Vallarta waters; the world's record marlin—653 pounds—was caught in the same trench, 150 miles south of Puerto Vallarta near Manzanillo. Fishing charter operators encourage (and usually insist on) catch-and-release fishing to avoid depleting the sport fisheries they depend on for their livelihood. When you land a marlin or sailfish, the captain will measure it and photograph it, then submit the information to a taxidermist who will make an exact replica of the fish in fiberglass for your wall.

Among the most majestic denizens of Banderas Bay are giant manta rays, commonly seen by scuba divers at the popular dive sites of El Morro, Corbeteña, Sequial and Chimo, and sometimes encountered even in the shallow surf off the beach at Bucerias. These huge, solitary, graceful creatures average 22 feet wide; the largest reach 30 feet wide and weigh up to 3000 pounds. Although they are closely related to sharks, they are harmless, eating only plankton and small fish and crustaceans, which they funnel into their mouths using the two large flaplike lobes that protrude beside their mouths. They do not have teeth, nor do they have poisonous spines like some smaller rays.

Sharks are rarely encountered in Banderas Bay. Some fishermen claim this is because there are only a few channels where sharks can swim through the barrier of undersea mountains from the open ocean; this has evolved into a New Age theory that dolphins prevent sharks from entering the bay. In reality, though, sharks were abundant in the bay as recently as the 1940s, when large schools of sardines attracted the creatures. Shark fishing became profitable for locals when, during World War II, the U.S. Army added shark liver oil to meals for its combat troops as a dietary supplement and preservative. After the war, the fishermen sold shark fins to Chinese restaurants in the United States. By the early 1950s, the shark fishery in Banderas Bay was depleted. Why sharks have never returned to the area remains a mystery, especially since even larger ocean animals such as manta rays and even whales often enter the bay.

The ocean dwellers that attract the most interest from human wildlife watchers during the winter months are humpback whales. Migrating south from their feeding grounds off the coast of Alaska, Canada and the U.S. Pacific Northwest, they spend two to three months traveling down the coast to the Bay of Banderas, where they breed or give birth but do not eat. The reason for the migration is that newborn whale calves have only a very thin layer of blubber and would not be able to survive in the colder northern waters before they have fattened on mothers' milk. The first humpbacks arrive in mid-October and the last ones leave in mid-March, with the largest numbers during the last two weeks of January through the first two weeks of February. At least 300 whales visit the bay each winter, some staying only a day and others staying as long as five weeks. Whale watchers can often see the giant beasts breaking the water's surface in playful behaviors called breaching, fin and tail slapping and spy-hopping, and sometimes in dramatic courtship battles during which two to as many as eighteen male whales will push, shove and strike each other for the right to get close to a single female. A courtship battle can last for many hours before the strongest male drives off the competition and succeeds in breeding with the female.

Also spotted in Banderas Bay from time to time are ziphius and mesoplodons (beaked whales), both rare deep-water whales that feed on squid. The bay has a resident population of Pacific bottlenose dolphins. It is also visited by spotted dolphins and by spinner dolphins, the most acrobatic of all dolphin species.

BIRDS   The forests east and north of Puerto Vallarta have attained an international reputation as a great place for bird watching. Ornithologists in the region have confirmed 173 bird species as living in Puerto Vallarta year-round, while 180 more species migrate here for the winter.

Some of these species are the kind of rarities that serious birders come from far and wide in hope of glimpsing. For instance, Puerto Vallarta's mountains are one of the last sanctuaries of the large, spectacularly colored, endangered military macaw, and this is the only region where you can see a black-throated magpie jay. Among the many other exotic species are green jays, pygmy owls, snail kites, elegant trogons, crested guans, golden-cheeked woodpeckers, collared forest falcons, tropical kingbirds, crested caracaras, russet-crowned motmots, streak-backed orioles, rufous-bellied chachalacas, orange-fronted parakeets and numerous species of parrots and loros.

The Puerto Vallarta region boasts 15 species of hummingbirds. Some, such as broad-tailed, broad-billed, black-chinned and rufous hummingbirds, spend the summer in the western United States and migrate to the central Sierra Madre Occidental for the winter. Others—the calliope hummingbird, Costa's hummingbird, dusky hummingbird, green violet-ear hummingbird, cinnamon hummingbird, beryline hummingbird, white-eared hummingbird, amethyst-throated hummingbird, lucifer hummingbird, sparkling-tailed hummingbird and the tiny bumblebee hummingbird—are rare north of the border. Hummingbirds may appear anywhere in the PV area but are especially abundant in the remote pine-oak high country of the Sierra Madre, where they are attracted by the numerous species of trumpet-shaped flowers on whose nectar they feed.

As for large birds, the sierra above Puerto Vallarta is home to the golden eagle, known locally as the *aguilla real,* or royal eagle, which is revered by the Huichol Indians as a protector of the passageway between the earth and the spirit world and a guide for shamans. Its feathers are used in Huichol healing ceremonies. Another dark-colored, eagle-sized bird, which you're more likely to see on out-of-town driving tours, is the *zopilote,* or black vulture. Their presence is virtually constant along the region's highways, since their most important source of food is road kill. They can also be seen circling overhead for hours on end; you can recognize them because, unlike eagles, they hold their wings upswept into a V instead of straight across, rocking from side to side and rarely flapping their wings as they fly. These somewhat repulsive avian sanitation workers possess two remarkable superpowers: their amazingly keen eyesight lets them spot small rodents from up to two miles in the air, and their remarkable immune system can withstand 10,000 times the quantity of toxic bacteria that would cause a human to die of food poisoning.

Wading birds are common along all beaches, ponds and estuaries throughout the region. They include sandpipers, sanderlings, willets, whimbrells, oystercatchers, long-billed curlews, snowy egrets, green herons, cinnamon herons, boat-billed herons, yellow-crowned night herons, bare-throated tiger herons, white-faced ibis, roseate spoonbills and wood storks, among many others. Ponds and wetlands also play host to many kinds of endemic and migratory waterfowl such as masked ducks, Muscovy ducks, black-bellied whistling-ducks, least grebes and blue-winged teals.

Along the beach, you can hardly look skyward without glimpsing such sea birds as Heermann's gulls, royal terns, magnificent frigates and neotropic cormorants circling overhead, while brown pelicans skim along just above the water's surface. Serious birders will take the long boat trip out to the Marieta Islands at the mouth of the bay just to get a look at the rare blue-footed booby.

While you can while away whole days watching the birds anywhere in the Puerto Vallarta region, the area that birding enthusiasts from all over the world come to visit is an easy 100-mile drive to the north around the small town of San Blas (see Chapter Five).

The reptile you're most likely to see in the Puerto Vallarta area is the green iguana. In the forests, these large, plant-eating lizards are everywhere. Iguanas keep growing throughout their lives and typically reach lengths of four to six feet, though some grow to seven feet long. Young ones are bright green and have smooth backs. They change color with age, becoming grayer each time they shed their skins, and grow comblike serrations down their backs, giving them a strange, primeval look. The males have a flap of skin called a dewlap under their chins, which they can inflate, making themselves appear larger to intimidate predators or impress female iguanas. Although they sometimes bask on rocks in the sunshine, iguanas spend most of their time in the forest canopy, where tree leaves provide abundant food. They can dive into water from as high as 50 feet, and can fall to the ground from the same height without injury. Iguana meat was traditionally considered a delicacy in the Puerto Vallarta region, but they have now been declared an endangered species in Mexico, and it is illegal to kill them.

Much smaller and even more common are geckos, which you may see scrambling up the wall in even the fanciest hotel room. These tiny, fast lizards are believed to bring good luck, and that is certainly true if you're visiting Puerto Vallarta in the summer, when there are mosquitoes. Geckos emit occasional quick chirping sounds that attract mosquitoes, which they then catch and eat. A single gecko can keep a whole room insect-free.

There are 82 species of snakes found in coastal and forest areas of Jalisco and Nayarit. Of these, 15 are venomous to man, including the small but deadly fer-de-lance and the cascabel, or Mexican rattlesnake. Poisonous snakes have been pretty much eradicated from populated areas. It is possible to encounter a coral snake in a residential garden, but highly unlikely. Three species of these small, brightly banded snakes, differing in color, are native to the area. They are shy and reclusive, but their bite can be fatal. The yellow-bellied sea snake, which is occasionally seen offshore in isolated, rocky areas of Banderas Bay, can also inflict a painful or even fatal bite. Most snakes, though, from small garden snakes to boa constrictors, are benign and useful in the control of insects and rodents. When traveling in wild forest areas, remember that poisonous snakes do not attack humans. They swallow their food whole and can tell that you're too big to eat, so they will only use their venom against humans in self-defense. When snakes may be present, walk loudly and heavily and take care not to put your hands or feet where you can't see them (such as in holes, under rocks or in tall grass). If you do encounter a snake, don't try to scare it off with sticks or stones. Instead, keep a safe distance and retreat calmly.

Of the eight species of sea turtles that inhabit the world's oceans, the one that is most common in the Puerto Vallarta area is the *golfina* or olive Ridley sea turtle. Named for the color of its heart-shaped shell, it is a relatively small sea turtle, reaching about two-and-a-half feet in length and weighing 80 to 110 pounds. Other sea turtle species are also found here, including the Laud turtle, the largest of all turtle species. The turtles feed on shellfish, mollusks and fish, and can dive as deep as

500 feet in search of food. Female turtles nest up to three times per season at unpredictable intervals, laying about 100 eggs each time and leaving them buried in beach sand, where they take two months to hatch. The large number of eggs compensates for the fact that when they hatch, seabirds and other natural predators eat a large percentage of the baby turtles before they can make their way from their beach nests to the water. The turtle population is now in decline, though, because humans in Mexico have long considered sea turtle meat and eggs as delicacies and because they tend to get caught up in fishermen's nets. The Mexican government prohibits any harvesting or endangering of sea turtles or their eggs and has established a conservation program to protect key nesting areas along the coast, putting them off-limits during the June-to-December nesting season. The Puerto Vallarta Sea Turtle Conservation Program coordinates the activities of volunteer groups and resorts to protect the turtles. For instance, the Marriott in Nuevo Vallarta protects the turtles against danger from its guests' recreational activities by hiring specialized staff members to patrol the beach every night and collect the eggs, taking them to a protected hatchery where they are reburied in the sand. The hotel boasts that 87 percent of the eggs hatch—more than twice the number that would survive in nature—and that they release 12,000 baby turtles into the sea each year. Several local tour companies offer nighttime "turtle camp" tours of the nesting area and hatchery.

The most spectacular of the reptile species living in the Puerto Vallarta area is the river crocodile. One of the oldest surviving vertebrate species on earth, these crocodiles are more closely related to birds and dinosaurs than to alligators (which aren't found in western Mexico), iguanas or other lizard species. Compared to alligators, crocodiles are larger and more gray than green in color, with narrower, more pointed heads and long, sharp teeth that are visible even when their mouths are fully closed. Their backs are covered with armorlike plates. They live in freshwater estuaries and rivers, though they also are sometimes seen in golf course water hazards and on remote beaches along the Banderas Bay coast. Young crocodiles eat large quantities of insects, worms and leeches; as they mature, they hunt amphibians, birds, fish and mammals. They can swim or run quite fast, but they spend most of their time motionless. They can close their nostrils as well as their eyes and remain completely submerged underwater for up to an hour at a time. They can grow to lengths of up to 20 feet, though the record for a crocodile encountered in the Banderas Bay area is 13 feet. Your best opportunity to see full-grown crocodiles up close is the Cocodrilario, or crocodile preserve, located on a back road south of San Blas (see Chapter Five).

MAMMALS Since hunting is extremely restricted in Mexico, the main threat to mammal species is habitat destruction due to logging and agriculture. Because the mountains above Puerto Vallarta are sparsely populated and mostly roadless, they are home to an abundance of animal life. One-fifth of all mammal species in the area are found only in this region—mostly unique kinds of mice, rats, shrews and bats. Other mammals of the sierra include common North American forest animals such as raccoons, skunks, badgers, foxes, rabbits, squirrels, coyotes and white-tailed deer.

Although visitors are unlikely to glimpse one, the wilderness of the Sierra Madre in Jalisco and Nayarit is one of the last refuges in Mexico for the jaguar, or *tigre*, the largest, most majestic and mysterious jungle predator in Latin America. This and other wild cats, including pumas and the much smaller ocelots, jaguarundi and margay cats, are reclusive and nocturnal, but visitors to high mountain areas may hear a jaguar's roar or the blood-curdling scream of a puma or ocelot in the night. Jaguars and pumas, as well as deer, are key symbols in the shamanic tradition of the Huichol Indians who live in remote parts of the Sierra. The deer represents the shaman's spirit guide; eating peyote allows him (or her) to transform into a jaguar and hunt his own deer spirit. The puma is the guardian of the shaman's vows, and if he fails to keep those vows the puma will eat his spirit.

One of the most common mammals of the sierra, the nine-banded armadillo digs holes in the ground at the rate of several a day to unearth insects and worms to feed on as well as for shelter. Many other animals and birds make their homes in abandoned armadillo holes. This slow-moving creature with its hard shell of armor can curl up into a ball for protection from predators. Unfortunately, this protection is ineffective against cars and trucks, so armadillos are the most commonly seen road kill along the highways of Jalisco.

Other mammals that live in the sierra include *javelinas*, or collared peccaries, piglike animals that travel in groups; though they are vegetarians, they can attack people with their sharp tusks when upset. Coatimundis (known locally as *tejón* or *pisote*), long-nosed, sleek relatives of the raccoon, live in trees and descend at night to search for food ranging from fruit to eggs, lizards and insects. With a reputation for mischievousness and little fear of humans, they are often kept as house pets in Mexico.

Monkeys are rare in the forests above Puerto Vallarta since Jalisco is at the extreme northern edge of the habitat range; however, black-handed spider monkeys are occasionally spotted. Their presence is unmistakable, as they make loud rustling sounds when moving through the treetops.

INSECTS Puerto Vallarta itself is relatively mosquito-free during the dry winter season, but the rainy season is another story. Though mosquitoes don't like salt water and thus are rarely encountered on the beach, they can be a problem in the jungle at any time of year, so it's advisable to wear long sleeves and pants and take along insect repellent when going on a canopy tour, forest horseback ride or bird-watching expedition. What works for one person may not work for someone else. People who wish to avoid DEET, the active chemical in most commercial mosquito repellents, may want to investigate other methods. Herb shops and health food stores sell good-smelling and more or less effective insect protection lotions made from oils and herbal essences. Tests have found herbal repellents made with citronella (which is also contained in Avon's Skin-So-Soft lotion) to be about as effective as DEET but not nearly as long-lasting. Some people swear by daily doses of vitamin B or garlic, others by baby lotion or tobacco smoke. In San Blas, where tiny, ferocious biting gnats called *jejenes*, or no-see-ums, are a way of life, locals swear that you can make the most effective repellent by mixing 20 to 30 drops of pennyroyal extract (available at herb shops in the U.S. and Mexico) into a two-ounce bottle of commercial DEET product. It smells better and works wonders. Pennyroyal will boost the effectiveness of citronella, too.

Of course, if you find a mosquito net above your bed in a hotel room, there must be a good reason for it, so use it. Another trick I've found effective to keep mosquitoes at bay during the night is, soon after dark, to turn off all lights in the hotel room except the light in the closet and leave them that way for at least half an hour. Mosquitoes and other flying insects will be attracted to the light. Then shut the closet door, trapping them inside, and make sure all windows and doors in the room remain closed.

Speaking of biting bugs, outside the city it's not uncommon to encounter a tarantula or scorpion. In fact, it's almost impossible to take a long road trip without seeing a tarantula crossing the highway in front of you. These huge, hairy spiders are not deadly, just scary if you dislike spiders. Their bite is as painful as a bumblebee sting, but no more life-threatening. The good news is that tarantulas will not bite people except under extreme provocation. Mexican kids sometimes keep them as pets and handle them fearlessly. Scorpions are another matter. Their bites can sometimes be fatal. There are many theories holding that big scorpions, small scorpions, light-colored scorpions or dark-colored scorpions pack the most poison, but nobody really knows. When staying in lodgings outside the city, take the simple precautions of shaking your shoes out before putting them on and being cautious about turning over rocks.

Most other insects of the region are merely colorful or strange. In the first category are the thousands of varieties of butterflies you're likely to see any time you drive along country roads or hike, bike or ride horseback in the forest. In the latter category are several varieties of huge beetles, including four-inch-long elephant beetles, the largest in Mexico, and bomber beetles, which defend themselves by firing small shots of a noxious-tasting substance with a loud bang.

OUTDOOR ADVENTURES

Even if you don't spend a single hour sunbathing on Puerto Vallarta's legendary beaches, you can count on returning home tanned to a deep bronze or, if you're less cautious on the early days of your trip, fried to a flaming red. Just about everything there is to do in Puerto Vallarta, except for dining, dancing and shopping for art, happens outdoors.

Outdoor recreation in and around Puerto Vallarta falls into two broad categories: resort sports, which require specialized water sports equipment provided by your hotel or rented at the beach, and backcountry adventures, which generally involve taking guided tours. Although foot trails lead practically everywhere, it's still fairly rare for visitors to venture into the mountains on their own, partly because few trails are mapped and partly because the heat and rugged terrain make hiking a less attractive option than renting a mountain bike or horse, both of which usually come with a guide to make sure you don't get lost.

Although the whole concept of renting personal property is strange to people in most parts of Mexico, entrepreneurs in and around Puerto Vallarta have long since discovered that renting bicycles, sea kayaks, scuba equipment, wave runners, jet skis, golf clubs and just about any other toys your heart may desire can be a profitable business. Rentals are available at Playa del Muerto, the main city beach, as well as at Marina Vallarta and all resort hotels (though most resorts give guests priority in renting motorized water sports equipment and, especially at all-inclusive resorts, may reserve nonmotorized equipment for guests' use only). Tour operators, especially the big, diversified tour company Vallarta Adventures, provide every kind of equipment imaginable as part of their trips.

If your plans involve boldly going where no tourist has gone before—the forest wilderness of the Sierra Madre, the swampy lagoons of Nayarit or the last undiscovered beach on the Riviera Nayarit—keep in mind that backcountry recreation is not the common pastime in Mexico that it is in the United States, so amenities like trail maps, trailheads and campgrounds just don't exist in these areas. Ask at the nearest hotel and you will have no trouble finding a freelance guide who can take you wherever you want to go and outfit you with the equipment you may need.

CAMPING

Tent camping is by no means the organized activity that it is up north. Most camping in Mexico takes place in a handful of national parks as well as in roadside RV parks, which in this area are usually attached to small hotels.

The most tempting places to camp are beaches. Beach camping is not permitted, nor is it safe, within the Puerto Vallarta metropolitan area. Some beaches along some bays south of Puerto Vallarta along the Costa Alegre offer wonderful camping, as does the beach near Sayulita. By law, all beaches in Mexico are public, but foreshore rights are privately owned—not necessarily by the same people who own the land adjacent to the beach—and often give resorts or other private owners the power to block public access to beaches. On favored tent camping beaches, someone may come around to collect a few pesos from you for the right to camp there. If a beach is empty and no other tents are pitched there, it's best to ask at the nearest village or lodging whether camping is permitted there.

Many beach campers prefer to eschew tents and sleeping bags in favor of hammocks strung under existing palapas. There used to be public palapas on many remote beaches for use by fishermen spending the night away from their villages. Many of them have now been destroyed to prevent long-term squatters from occupying the beach. If you discover an unused palapa, the same rule applies as for tent camping: ask around to find out whether it's okay to camp there. And if you decide to stay under a palapa that doesn't look like it's been used for a while, be sure to beat the roof soundly with a stick before hanging your hammock. Palm thatched roofs are a favorite hiding place for scorpions.

FISHING

Banderas Bay and the Middle American Trench, which runs from just outside the mouth of the bay south to Manzanillo, enjoy a world wide reputation for great fishing. The bay teems with red snapper, blackspot snapper, dorado, yellowfin tuna, mackerel, amberjack, grouper, wahoo and roosterfish, while in the trench beyond the bay some of the best marlin, sailfish and tuna fishing anywhere awaits. In general, the best fishing is during the months when the water is warmest, from April through November. Fishing licenses are required for all freshwater and saltwater fishing in Mexican waters, and every person, including minors, who is aboard a vessel where anyone is fishing must have his or her own fishing license. Either a Mexican fishing license or a valid U.S. saltwater fishing license will do. One-day fishing licenses can be issued by charter boat operators and cost US$12 per couple. No license is required for fishing from shore.

In ocean waters and estuaries, there is a daily ten-fish limit, with no more than five fish of a single species, except that only one marlin, sailfish, swordfish or shark and two dorado, shad, tarpon or roosterfish can be caught in a single day, and each of these species counts as five fish toward the ten-fish daily limit. There is no limit on catch-and-release fishing.

HUNTING

The Puerto Vallarta area attracts some duck, dove and quail hunters, but it's hardly worth the hassle. Since firearms are rigidly controlled in Mexico, burdensome restrictions apply. A permit to bring a rifle or shotgun into Mexico requires an official letter from your local police or sheriff's office certifying that you have no criminal record, along with eight passport-size photos of yourself for each gun. Firearms must be brought into Mexico with the trigger under seal, which can only be broken by a licensed hunting outfitter who is also responsible for resealing it after each use. You can only bring in 50 rifle or shotgun shells per weapon, limited to two weapons. Non-Mexicans can only hunt when physically accompanied by a registered local guide. The cost of hunting licenses for waterfowl, quail or other birds is about US$450 each. Applications for hunting licenses and firearm permits are time-consuming and complicated, and they must be taken care of before you head into Mexico. Once you cross the border with a gun or ammunition, it's too late to apply for a permit; if you don't already have one, you go directly to jail. All in all, it's better to forget the idea of a Mexican hunting trip and carry binoculars and a camera instead.

The Puerto Vallarta region is not known as a scuba diving destination, primarily because the rivers that flow down from the Sierra Madre into Banderas Bay often make the water murky near shore. But many diving enthusiasts are pleased to discover that the bay not only provides habitat for a great diversity of colorful tropical fish species but also offers unique undersea rock formations to explore, including coral reefs, sea caves and sheer rock walls that drop off thousands of feet. You might think that such depths would make no difference, since most human scuba divers descend to maximum depths of less than 100 feet. When ocean currents meet these virtually bottomless cliffs, though, they can create upward flows that carry strange, rarely seen sea life from great depths.

The most popular dive site in the bay is Los Arcos Marine Reserve, close to shore and just south of town. More remote, less crowded sites include Las Marietas Federal Marine Reserve, El Morro and Corbeteña. More information on these sights can be found in the Outdoor Adventures section of Chapter Four.

There are numerous dive shops in and around Puerto Vallarta and Manzanillo, and dive excursions can be arranged through the tour desk at any resort hotel. Scuba divers must have proof of certification. Those who aren't certified can take a short series of classes called a "resort course" at the larger hotels and qualify for easy guided scuba trips; some all-inclusive resorts include a free introductory scuba lesson in their swimming pool as part of the package. Diving lessons and excursions are not cheap, but if you savor beauty and mystery, skip a few movies back home and catch this show.

Snorkeling is another diving option that costs little or nothing, requires no certification and offers a view of at least the uppermost layer of the underwater world. It lets you float gently on the surface while viewing what lies below for extended periods of time. You can dive to depths of ten feet or so and stay submerged for as long as you can hold your breath, and even this limited experience can reveal a marvelous new world you can't see from above the water's surface. Snorkeling also works well in combination with sea kayaking, giving you access to uncrowded waters farther offshore or down the coast. Most all-inclusive resorts include complimentary use of snorkels, masks and fins as part of their packages, and some offer free shuttles to popular snorkeling areas such as Los Arcos.

The waves in most of Banderas Bay don't come big enough to support surfing, though Punta de Mita and some sheltered reefs far from resort areas have long peeling or barreling waves in the winter months. Surfers usually head north to Sayulita, where the surfing is said to be some of the best on the Pacific coast of North America. In summer, there is also great surfing at nearby San Pancho as well as farther up the Nayarit coastline around Chacala and Santa Cruz. With water temperatures around 75° to 78°F in the winter and 80° in the summer, wet suits are not needed.

Windsurfing is a popular activity in Banderas Bay. Many all-inclusive beach resorts in Puerto Vallarta and Nuevo Vallarta make sailboards available to guests at no charge. The best windsurfing is along the northern beaches around Punta de Mita, where sailboards can be rented from local entrepreneurs on the beach. Kiteboarding, a relatively new sport that involves using a parafoil-like kite to tow a surfer on a snowboard-like board and, with skill and a little luck, lift him or her into the air, is gaining in popularity around Puerto Vallarta. A major international kiteboarding competition is held in Puerto Vallarta at the end of June and beginning of July.

OCEAN SAFETY

The waters of Banderas Bay invite swimming, boating, scuba diving, fishing, kayaking, windsurfing and other recreational activities. The surf on the inner bay is usually gentle, but the same is not true of beaches outside the bay. Less than an hour to the north, for instance, the beach at Sayulita is famous for its big, rolling waves. Whether you're out for a morning swim, a day of sport fishing or a kayak expedition, it is prudent to be conscious of the ocean's risks. High winds off the ocean can bring big swells, overpowering waves and, in some places, treacherous undertows. Rip currents threaten open sections of the coast. These sudden, strong currents can be spotted by their ragged-looking surface water and foamy edges. They can drag you out to sea. If you get caught in one, don't panic and struggle against it or try to swim straight for shore; instead, free yourself from its inexorable pull toward the open water by swimming parallel to the shore until you have escaped the current, then swim in diagonally.

When swimming, remember that nature is in charge. In the ocean, conditions can change from good to bad in a matter of minutes. Erratic currents and powerful waves contain hidden pitfalls that can be avoided with a little awareness. Waves can be deceptive. They come in varying sets: one set may consist of seven small waves followed by seven big ones; or seven big waves followed by one calm swell; or a series of small waves overshadowed by a big, angry swell. If you get caught in a wave about to crash you onto the shore, try to roll up and tumble with it rather than thrashing against it. Remember that waves grow bigger and more surly during the full moon. Stay alert and never turn your back to the sea.

Above all, when you go swimming, use common sense in judging safety conditions. Strong surf, steep dropoffs at the tide line, whirlpools and eddies around rocky areas all signal danger. If in doubt, don't go. Avoid swimming alone.

There are also risks from sea creatures. Sharks are not common around Puerto Vallarta, and stingrays are sometimes reported but rarely cause injuries. (Still, it's not a bad idea to walk on shallow, sandy sea floors near shore with a "stingray shuffle," moving your feet forward through the sand instead of stepping downward, so that on the off chance you do cross paths with a stingray, it will scoot off to safety.) Porcupine fish, often seen around stands of coral in Banderas Bay, puff up when threatened, causing the bony inch-long spines that cover their bodies to stand straight out, and are sometimes rumored to inflict venomous stings, but this has never been proven; more likely, the belief comes from confusing them with puffer fish (also found in these waters), which are deadly poisonous if eaten without proper preparation but do not cause poisonous bites or stings. Divers on undersea walls around Puerto Vallarta must be watchful for moray eels, which can be aggressive, biting and holding on tenaciously. They are not poisonous, though. Yellow-bellied sea snakes, on the other hand, are venomous but not aggressive.

Jellyfish and sea urchins cause by far the most injuries from sea creatures in the Puerto Vallarta area. The common jellyfish around here look like small, transparent, squishy globules with blue on the bottom edge and a single long, thin tentacle that stings very painfully. A favorite food of sea turtles, jellyfish are not around all the time, and when they are they tend to travel in swarms. A simple precaution is to watch for any that may have washed up on the shore and, if you see them, avoid going in the water. Sea urchins are hard-shelled, round, black echinoderms with long, sharp spines, used for protection and locomotion, which can inflict painful stings. Neither jellyfish nor sea urchins are aggressive (they don't have brains), but if you come in contact with either one, you won't forget the experience. Soaking the affected area in very hot water for 15 to 90 minutes will draw the toxin out. Another remedy is to apply undiluted vinegar, ammonia or even urine. If these preliminary treatments don't work, consult a doctor.

Beware of sunburn, the trickiest ailment of the tropics. Tan slowly and use plenty of sunscreen on sensitive areas: lips, nose, shoulders, even the tops of your feet. Nude sunbathing is against the law in Mexico, and women sunbathing topless is not allowed on Puerto Vallarta beaches. To bask in the buff, head for a beach on a remote bay where there are no local people in sight, or, better yet, pick one of the few Puerto Vallarta resort hotels that has a clothing-optional rooftop sundeck.

If you do get a sunburn, you can get relief by using cool compresses soaked in equal parts water and milk. Aspirin also helps, and over-the-counter steroid creams sold in Mexican pharmacies can provide relief in serious cases. A cool bath also helps. Don't use bath oil, bath salts or bubble bath, though a half-cup of cooked oatmeal dissolved in the bathwater is soothing. Aloe vera, either directly from the plant or in a commercial cream, works wonders. A light moisturizer or baby powder will ease the discomfort of wearing clothes over a sunburn. Most important, stay out of the sun until the sunburn is completely gone. If the sunburn is severe, with bright red color and blisters, fever, chills, faintness or nausea, see a doctor immediately.

HISTORY
AND
CULTURE

More than almost any other place in Mexico, Puerto Vallarta is a cultural melting pot. An unfortunate history of brutal conquistadors and Indian resistance prevented large-scale colonization of the region for centuries, even after contact with seafarers brought diseases that wiped out the entire coastal Indian population. "Modern civilization" in the form of roads, electricity, telecommunications and such put in its appearance at isolated Banderas Bay only within the past generation or so. Since then, the influx of people to Puerto Vallarta has created a kaleidoscopic, multicultural population of Mexicans from many distinct regions of the country, some of the most traditional Indians in the Americas, part-time snowbirds and full-time expatriates from the United States and Canada, a lively international arts scene and a vibrant gay community. It's the people and their heritage, as much as the beaches, that make Puerto Vallarta a one-of-a-kind resort area.

HISTORY

As the heartland of western Mexico, the state of Jalisco relates to the rest of the country in much the same way that the American West does to the mainstream of United States culture. Isolated from the capital by distance, rough terrain, historical accident and violent confrontations with the native people, it was settled much later in history and developed its own unique character, symbolized by *charros* (cowboys), mariachis and tequila, achieving a mythical quality that is fundamental to the national identity today.

ANCIENT ONES   While American Indians almost certainly inhabited the Puerto Vallarta area and the rest of west central Mexico for at least 10,000 years, they lived lightly on the land and left no traces until around 200 B.C. This date has been ascribed to the earliest shaft tombs discovered in the Sierra Madre in what are now the states of Jalisco, Nayarit and Colima.

The people of the mountains and forests at that time lived in villages of wood huts with palm thatch roofs, now long vanished in the tropical climate. The only vestiges of their culture are the shaft tombs in which important people, probably tribal leaders or rulers, were buried.

The shaft tombs that have been unearthed at sites throughout the Sierra, including the Valle de Banderas and Mascota areas, are similar to those made around the same time in the mountains of Colombia and Ecuador and much earlier in Egypt's Old Kingdom (2686–2181 B.C.) and Mycenae in Greece (1650–1500 B.C.), though the Mexican ones tend to be deeper than those found in the Old World. They were dug down vertically to depths of 15 to 60 feet beneath the earth's surface, with one or several burial chambers excavated horizontally at the bottom. The chambers often contained entire families and sometimes their servants and dogs, along with funerary pots, plates and utensils, tools, weaponry and hollow clay figures depicting humans and dogs.

Burial goods found in Jalisco tombs contain many statuettes with distinctively long faces and prominent noses. In Colima, there are many naturalistic terracotta sculptures of people with Chinese-looking features, as well as unique statues of dogs at play, examples of which can be seen in Puerto Vallarta's Museo Arqueológico. In Nayarit, tombs often contained clay figurines of emaciated shamans—medicine men who fasted before rituals in which they crossed over to the spirit world for purposes such as healing, foretelling the future or finding lost items.

The last known shaft tombs date back to about A.D. 400. Except for the cryptic clues from contents of these tombs, nothing is known about the ancient people who made them, including whether they were ancestors of the Indians who lived in the region much later or whether they simply vanished. Archaeologists in the mid-20th century theorized the existence of a single widespread "shaft tomb culture," but because of the artistic differences between treasures unearthed in different areas, the theory has been rejected. Today the people that made the shaft tombs are referred to simply as the Nayarit Culture, the Jalisco Culture and the Colima Culture.

AZTLÁN   Around A.D. 1350, migratory people who became known as Aztecs migrated to Mexico's central valley. They settled on an island in the middle of a lake (now drained and filled) where modern Mexico City now stands. The warlike Aztecs achieved military dominance over the other native people of the central highlands and established a trade empire that reached from the Yucatán Peninsula to the northern desert.

Mexican legend says the Aztecs originally came from an island in the mythical land of Aztlán ("Place of the Herons"). Mexican Americans living in the U.S. today use the name Aztlán to refer to the land taken by the U.S. after the Mexican War in the 1840s—now New Mexico, Arizona and California. However, it seems unlikely that the name would be given to such an arid desert region. Although there is no archaeological evidence, Mexican schoolchildren learn that Aztlán was located in the coastal wetlands of Nayarit on an island called Mexcaltitán, less than a day's drive north of Puerto Vallarta. The Aztec language, Nahuatl, was a dialect of the Uto-Aztecan language group and closely related to that spoken by the Huichol people of Nayarit today.

Though they built the most powerful empire in Mexican history, the Aztecs could not control the Jalisco and Nayarit region, which included their ancient homeland, or even establish trade there. Their enemies, the fierce Purepecha (later called Tarascan) people who lived around

Lake Patzcuaro, stood between the Aztecs and the western lands. The Purepechas defeated the Aztecs in a prolonged war in 1479. As a result, the Indians of the Sierra Madre Occidental and the central Pacific coast remained isolated from the Aztec empire.

CONQUISTADORS AND NAVIGATORS The seminomadic people of Jalisco and Nayarit did not know about Spanish conquistador Hernán Cortés' arrival on the coast of the Gulf of Mexico in 1519. The story of Cortés' conquest is familiar to every Mexican student today: the Aztecs offered Cortés gifts of gold to go away and leave them in peace, but instead Cortés and his 500 men with horses, armor, steel swords and firearms marched on the center of the Aztec empire, Tenochtitlán, an island city of more than 300,000 people—the size of Rome at the time. Aztec ruler Moctezuma welcomed Cortés as a guest in his palace, believing him to be a descendant of the god Quetzalcoatl, but Cortés took Moctezuma hostage and tried to rule the Aztec empire through him.

In 1520, Cortés received word that the governor of Cuba, whom Cortés had defied by invading Mexico on his own, was sending another conquistador, Panfilo de Narvaéz, to arrest Cortés and take his place. Cortés set out for the coast to arrest Narvaéz, leaving Pedro de Alvarado in command of Tenochtitlán. Alvarado massacred many Aztecs during Cortés' absence, and soon after his return the Indians revolted and attacked the Spaniards, killing many and driving the rest off the island. Moctezuma was killed in the battle. His son, Cuauhtémoc, became emperor.

In 1521, Cortés laid siege to Tenochtitlán and, after three months, regained control of the city, imprisoning Cuauhtémoc. His troops demolished much of the Aztec city and, in its place, built Mexico City, which he envisioned as the capital of colonial Nueva España, or New Spain. Toward that end, he dispatched expeditions to assert control over the rest of Mexico.

In 1522, Cortés sent his loyal lieutenant, Gonzalo de Sandoval, to explore the Pacific coast and establish a shipbuilding port. The spot Sandoval picked was Playa de la Audencia, about 150 miles south of Banderas Bay. He spent a year there building ships and then sailed forth with his enlarged navy force to conquer the Philippines.

Two years later, Cortés sent his nephew, Francisco Cortés de Buenaventura, to continue exploring the Pacific coast. The younger Cortés landed at the site of present-day Puerto Vallarta, seeking to replenish his ship's supplies of food, water and wood. More than 18,000 natives awaited him and his crew. They displayed colored cloth banners ("*banderas,*" giving Banderas Bay its name) streaming from the tips of their bows and spears. Although his men numbered fewer than 100, Cortés brazenly demanded that the Indians surrender. They refused.

According to Cortés' official report, as he and his men prepared for battle, a monk on his ship led them in prayer to the Virgin Mary. The monk carried a flag bearing the image of the virgin, which was suddenly lit by a beam of heavenly light—whereupon both sides fell back in amazement and abandoned the confrontation. Cortés and his men beat a hasty retreat. Some people claim this legend is why the Virgin Mary was declared the patron saint of Puerto Vallarta centuries later.

GUZMÁN AND THE INDIAN WARS   Political treachery in Mexico City set into motion a chain of unfortunate events that would keep western Mexico isolated for nearly two centuries. Soon after sending his nephew to explore the Pacific coast, Hernán Cortés himself led an expedition eastward to Oaxaca, Guatemala and Honduras. He took Aztec emperor Cuauhtémoc along, fearing that the puppet ruler of the Aztecs would lead an insurrection in his absence, and later hanged him for treason.

Cortés was gone for two years. He and the remnants of his expeditionary force came straggling back to Mexico City in 1526 to find that his enemies had spread the word that he was dead. Unable to regain his position as military ruler of Mexico, Cortés withdrew to his hacienda while the usurpers of his power sent complaints back to Charles V, King of Spain and Holy Roman Emperor, charging him with atrocities against the Indians. Finally, in 1528, Cortés returned to Spain to face the charges (he was absolved) and request that he be named governor of New Spain (his request was refused, though he was dubbed Marquis of Oaxaca).

While Charles V summoned Cortés to Spain, an *audencia* (court of justice) was put in charge of New Spain. Two of the four members of the court died under mysterious circumstances, leaving the country in the hands of its surviving members—Bishop Zumárraga and lawyer Nuño Beltrán de Guzmán. The two men were very different: Zumárraga was committed to protecting the Indians, while Guzmán capitalized on his new position as head of the *audencia* by becoming the de facto dictator of New Spain, selling Indians into slavery and seizing the estates of Cortés' supporters.

Ultimately, Bishop Zumárraga managed to smuggle a letter complaining of Guzmán's misdeeds to Emperor Charles V, who immediately sent a new *audencia* to remove Guzmán from office and have him excommunicated. When Guzmán heard of their impending arrival, he embezzled funds from the colonial treasury and hastily mounted an expedition of 300 soldiers and 10,000 Indian slaves to "pacify" the largely unexplored interior of western Mexico (even though, except for Francisco Cortés de Buenaventura's confrontation at Banderas Bay, there had been no conflict with the western natives up to that time).

Guzmán established a fort and town which he named Guadalajara after his birthplace in Spain. He declared Guadalajara the capital of a new, unauthorized Spanish colony, Nuevo Galicia, which encompassed the modern-day Pacific coast states of Jalisco, Nayarit and Sinaloa. There he doled out vast land grants called *economiendos* to himself and his officers and proceeded to slaughter or enslave the Indians who lived on these lands. His exploits earned him the nickname Guzmán Sangriento ("Bloody Guzmán") and a legacy as the most despicable villain in Mexican history.

The Chichimac people, the only warlike Indians in the area, repeatedly raided Guadalajara, forcing Guzmán to move his capital to different locations twice, taking the name with it. Although each of his three capitals was called Guadalajara, none was at the site of present-day downtown Guadalajara.

Guzmán's retaliation against the Chichimacs was ruthless and massive. He ordered that all the Indians in the province be rounded up, branded as slaves, and divided between his estates and those of his supporters.

When Franciscan missionaries arrived in Nuevo Galicia to convert the Indians, they found a rising tide of hostility and learned of Guzmán's reign of terror. They reported Guzmán's brutality to his archrival, Bishop Zumárraga, who arranged for a military force to go to Guadalajara for the purpose of arresting him. Hearing this, Guzmán responded by assembling his army and hastily embarking on another "expedition," but he was intercepted, captured and brought back to Mexico City. Ultimately sent to Spain to stand trial on charges of cruelty to Indians, he died in prison.

The Viceroy of New Spain annexed New Galicia and in 1538 appointed a new governor, Francisco Vasquez de Coronado, the husband of the colonial treasurer's daughter and one of the wealthiest men in New Spain. Soon after taking office, however, Coronado applied to the Viceroy for authorization to make an expedition to the north to investigate rumors of wealthy Indian cities in what is now New Mexico. In 1540, he set out from New Galicia with 300 soldiers, 1000 Indian laborers and enormous herds of livestock.

Coronado would ultimately find that the "seven cities of Cibola" he sought were merely poor adobe pueblos of the Zuni people and that their treasure was nonexistent. Although he would earn a place in history by exploring the American Southwest from the Grand Canyon to Kansas, he would straggle back to Guadalajara with less than one-third of his original followers and, worse yet, no gold. The Viceroy would declare his expedition a total failure.

Coronado's expedition had taken virtually all the soldiers stationed in Nuevo Galicia, leaving the province defenseless. With Bloody Guzmán's brutality still fresh in his mind, Caxana Indian leader Tenamaxtli organized an uprising intended to drive the Spanish settlers out of western Mexico. This rebellion would be called the Mixtón War.

When the viceroy in Mexico City received news that Tenamaxtli and his warriors had captured several towns in Jalisco, including the capital, he sent an army under the command of aging conquistador Pedro de Alvarado (remembered in history for losing the Aztec city of Tenochtitlán in Cortés' absence and later conquering Guatemala) to fight the Indians. The army arrived just in time to retake Guadalajara in a decisive victory over the Indians. Alvarado himself was killed in the fighting.

When Coronado returned from his expedition in 1542, he resumed his post as governor and moved the town of Guadalajara once more, this time to the location of present-day downtown Guadalajara, where he held office for two more years. Peace would not last, though. In 1850, the Chichimeca people of northern Jalisco rose up against the Spanish in a guerrilla insurgency known as the Chichimeca War. The violence, as well as the rugged terrain of the Sierra Madre, put a stop to Spanish colonization of the area for the next 40 years.

The Chichimeca War ended with a whimper as the majority of the Indians in Jalisco died in epidemics of measles, smallpox, diphtheria, influenza, scarlet fever, typhoid, mumps and other European diseases to which they had no natural immunity. Along the coast, particularly in the heavily populated region around Banderas Bay, virtually all the Indians died. In the end, the Viceroy sent thousands of Nahuatl-speaking Indians from central Mexico to re-colonize Jalisco and serve "as a frontier militia and a civilizing influence." By the year 1600, all the native tribes of Jalisco except the remote, isolated Huichols had vanished as distinguishable cultural entities.

FIRST COASTAL SETTLEMENTS   In 1541, launching his campaign in the Mixtón War, conquistador Pedro de Alvarado chose Banderas Bay as the place to disembark his army for the trip across the mountains to Guadalajara. He named the spot where he landed Las Penas ("The Rocks"), referring to the formation now known as Los Arcos. Although several Spanish explorers over the following years proposed establishing towns on Banderas Bay, no permanent town would be built there for another three centuries.

In 1644, Bernardo Bernal de Pinadero set up a small shipyard in the vicinity of present-day Mismaloya. Using timber from the lush hardwood forest of the Sierra Madre, it produced only two ships before it was abandoned. Over the centuries, Spanish galleons, pirate ships, fishing vessels and whalers all used Banderas Bay for shelter from tropical storms, as a place to forage for supplies and sometimes to hide from their enemies.

The first permanent port on the central Pacific coast was established a hundred miles to the north at San Blas, Nayarit, in 1768. The same year, Father Junipero Serra set out from San Blas on his northward journey to establish missions on the California coast, including the original settlements at San Diego, Los Angeles and San Francisco. San Blas soon grew to a population of 30,000.

In 1825, another port and shipyard was established 150 miles the south of Banderas Bay on Bahía Santiago de la Buena Esperanza. The port was named Manzanillo, and the name of the bay was changed to that of the city.

In the Sierra Madre east of Banderas Bay, another large population center had appeared. The discovery of silver and gold in the mountains gave rise to the isolated town of San Sebastián del Oeste, which become one of the major mining centers of Mexico and grew to 40,000 people. At Banderas Bay, ships from San Blas unloaded supplies, construction materials and huge quantities of salt needed for refining precious metals, all of which were carried overland to San Sebastián and the other mining towns of the Sierra. A small makeshift port, consisting of palm-thatched lean-tos to provide shade, was located along the beach of Banderas Bay.

In 1851, trader Don Guadalupe Sánchez Torres, who was in the business of transporting salt for the mines from San Blas in his small boat, decided to move his family into a hut he built on Playa del Muerto, the site of present-day Puerto Vallarta's Zona Romántica. Little by little, other traders, farmers and ranchers arrived and the settlement grew to around 1500 people. The new town was named Puerto Las Peñas de Santa María de Guadalupe. "Las Peñas" came from Pedro de Alvarado's name for his landing site. Taking Santa María de Guadalupe as the town's patron saint may be due in part to the legend of the miraculous apparition of the Virgin that prevented a battle between Francisco Cortés de Buena ventura and the local Indians back in 1524; a more likely explanation is that Don Guadalupe's family arrived to occupy their new home on December 12, 1851—the feast day of the Virgin of Guadalupe.

FISHING VILLAGE Pirates are said to have raided Puerto Las Peñas from time to time in the hope of stealing shipments of gold and silver shipments from the mines of San Sebastián, though nobody seems to know the specifics of these attacks. The rest of the time, the village slumbered in the tropical sun.

The Mexican government officially opened Puerto Las Peñas to international shipping in 1885 and established a customs house there. In 1888, a fire destroyed half the town; firefighting was hampered because most of the men were away attending a cockfight at the time. Five years later, a tsunami washed away much of the newly rebuilt town.

Puerto Las Peñas never developed into a busy port because in 1889 a railroad was completed between Mexico City and Colima, the capital of the state south of Jalisco. The rail terminus was a short trip from Manzanillo, making it far easier to transport goods to the interior from Manzanillo than from Banderas Bay. The railroad would be finished all the way to Manzanillo 20 years later.

On May 31, 1918, following the end of the Mexican Revolution, the federal congress approved a municipal charter for the village. At the same time, Puerto Las Peñas was renamed Puerto Vallarta in honor of Don Ignacio L. Vallarta, a lawyer and former governor of Jalisco, who had helped draft the Mexican constitution 71 years earlier.

In 1922, much of Puerto Vallarta's population was wiped out by a yellow fever epidemic. A few years later, when the U.S.-based Montgomery Fruit Company bought up expansive acreages in the region, workers began to move to the nearly abandoned town to take agricultural jobs and build a railroad line to carry bananas to the coast.

In 1935, Mexico passed land reform legislation that barred non-Mexican companies from owning agricultural property, and the Montgomery Fruit Company was forced to shut down their operations. From that time on, the village of Puerto Vallarta looked mainly to fishing and cattle ranching for its economic life. Prosperity returned during World War II, when the U.S. Army used shark liver oil as a nutritional supplement and preservative in rations for its millions of troops, and shark fishing in Banderas Bay became a lucrative business.

TOURISM ARRIVES Puerto Vallarta's 40-year run of bad luck ended in the early 1930s, when the first international tourists arrived in Puerto Vallarta via a charter plane that landed on a makeshift dirt airstrip. From then on, word leaked out slowly about this hidden tropical paradise, which could not be reached by road. The trickle of visitors picked up a little in the early 1950s, when first Aeroméxico and then Mexicana Airlines started regularly scheduled air service to Puerto Vallarta.

Film director John Huston recalled the Puerto Vallarta of that era in his autobiography, *An Open Book*. "When I first came here, almost 30 years ago . . . there was one road to the outside world—and it was impassable during the rainy season. I arrived in a small plane, and we had to buzz the cattle off a field outside town before setting down."

It was Huston's 1964 motion picture adaptation of the Tennessee Williams play *The Night of the Iguana*, along with the presence of Elizabeth Taylor and the film's star, Richard Burton, that catapulted Puerto Vallarta into the public consciousness overnight. The film's images of tropical jungle and crystalline waters were captivating, and Burton and Taylor's spicy, scandalous affair created an image of the little fishing village as an "anything goes" kind of place beyond the limits of conventional morality.

Tourists began to flock to Puerto Vallarta in such numbers that the travel infrastructure was quickly overwhelmed. In 1970 the governor of Jalisco, Francisco Medina Ascencio, asked the federal government to fund public utilities, paved roads and an international airport to sustain Puerto Vallarta's growth as a resort area. At the same time, he approached major hotel chains around the world, pitching Puerto Vallarta as an ideal location for resort development. Ascencio's plan worked, and the long stretch of beach north of town, which fishermen had been using to tie up their *pangas*, was transformed within a few years to the high-rise Hotel Zone.

The last resort in the Hotel Zone was completed in 1980, but growth continued. In 1986, construction began on an ambitious planned development known as Marina Vallarta. Besides attracting a yacht crowd, the project incorporated a maritime dock for cruise ships, and soon several major cruise lines decided to include Puerto Vallarta as a port of call on their "Mexican Riviera" cruises.

Construction never slowed after the completion of Marina Vallarta. The 1990s saw resort and condominium development extend northward along the shore, creating a new area called Nuevo Vallarta. This growth continues today, as part-time and full-time residents come from the United States, Canada and other parts of Mexico in such numbers that many condominium complexes are sold out before they are even built. Growth is expected to extend around the north shore of the bay, engulfing Bucerías, Cruz de Huanacaxtle and Punta Mita within the next decade or so.

History in the Streets

Many of the streets in Puerto Vallarta are named after historical figures who are well known to Mexican schoolchildren but unfamiliar to most U.S. and Canadian visitors. Here are some of them:

Ignacio L. Vallarta, governor of Jalisco in the 1850s and chief justice of Mexico's supreme court during the rule of Benito Juárez, was one of the drafters of the Mexican constitution in 1857.

Basilio Badillo, governor of Jalisco in the years following the Mexican Revolution, was a founder of the Partido Revolucionario Institucional (PRI), the political party that controlled the Mexican government for more than 70 years.

Lázaro Cárdenas, Mexico's president from 1934 to 1940, was a controversial figure best known for land reforms creating the ejido (agricultural commune) system and nationalizing the petroleum industry.

Pino Suárez, a journalist from Yucatán, was vice-president under Francisco Madero from 1911 to 1914, when both men were executed after a coup d'etat.

Díaz Ordaz, Mexico's president from 1965 to 1970, hosted the Olympic Games, but his presidency was tarnished by his heavy-handed methods of dealing with student unrest, leaving at least 45 demonstrators dead.

Francisco Medina Ascencio, governor of Jalisco from 1966 to 1971, championed the idea of large-scale tourism development in Puerto Vallarta and created the Hotel Zone.

CULTURE

PEOPLE

Former Mexican president Gustavo Díaz Ordaz once wrote, "The more I see of this land, the more I love Jalisco. It is a mirror in which you can see all of Mexico." Today this is even more true, at least in the microcosm of Puerto Vallarta.

Puerto Vallarta is a young city, so the vast majority of its residents come from other parts of Mexico. Most of them are *mestizos* (often called *mexicanos*), a synthesis of Spanish and Indian cultures that has evolved over nearly five centuries. Under the strict caste system of Spanish Colonial Mexico, mestizos were considered the lowest status in society, denied the protection of the law and often enslaved or banished to rugged frontier areas. In spite of that marginalization, the mestizo population eventually became dominant by sheer numbers. When the Spanish withdrew after ceding Mexico its independence, there was a cultural movement to get rid of all things Spanish. Mexicans tend to reject their Spanish roots and glorify their Indian heritage, proudly claiming descent from the ancient Toltecs or Aztecs. At the same time, many mexicanos view Indians (called *indigenas* or, more disparagingly, *indios*) with disdain as rural bumpkins or menial workers. The difference between mestizos and Indians today is mainly cultural, not racial; *indigenas* can gain acceptance as mexicanos through education and lifestyle changes, and many prominent politicians in Mexico have been Indians.

Americans often view Mexico as a Third World country and stereotype the Mexican people as poor, uneducated and superstitious. This is far from the truth. Although Mexicans' per capita income—US$12,500 a year—is only about one-third that of the United States, it is about 50 percent higher that of the world as a whole and 75 percent higher that of all Latin American countries. The World Bank ranks Mexico among the world's "high income nations." What appears as poverty is actually a wide disparity between rich and poor, with a relatively small, though growing, middle class. *Forbes* magazine reports that Mexico has more billionaires (in U.S. dollars) than any other country except the United States, Japan and Germany; in the number of millionaires, it has recently surpassed Germany. The unemployment rate is only 3.7 percent—lower than in the U.S.

But some 25 percent of Mexico's population is underemployed, mostly in subsistence-level farming, and Mexico's minimum wage is only 53 pesos (US$4.80) a day—less than one-tenth that in the U.S. The top 20 percent of income earners make almost two-thirds of the income in Mexico. This unequal income distribution makes for a highly visible, huge number of people living in poverty. The literacy rate in Mexico has risen tremendously in the last two generations and now stands at 91 percent (compared to 99 percent in the U.S.). The number of children per family—now about 2.4—has declined drastically in the past 20 years (in 1965, the average Mexican family had seven children), and the number of women working outside the home has more than doubled. However, these sweeping changes have taken place mostly in the U.S. border areas and in the major cities, especially Mexico City and Guadalajara. In many parts of the country, social and economic conditions have actually worsened since the advent of NAFTA in 1994, and it is from these areas, such as Oaxaca and Chiapas, that many laborers have migrated to seek work in Puerto Vallarta, one of the most prosperous communities in the country.

The surviving native people of the Puerto Vallarta region are the Huichols, who live in Nayarit in remote areas of the Sierra Madre. Against all odds, rugged terrain has sheltered them from the outside world, and much of their culture and belief system has survived intact since pre-Columbian times. They number around 15,000 and live in extended-family groups in compounds of wood houses known as *ranchos*; they have no permanent tribal structure beyond the family. In the past 40 years, Huichol artists have developed distinctive new art forms, decorating wood carvings and eggs with brightly dyed yarn or beads in elaborate, symbolic patterns. These works are widely sold in Puerto Vallarta and are among the most collectible folk *artesanía* to be found in Mexico today. *Artesanía* provides cash income for many families in the Sierra Huichol as well as those who have been displaced to urban areas. The Huichol culture is being eroded today by many factors, including poverty, disease, missionaries and tourism, as well as increasing outsider access to the traditional Huichol homeland. Nongovernment organizations such as **The Huichol Center** (Huejuquilla Calle Victoria #24, Huejuquilla El Alto, Jalisco, Mexico; 333-983-7054) support the Huichol way of life by helping conserve traditions and providing aid to the impoverished and to Huichol religious practitioners, as well as offering health care and educational opportunities.

Besides mexicanos, both poor and wealthy, and a small number of Indians, the multicultural population of Puerto Vallarta includes about 25 percent full-time and part-time residents who are non-Mexican expatriates from the United States and Canada. This gives rise to encounters between the two very different cultures—in areas ranging from certain aspects of the Mexican creed of machismo to different driving customs, hand gestures and beliefs about health. For example, Anglos have transformed Puerto Vallarta's public areas in the past decade by implementing spay-and-neuter programs to eliminate stray dog problems and by forming beach cleanup groups. On the other hand, the presence of so many Anglos has suppressed some Mexican traditions, for instance, introducing American Halloween customs into local Day of the Dead observances.

One practice you're likely to encounter if you spend enough time in Puerto Vallarta to get to know a Mexican family is the godparent system. The government and the church have failed the Mexican people in many walks of life, and they have traditionally turned to extended family as a social and economic safety net. In the Puerto Vallarta area, this has resulted in the practice of including Anglos in the family by inviting them to become godfathers and godmothers of one or more children. This has nothing to do with baptismal customs. A child can have literally dozens of godparents. If you are invited to be a child's godparent, be aware that this honor comes with a price tag. As a "wealthy relative," you may be called upon to pay for a birthday party or school supplies, or even to provide a monthly allowance. In fact, godparenting can get pretty expensive if you let it. Yet the motive is not solely financial; an Anglo godparent becomes a permanent part of the family. Every family member stands ready to help them understand and adapt to Mexican culture and can be relied on to help out with day-to-day problems and look out for their best interests.

CUISINE

Eating authentic Mexican food lets you experience tastes that aren't often found in many parts of the United States and Canada, though some are becoming more familiar there. The traditional fare of Puerto Vallarta locals is seafood in all its various forms, from oysters to jumbo prawns to swordfish. The preferred methods of preparation along Mexico's Pacific coast are often different than in the United States. Lobster tails (*langosta*) are sliced lengthwise and cooked shell-side-up on a grill. Shrimp (*camarones*) may be peeled and pan-fried with garlic and butter (*al mojo de ajo*) or in a piquant chile sauce (*a la diabla*). Large fish such as tuna (*atún*) and mahimahi (*dorado*) are cut into thick fillets and grilled on a wood plank (*a la plancha*), while plate-size fish such as red snapper (*huachinango*) are cleaned, breaded, grilled and served whole—eyes and all. A distinctive regional fish dish is *pescado sarandeado*, fillets of snapper or pargo that are marinated in lime juice with finely chopped fresh serrano chiles, slow-grilled and served with onion, tomato, cucumber and a special salsa. Fillets of fish are often served with a spicy tomato sauce (*a la veracruzana*), or with various other sauces such as butter and garlic. Fish, shrimp and other seafood are also rolled into warm corn tortillas to make tacos, or shredded, marinated overnight in lime juice and served uncooked in tall glasses as *ceviche*, or seafood cocktails.

Since the vast majority of Puerto Vallarta's residents have moved here from other parts of Mexico within the past decade or so, families and some *comedores* and neighborhood restaurants serve foods that originated in other regions of the country such as Puebla, Oaxaca and Chiapas. Corn, beans and chile are common ingredients in most home-cooked meals, but that's where the resemblance to most American-style "Mexican" restaurants ends. The skin of traditional Mexican corn kernels is tough, so instead of eating it on (or off) the cob as a vegetable, Mexicans usually grind it into meal to make tortillas—the fat kind called *gorditas*—or else marinate the kernels in lime to make a kind of hominy called *posole*, which is cooked into a stew of the same name. Corn that is harvested while young, before the sugar in the kernels has turned to starch, is roasted to make *chicos*, which are considered something of a delicacy. Beans are a staple at every meal in many households. In southern Mexico, black beans are preferred, and residents who come from the northern part of Mexico use pinkish *flor de mayo* beans; both kinds are found on Puerto Vallarta tables, either refried to the consistency of mashed potatoes or cooked *de la olla* in big pots, seasoned with bacon or chorizo sausage drippings and epazote, a pungent herb that has the side benefit of reducing gas and making beans more digestible. Chiles, which come in dozens of types, are the essence of Mexican cookery. Although some visitors have trouble getting past the "hotness" of chiles to savor the subtle nuances, the Mexican palate is trained to distinguish the unique tastes of even small amounts of serrano, poblano, negro, *xcatic*, jalapeño, ancho, *guajillo*, habanero, *arbol* and other kinds of fresh chiles, as well as smoked chiles such as chipotle and dried chiles such as *pasilla*, with as much sensitivity as Americans can tell the difference between nutmeg, rosemary, cloves and dill.

Casual foods eaten by Mexican residents include dishes that are familiar north of the border, such as tacos, burritos, quesadillas and enchiladas. These items may not look quite the same as at your local Taco Bell, though. Tacos are served flat on warm, soft corn tortillas, which you stuff with condiments and then roll up like cigars. Enchiladas come in many varieties, the common element being that they're smothered in chile; there are enchiladas *suizas* (in tomato, red chile and sour cream sauce with grated Swiss cheese), enchiladas *verdes* (in tomatillo and serrano chile sauce), enchiladas *en mole poblano* (in chocolate, peanut and poblano chile sauce) and many others. Especially in rural areas, chicken, pork, cheese and even bananas are used as fillings; you'll also find seafood given the same treatment.

Some Mexican dishes are traditionally eaten on fiesta days and other special occasions. These include main dishes of chicken, pork or turkey in chocolaty *mole poblano* or one of many other *mole* sauces such as Oaxacan-style *mole negro*, *mole de cacahuate* (peanut *mole*) or Teloloapan-style *mole* of red chiles almonds, peanuts, pumpkin seeds and sesame seeds. During the Christmas holidays it is traditional to make tamales, which are time-consuming and best made in large quantities and eaten freshly steamed; fruit tamales or other tamales with sweet fillings are seasonal favorites. One of the most unusual holiday dishes is chiles *en nogada*—fat poblano chiles stuffed with meat, fruit and nuts, covered in a creamy white walnut sauce and topped with pomegranate; it is eaten on Día de la Independencia because it is green, white and red, the colors of the Mexican flag.

You'll find such vegetables as *nopalitos* (sliced, marinated prickly pear cactus leaves), chayote (a hard, wrinkled, tasty light green squash) and jicama (the white meat of a root vegetable, which is grated, diced or cut into french fry–shaped sticks that are as crisp as water chestnuts); tropical fruits including tunas (cactus fruits), mamey, chirimoya, tamarind, guava and zapote (which is mildly narcotic); herbs and spices like achiote (a bright orange-colored seed), cilantro (coriander leaves), lavender and huitlacoche (a corn fungus reminiscent of truffles); and countless more culinary novelties. You may even find your meal brightened with edible flowers like *obelisco* (hibiscus) or *flores de calabaza* (squash blossoms).

While many Mexicans finish meals at home with candies or caramel-like *dulce de leche* instead of American-style desserts, the desert commonly served in restaurants is *flan*, a baked egg custard that is often topped with caramel but may also come in other flavors such as vanilla, coffee, chocolate or even citrus fruit. Another popular, very rich dessert is *pastel de tres leches*, a sponge cake soaked in evaporated milk, condensed milk and cream. On the street, vendors and small shops sell *helados*, ice cream bars on sticks that are quite different from their North American counterparts and come in more flavors than Baskin-Robbins.

Among the traditional nonalcoholic beverages are coconut milk, *horchata* (a cinnamon-flavored rice drink) and various vegetable juices such as *jugo de apio*, or celery juice. As a beverage, *atole* is in a class by itself. This soupy concoction is made by dissolving very finely ground corn flour—usually blue corn—in water and boiling it with flavorings, which can range from honey and chile to squash blossoms or lavender. Drunk since pre-Hispanic times, *atole* is still the main food of many traditional Indians and is prescribed like chicken soup to recuperating patients by *curanderas*, or healers.

In Puerto Vallarta you'll find plenty of places to order standard American-style bacon-and-eggs breakfasts, but don't pass up the opportunity to try Mexican-style breakfast dishes. Most Mexicans start their morning with a fruit salad, typically sliced papaya, *sandia* (watermelon), *melón* (cantaloupe) and *piña* (pineapple); in fact, a large fruit plate often serves as the entire morning meal. The most common traditional Mexican breakfast dish is *chilaquiles*, strips of tortillas cooked with ranch cheese, salsa verde and sometimes chicken, which originated as a recipe for using tortillas left over from the day before. Egg dishes include not only *huevos rancheros* (the fried eggs on tortillas smothered with salsa that have become a standard item on many breakfast menus in the United States), but also other fried egg and tortilla dishes like *huevos motuleños*, topped with green peas and diced ham. Breakfast meats commonly served in the Puerto Vallarta area include *machaca* (finely shredded, spiced beef) and chorizo (a crumbly sausage often added to scrambled eggs). And, of course, no Mexican breakfast would be complete without a steaming puddle of refried beans on the side.

TEQUILA

Tequila is the official national liquor of Mexico; in the state of Jalisco, it is almost a religion. (I once met a 90-year-old healer who attributed his longevity to "drinking a glass of tequila while praying to the Virgin three times a day.") Tequila represents a tribute to *mestizo*, the merger of Indian and Spanish heritage. Native people throughout Mexico made a fermented alcoholic beverage called *pulque* from the hearts of agave plants for some 9000 years before the Spanish conquistadors arrived. The Spanish brought the technology for distilling spirits; while the technique had been practiced on a small scale in Europe for centuries, distillation only became popular around the time of Cortés.

Distillation was widely used by Europeans to concentrate the alcohol content of wine into brandy, which was less bulky for carrying on ships. When Cortés and his men ran out of brandy, they struck on the idea of distilling the native *pulque*. The product was *mezcal*, of which tequila is the finest type.

Tequila is distilled from the fermented sap of the blue agave, a hardy succulent plant cultivated in the dry highlands of the state of Jalisco. The Mexican government takes tequila very seriously. By federal law, it can only be manufactured in Jalisco, where it is a source of great pride, made under tight government regulation. The aging process, for instance, takes place in kegs officially sealed by a federal inspector, and only he can remove the seal when the time comes for bottling. All tequilas are double-distilled. Some of the pricier ones are triple-distilled, though connoisseurs differ as to whether it makes a real difference or not.

In every small grocery store in Puerto Vallarta and surrounding small towns, as well as in boutique-style tequila stores, you'll find a rack of different tequilas, with price tags ranging from a few dollars to US$80 or $100. Several factors affect the price. Inexpensive tequilas, priced under about US$20, are *mixto*—distilled from a half-and-half blend of agave and sugar cane or corn syrup. Better-quality tequilas are *puro de agave*—100 percent from blue agave.

Four basic kinds of tequila are sold. *Plata* (silver) tequila, more popular among Mexicans because it is considered more pure, is the first liquid to come out of the still after the second distillation. It is aged for two weeks in kegs lined with banana leaves. *Joven abocado* (gold) tequila, popular in the United States, is the same as silver, with additives to soften the flavor and give it a whiskylike color; it is not aged.

Finer tequilas are aged in huge oak barrels to enhance their flavor and make them mellower. The aging process also results in a darker color. Tequila that have been aged for a year or less are called *reposada*, and those that are aged more than a year are called *añejo*. *Añejos* are produced in limited quantities and are the most costly.

Specialty tequilas, made mostly for tourist consumption, are infused with flavors ranging from tamarind to almond.

Most tequila today is made in factories in the town of Tequila, between Puerto Vallarta and Guadalajara, using modern distilling methods. A few boutique tequila makers use traditional methods, which some people believe improves their flavor—and certainly raises their price. Increasingly, tequila makers are selling *añejo* in fancy collector bottles, sometimes individually numbered. This marketing ploy is designed to push the price of a bottle up to around US$100. However, the tequila itself is about the same quality as brands selling in the $30 to $50 range.

In Jalisco, people don't often drink tequila with lime and salt or mixed into margaritas, as is the practice in some other parts of Mexico. And of course, tequila "slammers"—shot glasses of tequila and ginger ale, which are slammed on a bar or table to make them fizz, then chugged down in a single gulp—are considered blasphemous. The preferred way to drink fine tequila is as a *completo*—two shot glasses, one of tequila and the other of *sangrita* (not to be confused with the fruity wine drink sangria). You alternate small sips from the two glasses. The sangrita, a blend of orange juice, tomato juice, grenadine, chile and spices, cleanses the palate between sips so you can fully savor the tequila.

In the Sierra Madre towns east of Puerto Vallarta, locals prefer a kind of tequila called *raicilla,* a kind of moonshine, which is hand-distilled from the hearts of wild agave plants. Raicilla was illegal until recently. Today, several demonstration distilleries outside Puerto Vallarta have been licensed to make and sell it, mostly to tourists. This product is diluted to 78 proof, the highest alcohol content allowed by Mexican law. Old-fashioned raicilla, the kind that's sold under the counter at some highwayside food stands and from informal stores in people's homes marked with hand-lettered paper signs in villages around Mascota, may be as much as 150 proof—the kind of stuff that leaves you gasping for breath and unable to stand up.

LANGUAGE

The language barrier between English and Spanish should never be perceived as an obstacle to visiting Puerto Vallarta, which is almost certainly the most bilingual place in Mexico. Besides the large population of English-speaking U.S. and Canadian expatriates, almost all of the one million international travelers who visit Puerto Vallarta each year also come from north of the border. The key to getting a good job in Puerto Vallarta is to speak good English. In fact, most resort hotels require specific levels of English fluency to apply for different jobs such as waiter, desk clerk or concierge. Many Mexicans like to practice speaking English, so the language barrier you're most likely to run into is when you find yourself in a lengthy conversation *in English*—and can't understand a word.

Mexican students are required to attend school until the age of 14. Unless they drop out, they are required to take two years of English in high school. Students in Mexican universities must be reasonably fluent in English to graduate. So in general, educated middle-class Mexicans, including the majority of people who come to Puerto Vallarta for work, speak English well, while unskilled laborers usually do not (though many workers in Puerto Vallarta can understand a fair amount of English but are reluctant to try to speak it). When you travel away from the coast to any of the mountain towns and rural villages described in this book, you probably won't find anyone who speaks English, since those who do have moved to Puerto Vallarta to find jobs. Indian children who grow up on tribal land are not required to attend school, so adult Indians rarely understand English and sometimes cannot even speak much Spanish.

Speaking fluent Spanish enhances any trip to Mexico, of course. But what if, like most people who live in the United States, you don't? Many people who have never studied Spanish worry more than they ought to about traveling south of the border. One of the fundamental lessons of foreign travel is that people can communicate even though they don't know a word of each other's languages. Words help, but your tone of voice, the expression on your face, and gestures or sign language often count for more.

Even though English is widely understood in Puerto Vallarta, people will relate to you better if you attempt to speak Spanish, no matter how poorly. It pays in smiles if you study for your trip by practicing a few useful phrases like *"¿Cuánto vale esto?"* (How much is this worth?), *"La cuenta, por favor"* (the check, please), *"¿Tiene usted una habitación para la noche?"* (Do you have a room for the night?) and *"¿No habria modo de resolver la problema en otra manera?"* (Isn't there another way to resolve this problem?). Most of the time, if you start a conversation in rudimentary Spanish, more often than not the other person will try to answer you in English.

If your comprehension of Spanish leaves something to be desired, ask questions that can be answered with a yes or no, with one word, or with a number. It can be very frustrating to ask for directions and receive a cheerful reply so long, fast and complicated that you can't make sense of it. Better to ask questions like "Is this the right way to _____?" "How many blocks?" "On the right or left?"

Of the many books available for studying Spanish on your own, the one I've found most helpful and friendly is *Spanish Lingo for the Savvy*

Gringo (San Diego: Sunbelt Publications, 3rd edition, 2003) by Elizabeth Reid, who spent eight years teaching English to Mexicans.

Many people who have studied Spanish in school find themselves helpless when it comes to actually communicating in Mexico. Once you've learned it, the vocabulary stays stored in the deep recesses of the mind, but it's often hard to bring it to the surface after years of disuse. Before you leave for Puerto Vallarta, a few weeks using aids such as instructional cassette tapes or CDs can help attune your ear and tongue to the language. A painless way to tune into Spanish is to spend your TV-viewing hours watching Spanish-language channels or rented DVDs. The Mexican motion-picture industry has undergone a renaissance in recent years. Internationally acclaimed films such as *Como Agua para Chocolate* (*Like Water for Chocolate*, 1991), *Amores Perros* (*Love's a Bitch*, 2000), *Y Tu Mama También* (*And Your Mother Too*, 2001) and *El Crimen de Padre Amaro* (*The Crime of Padre Amaro*, 2002), as well as South American films like *María Full of Grace* and *The Motorcycle Diaries* (2004), are well worth watching in Spanish with or without the English subtitles. Most U.S. video rental stores have these titles in stock and can order other Mexican films. Many DVDs of popular Hollywood films have a Spanish-language option. Try watching movies dubbed in Spanish that you've already seen in English. Or opt for spoken Spanish with English subtitles.

MUSIC

Jalisco is the home of mariachis, the most familiar Mexican musical groups. These ensembles of musicians dress in big sombreros and tight clothes decorated with gold or silver piping. The bands, made up of five to eight or more guitar, *guitarrón* (bass guitar), *vihuela* (five-string guitar), violin and trumpet players, originated in southern Jalisco in the 1850s, and their ornate outfits represent the suits worn by *charros*, or cowboys, of that era on formal occasions. Though Guadalajara is the mariachi capital of Mexico, many of the best groups come to Puerto Vallarta, where they perform in clubs like Mariachi Loco (see Zona Romántica Nightlife in Chapter Four) or for free at the amphitheater on the *malecón* next to downtown. Mariachi music follows traditional forms, especially *rancheras*, cowboy songs that usually have to do with love or drinking, and *corridas*, folk songs that tell stories. Most of the standard *rancheras* sung by mariachis today were composed from the 1920s through the 1950s. The traditional dance associated with mariachi performances is the *jarabe tapatio*, known north of the border as the Mexican Hat Dance. (*Tapatio* is the word for any person who comes from Guadalajara.) Mariachis have their own union, which fixes prices for songs. If you request a song, the going rate is about five pesos per song for each band member, so a song from a large mariachi group costs as much as US$6.

Another kind of band, often encountered in restaurants, is the *trio romantico*, three musicians wearing business suits and playing a guitar, a *requinto* (a miniature guitar that sounds like a mandolin) and maracas or other small rhythm instruments. Their repertoire typically includes contemporary Mexican pop music, translations of American easy-listening tunes set to Latin rhythms and traditional Mexican songs.

If you hear one of these groups playing requests in a restaurant, you may get the impression that the only songs they know are "Guantanamera," "Cielito Lindo" and "El Rancho Grande." In reality, hundreds of traditional Mexican songs are included in the repertoire of every strolling musician. Get familiar with a few others and impress your companions when the musicians come around to your table. For starters, try the classic Mexican love song "Las Laureles" (The Laurels) or the haunting "Peregrina" (Traveler), written to honor a blonde American reporter with whom Mexican governor Felipe Carrillo Puerto had fallen in love.

A recent development in Mexican music, *narcocorridos* can be heard in bars frequented mostly by Mexicans. These are folk-style songs about drug smugglers, who are seen as heroes although they may wind up dead or in prison by the end of the song. *Narcocorridos* glorify the smuggler's rise from poverty to power and wealth by operating outside the law and living a life of excess, challenging authority (both U.S. and Mexican) and flouting all risks, including death. Especially popular among poor Mexicans, these songs are available on countless CDs and make an unusual souvenir or gift for the right person. In some parts of Mexico, the government has tried to ban *narcocorridos*, for much the same reason that some in the United States have tried to restrict the sale of gangsta rap CDs, but with no noticeable success.

PUERTO VALLARTA

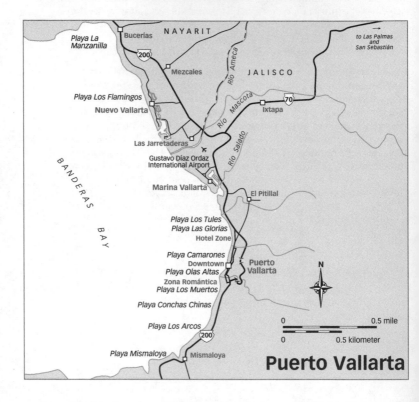

In an early, poignant scene from *The Night of the Iguana,* the 1964 film that put Puerto Vallarta on the map, a tour bus clatters down a narrow, dusty road. Richard Burton's tour guide character tells the driver, "Hank, stop on the bridge."

As the bus draws to a halt in the middle of the rickety wooden bridge over the Río Ameca, a petulant passenger demands, "What are we stopping for?"

Burton looks out the window at the village women washing clothes on the rocks of the river fringed with palm trees and lush rainforest while their laughing, half-naked children play in the water. "A moment of beauty," he muses. "A fleeting glimpse into the lost world of innocence."

Unimpressed, the passenger commands, "Drive on, driver."

Another woman prattles, "My brother-in-law in Abilene has a chain of 23 laundromats. He says all he wants on his tombstone is 'He liberated the women of Texas from the bondage of washing.'"

Today, the bridge where that scene was filmed has been replaced by an arched, traffic-clogged four-lane concrete span in the flight path of the nearby international airport. The river beneath the bridge marks the boundary between the states of Nayarit and Jalisco—and between the huge, modern resort and condominium developments of Nuevo Vallarta and Marina Vallarta.

Truly, the innocence of the 1960s has been lost, at least within the confines of metropolitan Puerto Vallarta. Yet even today, you don't have to drive very far outside the city to discover empty beaches, fishing villages lost in time and traditional Mexican mountain towns that have changed little since the Spanish colonial era. Within the city limits, "Old" Puerto Vallarta, with all its art galleries and gourmet restaurants, has somehow managed to preserve much of the historical small-town charm that first attracted visitors in search of a secluded tropical paradise. This is the Puerto Vallarta you see in travel posters and brochures, the one that looks like no other resort in Mexico. Here's where you'll discover the quaint old town with its landmark crowned church, its narrow cobblestone streets, its beachfront promenade, its wobbly wooden suspension bridges and its memorabilia of one of the most scandalous movie star romances of all time.

Old Puerto Vallarta extends for about three miles along the waterfront, but it is only four to six blocks wide and has not grown much in area since the first road reached it in the late 1950s. That's because it is almost completely boxed in on the inland side by the near-vertical, jungle-clad slopes of the Sierra de Vallarta. To take the highway bypass, or Libramiento, between the old town and the Hotel Zone, you drive through a tunnel under the mountains.

The purpose of this book is to entice you to check into a hotel downtown, within walking distance of all the best that the city has to offer, and even to rent a car and explore those hidden places within day-trip distance.

But before we go there, let's survey "New" Puerto Vallarta, the expanse of large resort hotels that lines the shore of Banderas Bay for some ten miles north of the old downtown area. More than 90 percent of international visitors to Puerto Vallarta stay in these resorts, and many spend their entire vacations without ever leaving the premises except, perhaps, for an occasional guided tour or a shopping spree to a nearby mall. They can bask on picture-perfect beaches under the glorious tropical sun to their hearts' content without ever having to encounter local, Spanish-speaking people. And for some tourists that's just fine.

If you're not one of them—if you're sure you have no intention of staying in a big resort—feel free to skip past the first part of this chapter. Flip forward to the more human-size, atmospheric cobblestone streets of downtown and the Zona Romántica. Or for a genuine tropical castaway experience beyond the reach of roads, phones or wireless internet, stay in a remote village on the bay's south shore.

Then again, you might consider that the comfortable anonymity of a large beach resort can be a welcome, hassle-free home base from which to explore the best of Puerto Vallarta by car, public transportation or guided tours. This can be especially true for families with children, as well as travelers who are taking their first trip outside their own country (by which I mean the United States or Canada, where the vast majority of international visitors to Puerto Vallarta come from; there are also a relatively small but growing number of tourists who come to Puerto Vallarta from Argentina, Brazil and other South American countries).

Not all resorts are created equal. Some are operated with families in mind, offering all-day schedules of special activities for kids and teenagers as well as nursery or babysitting services. Others are "adults only," not usually in the nudity-and-hedonism sense, which is pretty rare in Puerto Vallarta, but designed for honeymooners, second-honeymooners and mature couples who find the racket of children at play anything but relaxing. Even though Puerto Vallarta is unrivaled in all of Mexico as a gay-friendly destination (see Chapter Five), none of the resorts in this chapter is expressly gay and lesbian oriented; however, some adults-only resorts make a point of welcoming couples regardless of sexual orientation.

The majority of the resorts in the Hotel Zone and Marina Vallarta areas offer an all-inclusive option, and a few of them, as well as most resorts in Nuevo Vallarta, are all-inclusive only. "All-inclusive" means that the room rate includes all meals and many recreational activities, including nonmotorized water sports equipment, and usually free use of exercise facilities and free admission to the hotel's nightclub, if it has one. You will be charged extra for such activities as scuba diving, parasailing and horseback riding.

When it comes to meals, every all-inclusive resort has a free buffet restaurant, and most also have à la carte "specialty" restaurants where meals may or may not be included in the room rate. Be sure to check. Also, all-inclusive plans include alcoholic beverages in the room rate, but for many this amounts to only "domestic" liquor—that is, house-brand well drinks—and make you pay for all drinks using American, Canadian or European brand names. Again, it pays to check if booze on the beach plays an important role in your vacation plans.

Although I often refer to all the beachfront hotels in the Hotel Zone, Marina Vallarta and Nuevo Vallarta as "big resorts," some are a lot bigger than others. You'll usually find the beach and pool areas smaller but much less busy at places that have 100 rooms than at those that have 600 or 700.

Of course, while almost all beach resorts in this chapter charge room rates in the "deluxe" or "ultra-deluxe" range, some are much more expensive than others, ranging from around US$150 to $600 a night all-inclusive in season. The good news is that many guests stay at these resorts, regardless of price range, for a fraction of the stated rate by taking advantage of package deals that include airfare or special internet offers advertised on the hotel's website or through online booking agents.

And even though it doesn't seem possible that much could be "hidden" in this world of big-name beach hotels, this chapter does contain a number of tantalizing bed and breakfasts, local restaurants and sights that are tucked away inland from the ocean. Even in one of Mexico's largest megaresorts, by exploring off the beaten path you can find its local, human side.

MARINA VALLARTA

When Puerto Vallarta's new Hotel Zone had been completed and was operating at full capacity, developers unveiled plans for a new, in some ways even more ambitious, project. Centered around Mexico's largest yacht basin and a cruise ship dock, Marina Vallarta would include shops, restaurants, nightclubs, resort hotels and a championship golf course, along with hundreds of condominiums and private villas. Construction was started in 1986 and completed in just five years.

A disadvantage of staying in the Marina Vallarta area instead of the Hotel Zone is that it's farther from the colorful old city center. A one-way taxi fare can run US$11 to $17; otherwise, sightseers without rental cars have the choice of taking municipal buses, which stop frequently, or relying on the shuttles and organized tours provided by some resorts.

SIGHTS

MARINA VALLARTA The largest in Mexico, with over 500 slips for yachts, sailboats and sportfishing boats, ranging in length from 30 to 140 feet—and the surrounding 500-acre development, which includes stores, restaurants, spas and health clubs, resort hotels along the beach, villas and condominiums (including several condo complexes strategically arranged to form a wall sheltering boats in the marina from the wind), tour offices and water sports equipment rentals, as well as a school and a hospital.

MARINA MALECÓN The boardwalk follows the perimeter of the marina, providing a close-up look at the yachts and sailboats. It is lined with shops, many of them seemingly aimed at the cruise ship trade, and more than two dozen restaurants. The centerpiece of the *malecón* is **El Faro** (The Lighthouse), 110 feet tall, with an outside elevator that takes visitors to the circular bar on top, with its panoramic view of the entire Banderas Bay area. At the base of the lighthouse is a small aquarium.

ISLA IGUANA Between the Maritime Terminal and the marina is a manmade island that serves as an exclusive community of palm-shrouded waterfront villas and townhouses, built around a community swimming pool and tennis courts and fringed with more boat slips. It's one of Puerto Vallarta's most prestigious neighborhoods. Unless someone is expecting you, the guard at the gate won't let you in.

MARITIME TERMINAL At the entrance from the ocean to Marina Vallarta, the Terminal Maritima is where cruise ships dock and passengers disembark. When a ship is in port, which is most of the time, it's impossible to miss because it's the most massive thing in sight. In fact, a single cruise ship carries a far greater number of passengers than any resort hotel in the city could possibly accommodate. About 200 cruise ships, carrying over 400,000 visitors, put in at Puerto Vallarta—most of them weeklong cruises that depart from the San Pedro Docks in Los Angeles, California, and stop at Ensenada or Cabo San Lucas, Baja California, en route. At this writing, the Maritime Terminal can only dock two ships at a time. Occasionally as many as six or seven cruise ships arrive at Puerto Vallarta on the same day, exceeding the capacity of the docks, so it becomes necessary to shuttle passengers ashore on tender boats. A $16 million expansion project is underway that will let the terminal dock three and eventually four cruise ships at once. Many land and sea tours to Old Puerto Vallarta and other points of interest in the

HIDDEN LISTINGS

Marina Vallarta

CASA VELAS HOTEL BOUTIQUE

THE WHALE WATCHING CENTER/ OPEN AIR EXPEDITIONS

ARTE DE LAS AMÉRICAS

CASA VELAS HOTEL BOUTIQUE
PAGE 85

Elegant balconies and luxurious, sprawling accomodations at a prestigious adults-only resort

THE WHALE WATCHING CENTER/OPEN AIR EXPEDITIONS
PAGE 158

Expert-led tours offering an up-close and personal experience with whales and dolphins in their natural habitat

ARTE DE LAS AMÉRICAS
PAGE 89

Abstract contemporary sculpture and paintings by established and emerging Mexican artists

area depart from the Maritime Terminal on schedules coordinated with the cruise ship arrivals.

LA PALOMA PLAZA DE TOROS

✉*Maritime Terminal* ✆*322-224-1175* Visitors who wish to experience the Mexican cultural tradition of bullfighting can do so at the local bullring, located inconspicuously across the boulevard from the cruise ship terminal. The matadors with their capes and "suits of lights" are here, and the danger is genuine, but for several years this venue held "bloodless" exhibition bullfights, merely tormenting the bulls with lances until they were fighting mad. The no-kill *corridos de toros* failed to attract droves of *norteamericano* tourists, though, and local Mexican crowds dwindled, so traditional bullfights were brought back, and now you can watch the bulls stagger through their final agony or just drop at the matador's feet like a sack of raw meat. As this book goes to press, the bullring is up for sale to anyone who wants to build condominiums in its place, but for the time being, bullfights are held on Wednesdays at 5 p.m. from November through April. Admission is about US$25 per person.

EL PITILLAL

✉*There are two ways to get there. To take the old route, used by green buses, turn right on the main boulevard, cross the river and turn left on Francisco Villa, the main road that goes behind Sam's Club. The new route starts directly across the boulevard from the Maritime Terminal and is used by blue and white buses.*

For a complete change of pace from the manicured glitz of Marina Vallarta—and for an authentic taste of the "real" Mexico—take a 15-minute side trip from the Maritime Terminal to see Puerto Vallarta's largest residential area, where many of the construction workers and hotel and restaurant staffers live. Until recently it was a separate village and rather hard to reach until the road was paved and the new bridge was built (during the rainy season you had to cross the river by six-passenger ferry). Now a suburb with a population of more than 100,000, it's still pretty much a tourist-free zone of *tienditas* (little stores), *comedores* (Mexican fast-food stands) and homes that are tiny by North American standards. Although you could easily get lost among the dirt back streets in this maze of more than 200 square blocks, you don't really need to wander far from the main thoroughfare, Francisco Villa, which crosses the new bridge over the Río Pitillal and takes you directly to the pretty main plaza. Here, ringed with benches and shade trees, is a bandstand where Mexican musicians perform concerts on weekend evenings. On one side of the plaza is the beautiful, twin-towered **Church of San Miguel Arcángel**, whose most striking feature is a 26-foot, five-ton hand-carved wooden statue of Christ resurrected, backlit in blue. To get there, you can take a taxi, take a bus marked "Pitillal" (of which there are literally hundreds running up and down the main boulevard all day and evening) or drive your own car and follow a bus.

LODGING

The major resort hotels at Marina Vallarta line a wide, straight stretch of beach south of the ship channel. But about half the Marina Vallarta district is away from the beach, and with one unique exception lodgings here are much more affordable than those that front on the ocean.

CLUB EMBARCADERO PACIFICO

$$$ 253 ROOMS   ✉Paseo de la Marina Sur s/n   ☎322-221-1177   ✆322-209-0199
🖫www.embarcadero.com.mx, info@embarcadero.com

On the marina side, an easy walk from the beach, Club Embarcadero Pacifico has guest rooms and suites in white buildings with red-tile roofs, built around four swimming pools, two kids' pools, two tennis courts and volleyball and basketball courts. The rooms, most of which have large windows overlooking the marina, are decorated in nautical themes and feature marble floors and a choice of one king-sized or two full-sized beds. An optional all-inclusive plan includes free sea kayaking, windsurfing and sunfish sailboats.

FLAMINGO VALLARTA

$$ 96 ROOMS   ✉Carretera al Aeropuerto, Km. 6   ☎322-221-0880   ✆322-221-0888
🖫www.flamingohotels.com, flamingovallarta@pvnet.com.mx

Across the marina channel, close to the main boulevard and the causeway to Iguana Island, this family-friendly hotel makes up for the fact that it is far from the beach by operating a free water-taxi service that takes guests to different beach areas every day. The spacious, air-conditioned

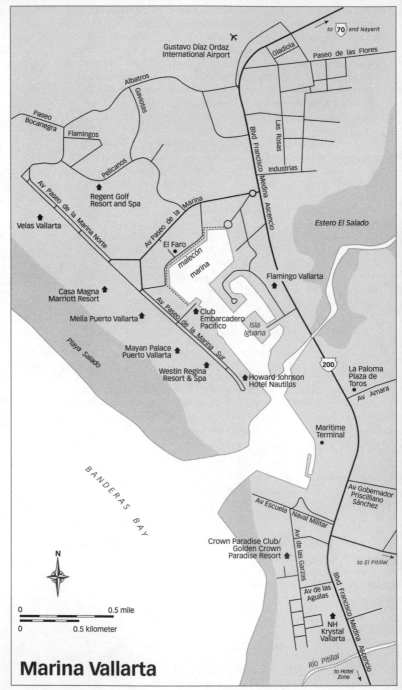

Marina Vallarta

guest rooms have one king-sized or two queen-sized beds, and all have balconies or terraces with views of the marina. The walls are not very soundproof and the decor, accented in clashing blue, green and orange hues, takes some getting used to. As an affordable home base for explorations around Puerto Vallarta, though, it's the best bet in the marina area. It's also one of the closest lodgings to the airport—just five minutes away, convenient for travelers returning from excursions to other parts of the region and preparing for a morning departure.

CASA VELAS HOTEL BOUTIQUE

$$$$ 80 UNITS ✉ *Pelicanos #311* ☎ *322-226-6688, 866-529-8813*

📠 *322-226-6699* 🖱 *www.casavelas.com, contactcenter@casavelas.com*

The most prestigious lodging in the area is tucked discreetly between the first and eighteenth holes of the Marina Vallarta Golf Club. Although this adults-only resort is not very close to either the marina or the beach, the luxury suites are designed with privacy in mind. Elegance is all-pervasive: In the lobby, a golden glow lights arches, columns and overstuffed couches; the spacious guest rooms, decorated in subtle hues, have beamed ceilings and windows running the full length of one wall, as well as sliding glass doors that open onto broad terraces or balconies. While golf is the central activity, there are also two swimming pools, tennis courts and a full-service spa, in addition to a complimentary shuttle to the resort's private beach club.

WESTIN RESORT & SPA

$$$$ 280 ROOMS ✉ *Paseo de la Marina Sur #205* ☎ *322-226-1100* 📠 *322-226-1144*

🖱 *www.starwoodhotels.com, reservations.01090@westin.com*

At the south end of the beach at Marina Vallarta, the Westin offers brightly colorful guest rooms and suites with modern furnishings including king-sized beds, couches, armoires and potted palms. All have individual balconies with full or partial ocean views, and premium suites offer such features as outdoor jacuzzis and plasma TVs. On the beach are wood-frame pergolas, each spacious enough for three people to lounge, with curtains that can be drawn for private sunbathing. The four swimming pools are landscaping masterpieces, with underwater benches and palm tree islands. There are also an outdoor whirlpool bath, a sauna, a steam room, tennis courts and a health club with cardio workout equipment, as well as fitness classes and personal trainers.

MAYAN PALACE PUERTO VALLARTA

$$$ 200 ROOMS ✉ *Paseo de la Marina Sur #220* ☎ *322-226-6002* 📠 *322-226-6050*

🖱 *www.grupomayan.com/mayan-palace/puerto-vallarta/index.html, conciergepvr@mayanpalace.com.mx*

One of three Mayan Palace properties along Banderas Bay, this resort offers a full range of guest accommodations. The majority of them are one-bedroom suites with king-sized and pull-out beds, making this a good high-end choice for families and groups. A standard suite can sleep four adults and two children, while a master suite sleeps six adults and two children. All suites have kitchenettes. Standard rooms with two full-sized beds are also available. All rooms and suites have air conditioning, ceiling fans and marble bathrooms. The hotel has a two-level swimming pool and a series of interlocking canals for kayaking, as well as a workout gym, tennis courts and a full schedule of children's activities.

MELIÁ PUERTO VALLARTA

$$$$ 321 ROOMS   ✉Paseo de la Marina Sur #7   ✆322-226-3000, 866-436-3542
📠322-226-3030   ✐www.melia.puerto.vallarta.com, melia.puerto.vallarta@solmelia.com

This family-oriented all-inclusive resort boasts the largest swimming pool in the city. Its standard guest rooms and luxury suites in five-story buildings and nine-story towers have balconies overlooking the ocean or the hotel gardens. The hotel is family-oriented, with Flintstones motifs popping up in the restaurants, playgrounds and shopping areas. The recreation program, one of the most complete in Puerto Vallarta, includes the use of lighted tennis courts, a game room, an exercise room and a jogging track, as well as all nonmotorized water sports equipment. There are aerobics classes, fun workshops and three kids' clubs—one with certified nannies and educational activities for children ages four and under; one for grade school–age kids with an outdoor playground, arts and crafts, a mini-disco and a campground; and one for teens with a climbing wall, batting cage, tennis clinic, disco and supervised activities. Also covered in the all-inclusive rate are meals and drinks at the resort's four restaurants and four bars, as well as ubiquitous snacks throughout the day. Wireless internet access is available in public areas and premium suites.

CASA MAGNA MARRIOTT RESORT

$$$$ 433 ROOMS   ✉Paseo de la Marina #5   ✆322-226-0000   📠322-226-0060
✐www.marriott.com

The largest beach resort at Marina Vallarta features luxurious European-style beds with cozy floral comforters and lots of plump pillows in its softly lit guest rooms and suites. Each accommodation has marble floors and a balcony overlooking the free-form swimming pool, tropical gardens and ocean beach. There are tennis courts, a health club and a sauna on the premises, and activities available at the private beach include jet skiing, water skiing and sailing.

VELAS VALLARTA

$$$$ 339 UNITS   ✉Avenida Costera s/n   ✆322-221-0091, 866-867-2593
📠322-221-0755   ✐www.velasvallarta.com, contactcenter@velasvallarta.com

This stylish hotel is built in a sweeping curve that surrounds its three swimming pools with artificial waterfalls and opens onto the beach. Designed to host conventions, Velas Vallarta has Marina Vallarta's most complete business center, including wireless internet access from anywhere in the hotel, video conferencing, secretarial services and photocopying. All guest accommodations are suites, ranging from studios to three-bedroom units. Huichol art and Mexican textiles make a pleasant counterpoint to the ultramodern teak furnishings, flat-screen TVs and parquet wood floors. All suites have ocean-view balconies or terraces, as well as kitchens or kitchenettes. Also on the premises are a spa, a gym and a beauty salon.

SUZIE WONG'S

$$ CHINESE ✉*Marina Vallarta, local 124* ☎*322-221-2057*

Right on the Marina Vallarta boardwalk, near the lighthouse, you'll find some of the best Chinese food in town. Diners can choose between eating outdoors under an open-air palapa or in the air-conditioned indoor dining room, where grass-green walls and gold-tinted windows set the mood. The menu features over 50 entrées, including such specialties as mu shu prawns, Peking duck, Mongolian-style chicken and shrimp skewers and lobster with Chinese vegetables in ginger sauce.

PORTO BELLO

$$$ ITALIAN ✉*Marina Sol #7* ☎*322-221-0003*

This restaurant offers fine dining Italian-style, with seating on a patio overlooking the yacht basin and the mountains. There is also air-conditioned indoor seating in a dining room with pastel art nouveau decor. The house pasta specialty is fusilli portobello with artichokes, black olives and basil. Other temptations on the menu include veal scallopini in white wine cream sauce, seafood and sautéed fish filet with shrimp and clams in saffron tomato sauce.

BRANDO'S BAR

$ BARBECUE ✉*Condominiums Marina del Rey, local 10* ☎*322-221-2721*

Set on a sandy shoreline overlooking the marina, this thatch-roofed restaurant-and-bar complex run by a pair of expatriate entrepreneurs from California was opened the day Marlon Brando died (July 1, 2004). The friendly, ultra-casual pool hall atmosphere and affordable prices have made it the local hangout of choice for Marina Vallarta condo dwellers. The house specialty is ribs.

BENITTO'S

$$ DELICATESSEN ✉*Plaza Neptuno* ☎*322-209-0287*

This casual café inside the shopping mall at the entrance to Marina Vallarta is a labor of love run by the former hotel manager of the Fiesta Americana. It features big, overstuffed sandwiches on focaccia or your choice of other fresh-baked breads. Try the corned beef with *vitetorne* sauce or the tuna with Spanish manchego cheese. There are also assorted salads, fondues and unusual juice blends such as carrot with almond or pear and basil.

ESTUDIO CAFÉ

$ MEXICAN ✉*Paseo de la Marina, local 31* ☎*322-297-0825*

This small patio eatery adjoins the studio-gallery of internationally renowned painter and muralist Federico León de la Vega, who is known for his lush-hued, larger-than-life depictions of fruits and other foods. The café run by his wife, Luly, is known primarily as a breakfast place, with heaping plates of huevos rancheros and delicious chilaquiles smothered in salsa verde. It stays open all day until early evening, with a limited salads-and-sandwiches lunch menu as well as seafood dinner specials. Open October through April, closed Sundays.

NIKKI BEACH

$$$ INTERNATIONAL ⌗Paseo de la Marina Sur #205 ☎322-226-1150

You've never seen a restaurant as chic and sexy as this "beach club" the Westin Resort & Spa (that is, unless you've visited one of the 13 other Nikki locations from Miami to Marrakesh). Set outdoors within a contained area of sand shaded by palm trees, the restaurant lets you dine reclining on a huge romantically lit futon, or on a stilted bed or one hanging suspended under a palapa, or even inside a private teepee. There is also more conventional seating in directors' chairs at hand-crafted wood tables, or at picnic tables with thickly padded benches. The menu has a short list of entrées—lobster, shrimp and scallop thermidor; New York strip steak; chicken satay; and seared sea bass. There are also impressive selections of seafood appetizers and sushi (including oddities such as a mole chicken katsu roll and a vegetable roll of asparagus, avocado and mango), and a raw bar including beluga caviar and shucked oysters.

ARGENTINA

$$$ ARGENTINEAN ⌗Paseo de la Marina Sur #220 ☎322-226-6028

Visitors from Buenos Aires, who are notoriously loyal to their own country's culinary traditions, claim this steakhouse in the Mayan Palace is the most authentic of the several Argentinean restaurants in Puerto Vallarta. Beefsteaks grilled over oak embers are the house specialty. Dining is alfresco on a terrace surrounded by lush gardens and whispering palm trees, and the sunset view is exquisite. Reservations required. Dinner only.

MIKADO

$$$ JAPANESE ⌗Paseo de la Marina #5 ☎322-221-0004

The exotic Japanese specialty restaurant in the Casa Magna Marriott, showcases fresh sushi and teppanyaki (meat or seafood dishes that a chef cooks in front of the guests on a grill built into the table), as well as a range of à la carte items including tempura and yakitori. Red walls, dark wood ceilings and trim, hanging kimonos and Asian sculptures, koi ponds and traditional background music all come together to create a relaxing ambience. Dinner only.

ANDREA GOURMET

$$$ INTERNATIONAL ⌗Velas Vallarta, Avenida Costera s/n ☎322-221-0091

The posh à la carte restaurant in the Velas Vallarta resort is an "international" restaurant with multiple personalities. On Monday the menu is all French; on Tuesday it's Asian; and on Thursday it serves gourmet Mexican dishes. The other days of the week, the fare is Italian, with an emphasis on the cuisine of Tuscany. There's elegant white-tablecloth dining both indoors and out, and live music accompanies the experience. Reservations required.

MARISCOS TINO'S

$$ SEAFOOD ✉*Avenida #333* ☎*322-225-2171*
For authentic Mexican-style seafood in an off-the-beaten-path location, head over to the El Pitillal neighborhood, where this no-frills family restaurant cooks fresh fish right off the boat. A specialty is the Puerto Vallarta local favorite, *filete sarandeado*—barbecued fillets of red snapper in a spicy cream sauce. The restaurant is hard to find; your best bet is to take a taxi there.

SHOPPING

GALERÍA EM

✉*Marina Las Palmas II, local 17* ☎*322-221-1728* This studio-gallery exhibits fine blown glass, stained glass and art mirrors by partners Estella, the artist who creates the designs, and Mariano, the production supervisor.

ARTE DE LAS AMÉRICAS

✉*Marina Las Palmas #17* ☎*322-221-1985* This sister gallery to Galeria Uno downtown features abstract contemporary sculpture and paintings by established and emerging Mexican artists.

PLAZA MARINA ✉*Carretera al Aeropuerto, Km. 8* ☎*322-221-0490* Located north of the Marina Vallarta Golf Club, this is Puerto Vallarta's largest shopping mall. It's air-conditioned and has 219 stores, with a balanced mix of tourist-oriented shops and others targeting an upscale local clientele. The Jalisco state tourism office is on the second floor.

PLAZA NEPTUNO ✉*Carretera al Aeropuerto, Km. 7.5* ☎*322-223-2500* This compact mall at the north entrance to the marina has additional recreational shopping opportunities. It is enhanced by tranquil garden resting spots. It also has an English-speaking hospital and pharmacy, as well as an internet café.

NIGHTLIFE

COLLAGE ✉*Boulevard Francisco Medina Ascencio s/n* ☎*322-221-0505* Near the entrance to the Marina Vallarta complex, Collage is the largest nightclub in PV. On winter weekends it is usually packed to its capacity of

2000 people. The music is international deejay disco. The Tuesday-night foam parties are a hit with the young-and-wild crowd. Open Tuesday, Friday and Saturday. Admission; open bar.

EL FARO ✉️*Paseo de la Marina #245* 📞*322-221-0541* The circular bar at the top of the 110-foot-tall marina lighthouse offers one of the most spectacular views in Puerto Vallarta—if you can get a window table. Late at night there's live, mellow folk music. Admission.

MAYAN PALACE CONCERTS ✉️*220 Paseo de la Marina Sur* 📞*322-226-6000* The Mayan Palace hosts free concerts at 8:30 p.m. on the first Thursday of every month, featuring performances that range from classical to jazz to mariachi.

CANDY'S GIRLS

✉️*Boulevard Francisco Medina Ascencio #2940-A* 📞*322-221-0633* Curiously enough, the area across the boulevard from posh Marina Vallarta has the highest concentration of *clubes caballeros*, or strip clubs, in the city. Candy's, one of the largest and best known, features not only the usual pole dancers but, on weekend nights, shower dancers, foam dancers and lesbian performances. Open all night. Admission.

LA HERRADURA

✉️*Hidalgo #296* Look for a local cultural adventure on Saturday nights in the working-class suburb of El Pitillal, where live Mexican *bandas* and *grupos* play dance music and the liquor is cheap and flows freely. You'll probably be the only out-of-towners there. Three blocks off the main plaza.

CINÉPOLIS

✉️*Avenida Francisco Villa 1642-A* 📞*322-297-6763* With 15 screens, this is one of the largest movie theater complexes in the Puerto Vallarta area. You'll find it near the south entrance to the El Pitillal neighborhood, in the shopping plaza adjoining the Soriana department store. Films in both English and Spanish are shown. Tickets cost about half as much as in the United States.

BEACHES

PLAYA SALADO
✉️*South of the Maritime Terminal ship channel*

🏖️ This broad, straight expanse of beach on the ocean side of the spit of land that protects Marina Vallarta is lined with resort hotels and condominiums, which restrict foreshore access so effectively that it's virtually impossible for nonguests to reach it by land. It's broken up by manmade rock obstacles to make "private" hotel beaches that are not good for long walks, and much of it is filled with chaise lounges and elaborate, curtained sunbathing platforms. All sorts of motorized and nonmotorized water sports are available through the hotels, and if non-guests really want to walk on this beach, they can do so by renting a kayak or jet ski at the marina and approaching Playa Salado by water. It's named *salado* (salty) because the area was a salt marsh before the marina was built.

HOTEL ZONE

The area known as the Zona Hotelera, or Hotel Zone (or sometimes the Zona Hotelera Norte, since the area south of town is also developing into a hotel zone, though one of a much different character), extends from the landmark Wal-Mart superstore and the maritime terminal to the northern edge of downtown. It was developed during the 1970s, realizing the vision of the Jalisco state governor, Francisco Medina Ascencio, who convinced the Mexican federal government to subsidize public utilities, paved roads and an international airport while simultaneously promoting the town to international hotel chains as a hot future tourist destination. With few exceptions, all of the Hotel Zone resorts stand between the broad, busy boulevard and the beach. The last major hotel was completed in 1980.

All of the large resort hotels are situated on side streets and cul-de-sacs between the main boulevard, which changes names from Avenida México to Avenida Francisco Medina Ascencio as it enters the Hotel Zone and the seashore. On the opposite side of the boulevard, accessible from a *lateral*, or frontage road, is an unsightly one-block-deep strip of businesses ranging from convenience stores and auto repair shops to superstores like Gigante and Wal-Mart. Hidden behind this commercial veneer are residential areas including the middle-class Mexican neighborhoods of Colonia 5 de Diciembre and Colonia Lázaro Cárdenas and, farther north, the quiet, pleasant and rather prestigious Colonia Versalles, inhabited by a mix of Mexicans and North American expatriates.

SIGHTS

UNIDAD DEPORTIVA ✉*Avenida Francisco Medina Ascencio s/n* ☎*322-222-0640* Across the main boulevard from the Sheraton Buganvilias Resort stands this large sports complex, which consists of a soccer stadium plus two other soccer fields, two baseball fields, a basketball court, a weightlifting and gymnastics gym, a skateboarding park, jai alai frontons and racquetball and handball courts. Besides local and regional events, the stadium hosts national and international soccer tournaments, two annual international softball tournaments and the Medio Maratón Internacional Puerto Vallarta, a 21-kilometer running race in which a 100,000-peso purse goes to the winner. Aerobic and martial arts classes at the sports complex are open to the public. Surprisingly few international visitors ever come to the Unidad Deportiva for classes

HIDDEN LISTINGS

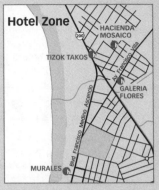

Hotel Zone

HACIENDA MOSAICO
TIZOK TAKOS
GALERIA FLORES
MURALES

HACIENDA MOSAICO

PAGE 95

Handmade mosaics and a swimming pool surrounded by mango, banana and guava trees in a secluded artists' retreat blocks from the beach

TIZOK TAKOS

PAGE 100

Homemade corn tortillas filled with *carne asada*, shredded pork, chicken or shrimp at one of the most authentic food stands in the area

GALERIA FLORES

PAGE 101

A showroom for a long-established gallery with a focus on bright, whimsical paintings

MURALES

PAGE 101

Upscale Mexican cuisine with an intimate, oceanview terrace— try the red snapper and scallops with baby cactus and bean sauce

or sporting events, many of which are free. You can see what's scheduled by checking the flyers posted on the wall of the main office.

LODGING

The hotels that follow are listed from north to south. None of them is within easy walking distance of downtown, though it's a short taxi or bus ride.

CROWN PARADISE CLUB AND
GOLDEN CROWN PARADISE RESORT

$$$$ 468 ROOMS ✉ *Avenida de las Garzas #1* ☏ *322-226-6800, 800-882-8215*
☏ *322-226-6855* ✎ *www.crownparadise.com, reservallarta@crownparadise.com*

Far from downtown but just five minutes from the maritime pier and Marina Vallarta, the family-oriented Crown Paradise Club and its partner hotel, the adults-only Golden Crown Paradise Resort, are twin medium-sized all-inclusive resorts in three-story buildings. The Crown Paradise Club has 254 guest rooms and suites with bright yellow walls and balconies overlooking the pool area, gardens or mountains; the "family rooms" have a special kids' area with a trundle bed, a bunk bed and its own TV. Many of the resort facilities are designed with kids in mind, including a water park with pirate ship, a castle and nine water slides, as well as family game and playground areas. The neighboring Golden Crown Paradise has 214 guest rooms and suites decorated in soft pink hues, with balconies overlooking the ocean or the pool area; the special "honeymoon suites" have jacuzzis—some inside, others on the balconies. There's a complete spa on the premises. The two hotels share the use of an exercise gym, tennis courts and a disco, and each has its own swimming pool. The nonstop schedule of activities at both resorts ranges from snorkeling, sea kayaking and windsurfing to aerobics, Pilates and tequila volleyball.

NH KRYSTAL VALLARTA

$$$ 433 UNITS   ✉ *Avenida de las Garzas s/n* ✆ *322-224-0202,* *888-726-0528* ✆ *322-224-0222* ✐ *www.nh-hotels.com/nhpuertovallarta,* *nhpuertovallarta@nh-hotels.com*

Concealed behind a grandiose, silver-domed portico at the north end of the Hotel Zone, the sprawling, low-rise NH Krystal Vallarta was Puerto Vallarta's first major beach resort. The hotel's location, close to the airport, is no coincidence. It was built in 1962, opening at the same time the first regularly scheduled air service to Puerto Vallarta began, when both the airport and the hotel were beyond the outskirts of town. Its 32 acres of grounds are lush with mature palm trees that all but hide most of the 433 guest units, which include rooms and suites in three-story villas without elevators; pricier villas are in one-story triplexes with individual plunge pools. The grounds are embellished with wrought-iron street lamps, brick paths, colonial-style fountains and aqueducts and tropical vegetation, making it the closest thing to a sightseeing highlight in the Hotel Zone. The newest section of the resort, the Krystal Club, features extra-spacious premium rooms with such amenities as terrycloth robes, 27-inch flat-screen TVs with premium channels, and a cluster of six shared eight-person hot tubs. The resort is in the final stages of a three-year, 17-million-dollar, top-to-bottom renovation.

HOLIDAY INN PUERTO VALLARTA

$$–$$$ 220 ROOMS   ✉ *Boulevard Francisco Medina Ascencio, Km. 3.5* ✆ *322-226-1700* ✆ *322-224-5683*

Towering over the beach and bay, this nine-story hotel has earth-tone guest rooms with private balconies and your choice of a king-sized bed or two double beds. Facilities include a swimming pool, a sauna, a fitness center and tennis courts. Except for the palm trees scattered liberally around the property, guests may feel that they haven't quite left the United States. For vacationers who like to gamble, the Holiday Inn has a sports book and bar. An all-inclusive option is available.

VILLA DEL PALMAR

$$$$ 568 UNITS   ✉ *Boulevard Francisco Medina Ascencio #1080, Km. 3* ✆ *322-224-8878, 877-845-5247* ✆ *322-224-8868* ✐ *www.villadelpalmarvallarta.com*

If spacious accommodations are a priority, the Villa del Palmar may fill the bill. This all-suite resort offers studio, one-bedroom and two-

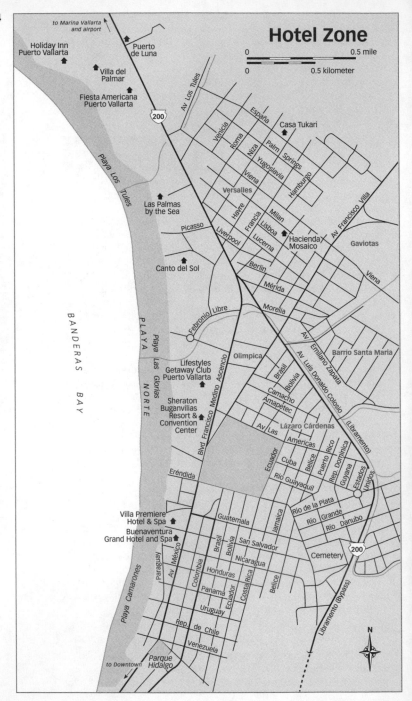

Hotel Zone

to Marina Vallarta and airport

Holiday Inn Puerto Vallarta

Puerto de Luna

Villa del Palmar

Fiesta Americana Puerto Vallarta

200

Av Los Tules

Playa Los Tules

Las Palmas by the Sea

Canto del Sol

Picasso

Venicia

Roma

Niza

España

Casa Tukari

Palm Springs

Yugoslavia

Hamburgo

Viena

Versalles

Havre

Milan

Francia

Lisboa

Liverpool

Lucerna

Hacienda Mosaico

Gaviotas

Av Francisco Villa

Berlin

Mérida

Morelia

Viena

BANDERAS BAY

PLAYA NORTE

Playa Las Glorias

Febronio Libre

Olimpica

Av Emiliano Zapata

Av Luis Donaldo Colosio

Barrio Santa Maria

Lifestyles Getaway Club Puerto Vallarta

Blvd Francisco Medino Ascencio

Brasil

Bolivia

Sheraton Buganvilias Resort & Convention Center

Camacho

Amapetec

Av Las

Lázaro Cárdenas

Americas

(Libramento)

Eréndida

Ecuador

Cuba

Belice

Puerto Rico

Rep. Dominica

Guyana

Estados Unidos

Río Guayaquil

Río de la Plata

Villa Premiere Hotel & Spa

Guatemala

Jamaica

Río Grande

Río Danubo

Buenaventura Grand Hotel and Spa

Brasil

Bolivia

San Salvador

Nicaragua

Cemetery

200

Paraguay

Av México

Colombia

Honduras

Panama

Ecuador

Costa Rica

Belice

Playa Camarones

Uruguay

Rep. de Chile

Venezuela

to Downtown

Parque Hidalgo

Libramento (Bypass)

N

bedroom guest units. All have furnished kitchenettes or full kitchens, satellite TV and central air conditioning, as well as private balconies overlooking the three swimming pools set along the edge of the beach. There are also tennis courts and a fitness center and spa. An internet café is located on the premises.

PUERTO DE LUNA

$$$ 110 UNITS ✉Boulevard Francisco Medina Ascencio #2500 ✆322-225-0480
✆322-225-0481 ✑www.puertodeluna.com, reservations@puertodeluna.com

One of the smallest, most intimate beach resorts in the Hotel Zone, this resort offers suites, somewhat frayed around the edges, in seven four-story colonial-style buildings across the highway from the beach. Most have one king- or queen-sized bed and one or two double-sized pull-out beds in a separate room, plus kitchenettes or full kitchens as well as balconies or patios, all making this a good bet for traveling families or adaptable groups of friends. The small grounds are landscaped with neatly trimmed lawns, a swimming pool and dense stands of palm trees. The staff speaks little English.

FIESTA AMERICANA PUERTO VALLARTA

$$$$ 291 ROOMS ✉Boulevard Francisco Medina Ascencio, Km. 2.5
✆322-226-2100 ✆322-224-2108 ✑www.fiestaamericana.com.mx

Part of Mexico's most prestigious hotel chain, this nine-story hotel is smaller than the company's highrises in Guadalajara and in other resort destinations such as Cancún, though the ambience in its public areas is hardly intimate. The exceptionally spacious guest rooms feature polished marble floors and one king-size or two queen-sized beds; all have balconies overlooking the pool area, the bay and the nearby forest of palm trees. One unique feature is a nursery where rescued sea turtle eggs are hatched during the July-to-January nesting season and guests can help release them into the sea. Choose between European and all-inclusive plans.

HACIENDA MOSAICO

$$–$$$ 7 ROOMS ✉Calle Milan #274, Colonia Versalles ✆322-225-8296,
866-263-9717 ✆322-224-8576 ✑www.haciendamosaico.com,
info@haciendamosaico.com

Tucked away in Colonia Versalles, a prosperous residential neighborhood east of the Hotel Zone that most Puerto Vallarta visitors never see, this is an artists' retreat with a walled garden. The location is a mile from the beach, on the other side of the highway, but you may be just as happy sunbathing by the hacienda's tranquil swimming pool, surrounded by mango, banana and guava trees. The guest rooms are all air-conditioned and individually decorated in bright colors. Fantastic furniture and mosaics handmade by the innkeepers add an extra touch of fun to the common areas. A full schedule of art workshops includes ceramics, beading and mosaics (of course). There is a three-night minimum stay.

CASA TUKARI

$$$ 4 ROOMS ✉Avenida España #316, Colonia Versalles ✆322-224-7177

📠322-295-2350 ✐www.tukari.com, info@tukari.com

In the same neighborhood, three blocks farther from the beach, stands a Mediterranean-style white B&B inn with arches and red-tile roof. Its individually decorated rooms, cooled with ceiling fans, surround a garden of lime, banana and guava trees. Sunbathers bask on chaise longues on a neatly groomed lawn beside the swimming pool. Massage therapy services are available on-site. No children under 12.

CANTO DEL SOL

$$–$$$ 550 ROOMS ✉Jose Clemente Orozco #125 ✆322-226-0123

📠322-224-4437 ✐www.cantodelsol.com, info@cantodelsol.com

With the best tennis club in the Hotel Zone and an abundance of activities for young and old, Canto del Sol Plaza Vallarta and its smaller companion resort, the recently renovated Villas Vallarta by Canto del Sol across the street, stand apart from other nearby all-inclusives. They keep guests busy with everything from bingo to dance lessons and from nightly movies to a beach sport called tequila volleyball (which, as you might expect, involves a lot of falling down). Their complete "Kids' Club" schedule of activities from 10 a.m. to 5 p.m. daily, offers everything from Mexican games and origami to sandcastle building and beach walks. The tennis club is equipped with four clay and four Laykold courts, all lighted for night play. The 270 standard guest rooms and 128 suites in the main hotel are decorated in soft and subtle earth tones and feature all the standard amenities as well as internet access, narrow balconies with pool or garden views and bathrooms with tubs. Villas Vallarta has another 152 rooms and one- and two-bedroom suites, most with fully equipped kitchenettes. Although neither resort fronts the bay, the beach is only a short walk away.

LIFESTYLES GETAWAY CLUB PUERTO VALLARTA

$$$$ 385 ROOMS ✉Boulevard Francisco Medina Ascencio s/n, Km. 1.5

✆322-226-3300, 800-718-7915 (within Mexico) 📠322-226-3350

✐www.getawayvallarta.com, rgarcia@getawayvallarta.com

If you like to sunbathe topless, one of the few places in town where you can do so is a rooftop area at this adults-only (over 18; straight and gay couples equally welcome) resort. The 385 rooms, mostly in a single 12-story building, are spacious and have one king-sized or two double beds. Facilities include two free-form swimming pools, a tennis court, a gym and a spa with sauna, jacuzzi and steam room. While it is all-inclusive only, the package includes all meals—breakfast and lunch in an ocean-view buffet or by room service, dinner in your choice of an international restaurant or an American-style steakhouse—plus unlimited drinks at numerous bars on the premises. Other amenities include a dance club, nonmotorized water sports such as sea kayaks, and introductory snorkel and scuba lessons in the pool. The beach is a little rocky.

LAS PALMAS BY THE SEA

$$$ 221 ROOMS   ⊠*Boulevard Francisco Medina Ascencio s/n, Km. 2.5*
322-226-1220, 888-790-5264 ✆*322-226-1268* ✐*www.laspalmasresort.com,*
reservaciones@laspalmasresort.com

Owned by a Mexican family, this resort boasts an unusually friendly, accommodating staff. Most guest rooms have balconies and views of the ocean; the other, more affordable units look out on the mountains and have no balconies. Facilities include two swimming pools and an exercise room with a sauna. There is an all-inclusive option, but the buffet food—the only choice besides the beachfront snack bar—tends to be blandly ordinary and non-Mexican, making the European Plan a better choice.

SHERATON BUGANVILIAS RESORT & CONVENTION CENTER

$$$ 600 ROOMS   ⊠*Boulevard Francisco Medina Ascencio #999* ✆*322-226-0404,*
800-942-6155 ✆*322-222-0500* ✐*www.sheratonvallarta.com,*
reservas@sheratonvallarta.com.mx

Big enough to overshadow its neighboring hotels, the Sheraton has a new, contemporary look, following a recent full-scale renovation. Its guest rooms, in nine towers that stand in a long row, overlook two huge swimming pools, grounds filled with lawns and dense stands of palm trees, and beyond them the beach and the bay. The spotless standard rooms have white walls, white tile floors, white ceilings and white furniture, as well as balconies (avoid the lower floors, where the views may be blocked by palm trees). The hotel strives to appeal to families with daily kids' activities and to businesspeople with large meeting spaces and a full business center, giving it something of a split personality. There's no all-inclusive option, and meals and drinks are expensive even by Hotel Zone standards. Fortunately, the restaurants and bars of downtown Puerto Vallarta are not far away.

VILLA PREMIERE HOTEL & SPA

$$$ 83 ROOMS   ⊠*San Salvador #117* ✆*322-226-7040, 877-886-9176*
✐*www.premiereonline.com.mx, reservations@premiereonline.com.mx*

Fairly close to downtown, the Villa Premiere is an attractive option for couples of all ages and sexual orientations. Children are not allowed. One of the downtown area's newest hotels, built in 1999, this smallish, pink eight-story establishment features vaguely Mediterranean architecture and a lobby filled with columns, fountains, big bird sculptures and bright paintings. The guest rooms and suites are modern with tropical pastel hues; they have balconies, many with ocean views. Perhaps because the hotel is too new for trees and large plants to have grown yet, the two parallel beachfront swimming pools have no landscaping. Only a few umbrellas provide shade, though the big double chaise longues are great for sunbathing. Unlike some Hotel Zone resorts, there are few planned activities. An optional all-inclusive arrangement covers the three restaurants on the premises, one open-air and the other two open only for dinner, as well as the poolside bar. Massages and other spa services are available for an extra charge.

BUENAVENTURA GRAND HOTEL AND SPA

$$–$$$ 221 ROOMS ✉ *Avenida México #1301* ☎ *322-226-7000, 888-859-9439* 📠 *322-226-3546* 🖅 *www.hotelbuenaventura.com.mx*

The closest of the Hotel Zone resorts to downtown Puerto Vallarta's picturesque old downtown area (one mile), this five-story hotel with standard rooms and suites has three swimming pools and is located by popular Playa Los Camarones. It's family-friendly, with lots of activities especially for kids. The main drawback for some guests is the overly firm beds—actually mattresses atop concrete pedestals, which are common in Mexican hotels but can be an unwelcome surprise to the Anglo spinal column. You can choose either a European plan (no meals included) or the all-inclusive option.

DINING

Every all-inclusive hotel has a primary buffet-style restaurant, included in the daily rate and designed to feed hundreds of guests efficiently and to offer a wide enough array of selections so that everyone will find something to their taste. Most also have one or more à la carte "specialty" restaurants. Guests sometimes have to pay to eat at these places; at other resorts, guests can eat there free a limited number of times and sometimes have their menu selections limited.

North American expatriates and seasonal residents in Puerto Vallarta tend to turn up their noses at the notion of dining out in the Hotel Zone. This attitude is partly because of a tourist-industry sameness that seems to pervade most big resort restaurants and partly because the prices are often exorbitant. Still, there are at least a few restaurants in the Hotel Zone that are worth considering as alternatives to the abundance of fine dining found downtown and in the Zona Romántica.

BOGART'S

$$$$ INTERNATIONAL ✉ *NH Krystal Vallarta, Avenida de las Garzas s/n* ☎ *322-224-0202*

A hallmark of the NH Krystal hotel locations at most of Mexico's famous beach resorts, Bogart's is all about ambience. The exotic, palace-like decor features white Moroccan-style archways and ornate filigrees, fountains, authentic North African rugs and tilework and high-backed wicker chairs. You almost expect the piano player to segue into "As Time Goes By" (and he sometimes does). The lighting is romantic, though so dim that you may have trouble reading the menu, which is long and international, ranging from shrimp flambé and lobster-stuffed chicken breast to wild salmon and *mixiote* (meat steamed in the paperlike outer layer of the *maguey*, or century plant leaf) and served with a julienne of leeks, snow peas, carrots, ginger, soy sauce and wild rice sautéed with pistachio nuts. Reservations required. Dinner only.

KAMAKURA

$$–$$$ JAPANESE ✉NH Krystal Vallarta, Avenida de las Garzas s/n
☎322-224-0202

This was the first Japanese restaurant in Puerto Vallarta and is still considered to be the best. The decor is clean and spare, with white walls, dark lacquer furniture and semi-opaque screens breaking it up into separate dining areas subtly enhanced by rock gardens and waterfalls in the corners of the restaurant. Seating is at *teppan* tables, fitted with hot, flat grills upon which a chef cooks your dinner right in front of you, slicing beef or chicken into strips and butterflying shrimp with a spectacular display of knife work. Kamakura also boasts the largest selection of sushi in Puerto Vallarta. For a happy ending to your dinner, try the crisp, hot-and-cold tempura ice cream. The restaurant offers a two-for-one special on Tuesdays. Dinner only. Closed Monday.

LAS GORDITAS NORTEÑAS

$ MEXICAN ✉Plaza Caracol, local 7A ☎322-293-1908

If it's no-frills, genuinely Mexican fast food you're after, stop in at this clean, bright, busy little eatery inside the Gigante (soon to become Soriana) supermarket across the boulevard from Los Tules condominium complex. Usually sold by street vendors, *gorditas* ("little fat ones") are thick corn tortillas, sliced open to form a pocket and stuffed with shredded beef, chicken, cheese or chile stew.

LA PETITE

$$$ FRENCH ✉Boulevard Francisco Medina Ascencio #2189 ☎322-293-0900

Located at the entrance to the Fiesta Americana but not affiliated with the hotel, La Petite is often hailed as the finest classic French restaurant in Puerto Vallarta—curiously enough, since owner-chef Nacho Cadena is Mexican born and trained. The menu changes (and usually improves) regularly but always includes savory renditions of standbys like paté, escargots, soufflés, duckling à l'orange with brandy and, for dessert, chocolate mousse. Formerly a disco, the restaurant has been completely transformed with dark wood furnishings and beam ceilings, two-story-high arched windows, soft lighting and reproductions of Toulouse-Lautrec paintings on the walls. A piano player entertains intermittently throughout the evening.

CITRUS

$$ INTERNATIONAL ✉Plaza Villas Vallarta, local C-46 ☎322-293-6381

This trendy beachside restaurant near the Villas Vallarta resort offers an eclectic menu of international dishes for breakfast, lunch and dinner in a modern setting. Start the day with a just-like-home breakfast of eggs over easy with bacon and hash browns or something more adventurous like *huitlacoche* crêpes filled with corn custard and topped with cilantro cream sauce. (*Huitlacoche* is a smoky-tasting fungus that grows on corn and is used like truffles.) Lunch focuses on soups, salads and sandwiches such as a Black Angus burger topped with avocado, mushrooms and goat cheese. Dinner entrées range from macadamia-crusted tuna to pad thai.

TIZOK TAKOS

$ MEXICAN   ✉*Boulevard Francisco Medina Ascencio at Calle Francia*

This hole-in-the-wall fast-food place with indoor seating as well as a walk-up window on the sidewalk is one of the best authentic taco stands in the Hotel Zone. Soft corn tortillas with assorted fillings such as *carne asada* (grilled beef), *pastor* (shredded pork), chicken or shrimp come with beans, cilantro, radish and grilled onion garnishes and four different salsas. You can also order mugs of Mexican-style beverages including *horchata* (a cinnamon-flavored rice drink) and *jamaica* (hibiscus tea).

PARADISE BAKERY

$ BAKERY / DELI   ✉*Sierra Aconagua at Prolongación Brasil*
✆*322-222-5133*

This long-time local favorite recently moved to a new, obscure location on a street corner two blocks east of Francisco Villa and a block south of the Highway 200 Libramento. Known for the best cinnamon rolls in town, owner Liana Turner also makes other irresistible temptations such as bittersweet triple chocolate brownies and mocha almond bars. The little café is open all day, serving sandwiches and salads. Doubles as a catering service for cocktail parties and private dinners, the Paradise can prepare anything from simple antipasto and pastry plates to full gourmet feasts.

100% NATURAL

$ VEGETARIAN   ✉*Boulevard Francisco Medina Ascencio #1630*   ✆*322-223-2974*

Organic and vegetarian (though, for the most part, not vegan) fare for breakfast, lunch and dinner can be found at 100% Natural, part of a franchise restaurant chain found all across Mexico. Breakfasts, all egg-based, include such creative items as *pochos,* poached eggs served over a bed of nopal cactus and spinach on bread, smothered in an almond, poblano pepper and cream sauce. For other meals, the menu includes a wide selection of salads as well as chicken sandwiches and soy burgers.

BISTRO LAS GAVIOTAS

$$$ SEAFOOD   ✉*Sheraton Buganvilias Resort & Convention Center, Boulevard Francisco Medina Ascencio #999*   ✆*322-226-0410*

This specialty restaurant in the Sheraton Buganvilias Resort, spotlights Mexican-fusion cuisine so noteworthy that it was selected as the headquarters for the 2005 Puerto Vallarta Festival Gourmet International.

The atmosphere is casual yet romantic, with white tablecloths, candle-light and folk art decor that includes a sculpture wall with large, backlit bronze discs that cast a soft glow. Live piano music completes the mood. The bill of fare offers such delights as scallops with asparagus and chorizo, chipotle seafood soup and pepper-sealed tuna with cilantro rice. Dinner only.

MURALES

$$$$ GOURMET MEXICAN ✉San Salvador #117 ✆322-226-7040

Intimate and decidedly upscale, Murales in the Villa Premiere Hotel takes its name from the classically Mexican mural art that decorates the walls. Seafood predominates, with such delights as red snapper and scallops served with baby cactus and bean sauce. Or try a non-seafood house specialty like roast duck marinated in dark beer and served in a tomatillo sauce with agave. Latin dinner music fills the air nightly. Besides the air-conditioned main dining room, there is an outdoor terrace with an ocean view. Reservations required. Dinner only.

SHOPPING

PLAZA CARACOL ✉Boulevard Francisco Medina Ascencio, Km. 2.5 The Hotel Zone has several shopping centers, of which the largest is Plaza Caracol in Colonia Versalles, across the main boulevard from the Los Tules and Fiesta Americana hotels. It is anchored by a large supermarket and the LANS Tienda Departmental, an exclusive department store. Also within the mall are **Deportes Marti**, the biggest sporting goods store in town, and banks, a multiscreen movie theater complex and an assortment of jewelry stores, home decor accessories and boutiques including **Etnica Boutique** (handwoven and embroidered resort wear), **Glamour** (women's fashion) and **Liquid Men** (men's fashion).

ALFARERIA TLAQUEPAQUE ✉Avenida México #1100 ✆322-223-2121 If you're shopping for collectible folk art, your best bet in the Hotel Zone is this beautiful store, which has been in business for more than 50 years, sells Talavera ceramics and other arts and crafts from Tlaquepaque, the famous artisans' village on the outskirts of Guadalajara, including handcrafted dinnerware and pre-Columbian replicas.

GALERIA FLORES

✉Francisco Villa #305 ✆322-293-1681 Pam and Fernando Flores's long-established gallery recently relocated from its smaller, chicer setting in Marina Vallarta to a sprawling showroom, classroom and studio spaces well hidden in the Colonia Olimpica neighborhood, a block north of the municipal sports stadium and across the street from the water company offices. Upstairs from Enmarcados GMC (also called Memo's), the framing shop used by most local artists and galleries, the gallery focuses on bright, whimsical paintings often featuring animals and other nature images, and offers art classes.

NIGHTLIFE

J&B SALSA CLUB ⊠*Boulevard Francisco Medina Ascencio #2043* ✆*322-224-4616* J&B features hot live Latin dance music—cumbia, salsa, merengue and bachata—by the house band Chevere. The band doesn't start playing until midnight, but free dance lessons are offered starting at 10 p.m. Thursdays and Saturdays. The crowd is mostly couples, in all age ranges. Closed Sunday through Tuesday. Cover.

BLANCO Y NEGRO

⊠*Lucerna y Niza* ✆*322-293-2556* Tucked away behind the Blockbuster video rental store, this small place is owned by internationally renowned singer/songwriter Mario Blanco, a master of a Cuban genre called Nuevo Trova that has become popular throughout Latin America. He usually performs after 11 p.m. and also opens the microphone to other top local musicians and poets.

CHRISTINE ⊠*NH Krystal Vallarta, Avenida de las Garzas s/n* ✆*322-224-0202* The longest established upscale dance club in the Hotel Zone and still one of the best, Christine has the same name and ambience as the nightspots at other Krystal resorts from Cancún to Ixtapa. This disco features techno music and a '70s-style light show with lasers, fog machines and big video screens. The dress code is casual. There's usually a long line to get in, and the cover charge, which varies from night to night, can be formidable—up to US$30 per person on weekends, though once you get in, it's an open bar. Open until 5 a.m. Women get in free on Wednesdays. Closed Tuesday. Cover.

THE FACTORY ⊠*Avenida de las Garzas #1* ✆*322-226-6800* This popular disco in the Crown Paradise Resort presents music-and-dance stage shows at 9:30 nightly, then opens its dance floor to the public. The action doesn't usually get going until around midnight, and the disco shuts down at 2 a.m. Cover; open bar.

MIRAGE SALSA Y MERENGUE ⊠*Boulevard Francisco Medina Ascencio at Liverpool* ✆*322-222-6050* This club starts the evening as a romantic piano bar. At 10 p.m. the Cuban house band Coco Hache fires up with hot Latin rhythms all night long. This place is a bit dressy—no shorts or sandals. Not to be confused with the old *club caballeros* of the same name.

HYSTERIA

⊠*Avenida Luis Donaldo Colosio #126* ✆*322-222-0698* For male visitors whose idea of a good time in Mexico involves something a little more on the raunchy side, there are a number of *clubes caballeros* (gentlemen's clubs), otherwise known as strip joints, well concealed to avoid offending Puerto Vallarta's family visitors. One of the most popular is Hysteria, on the highway that bypasses the southern part of the Hotel Zone, two blocks south of Avenida Francisco Villa. Like other clubs of its type in town, it has recently gone from topless to totally nude.

BEACHES

PLAYA NORTE

✉*From the edge of downtown along the Hotel Zone to the Marina Vallarta yacht basin entrance*

Also known as Playa Las Glorias and Playa Los Tules and Playa del Oro, this wide three-mile length of medium-grained, cream-colored sand is segmented not only by shallow water flows where a nameless creek and the small Río Pitillal meet the bay, but also by man-made rock jetties every 500 yards, designed to keep the big hotels' beachfronts private and to protect the beach from erosion. These jetties make good places for fishing from shore but also turn long walks on the beach into rock scrambles. Hotels use security guards to restrict beach access, too. (Under Mexican law, all beaches are public property up to the high-water mark, but privately owned foreshore or beach frontage rights, which are property rights independent of the adjacent real estate itself, give owners the right to block access to the beach.) Generally, the hotels only allow their guests, and those of other hotels who have special arrangements with them, to use their stretches of beach. This keeps souvenir vendors from bothering the guests but also bars locals and nonguests from using the beach. If you're staying in one of the downtown hotels and want to experience the Hotel Zone beaches, the best way is to go to the activity desk at one of the big hotels and sign up for a water sports activity such as parasailing or a jet ski rental. Camping is not permitted here or on any beach along Banderas Bay.

DOWNTOWN PUERTO VALLARTA

Downtown (*Centro* in Spanish) Puerto Vallarta is where you'll find banks and ATMs, as well as plenty of places to spend your pesos. This part of town is known for its outstanding art galleries—nearly two dozen of them in ten blocks—as well as quality arts and handicrafts stores offering the amazing bead and yarn work of the Huichol Indians, pottery from Guadalajara area artisans' villages and countless stores whose showcases gleam with silver Taxco jewelry. But the most entertaining activity in the Centro may be people-watching. Old Puerto Vallarta, for all its touristic veneer, remains a living, vibrant, authentic Mexican town where tradition runs deep and often comes face-to-face with contemporary global values in a spirit of lively, thoroughly bilingual celebration.

With its tangle of little back streets and signs in Spanish, it's possible to get lost in Old Puerto Vallarta. Don't panic; enjoy it. Sandwiched between the ocean on the west, the mountains on the east and the river in

CHEZ ELENA

PAGE 113

A local secret for international cuisine—Indonesian skewers with peanut sauce are the house specialty

LOS CUATRO VIENTOS

PAGE 109

Simple, cheerful guest rooms with handpainted Mexican ceramics, tropical gardens and a rooftop terrace perfect for sipping margaritas

HUICHOL COLLECTION GALERÍA MUSEO

PAGE 115

Huichol artists at work—brightly colored yarnwork, beads and woodcarvings by local indigenous people

TEQUILAS

PAGE 119

A casual atmosphere with a strolling mariachi band and one of the largest tequila menus in town

GRINGO GULCH

PAGE 107

A hint of Old Hollywood—the private enclave that Elizabeth Taylor, Richard Burton and others called home

the center of town, it's just about impossible to stay lost for very long. Take a map along whenever you go exploring. Besides the one in this book, maps are available from the tourist information office in the municipal palace on the Plaza de Armas.

Old Puerto Vallarta's streets are not designated as *calles* (streets) or *avenidas* (avenues). They are simply called by their names—Morelos, Hidalgo, Lázaro Cárdenas, Ignacio Vallarta and so forth. Most are named for Mexican heroes and local founding fathers, which can occasionally present problems because some historical figures share the same last names. For example, there are different streets called Francisca Rodríguez and Agustín Rodríguez, with the first names abbreviated in small letters on the street signs.

SIGHTS

PLAZA DE ARMAS ✉ *Paseo Diaz Ordaz between Iturbide and Zaragosa* The place to start your exploration of downtown Puerto Vallarta is the main downtown plaza, where locals and visitors alike linger on benches beneath a few shade trees, their trunks painted white to deter insect pests. Typical of most towns in Jalisco, there is an ornate gazebo surrounded by flocks of pigeons. Fronting on the north side of Plaza de Armas, the **Presidencia Municipal** (City Hall) is a modern structure with a pillared front portal and a balcony from which the mayor can make speeches. It's worth a visit to see the large mural by Manuel Lepe (1936–1981), the self-taught painter who is hailed as the founder of the city's art scene and dubbed a National Artist of Mexico by President Luís Echeverría. Though hard to find in Puerto Vallarta since his daughter closed her gallery in the year 2000, his naïf-style paintings filled with colorful arrays of angels, children, animals, airplanes and boats have made their way into museums and private collections around the world. The city hall mural, in the building's main stairwell, depicts the founding of the port of Puerto Vallarta. Lepe painted it just a year before he died suddenly of a brain aneurism. On the ground floor at the east corner of the Presidencia Municipal, the city **Tourist Information Office** has truckloads of tourist brochures and friendly, bilingual staffers to hand them out to you.

ANFITEATRO LOS ARCOS ✉ *Across Díaz Ordaz from the Plaza de Armas* Overlooking the bay is a Greek-style open-air theater where free music concerts are presented on Sunday evenings and during community celebrations. The name comes from the row of stone arches supported by free-standing columns between the theater and the sea. The amphitheater used to mark the midpoint of the *malecón* until it was extended farther south recently.

THE MALECÓN ✉ *On the waterfront* The paved promenade runs the entire length of the downtown area, over the Río Cuale on a pair of footbridges and down along Los Muertos Beach to the pier where the water ferries to Yelapa depart. The total length is presently about four kilometers. There are plenty of benches along the way for resting and watching the sea. The *malecón* is one of the liveliest places in town after dark. This is especially true on Sundays, when painters line its whole length to display their works for sale, but on any evening of the week you can count on finding plenty of street performers, such as a mime painted like a gold robot, a weightlifter who balances stacks of 200-pound rocks by the shore or a man caked with mud who stands absolutely still for half an hour and then comes to life to spout Spanish poetry.

Among the *malecón's* most remarkable features are its many large bronze sculptures. Starting at the north end, you'll see the newest sculpture, **Los Milenios**, Mathis Lidice's modernistic depiction of the passage of time. Farther along stands **La Nostalgia**, a pair of abstract figures seated by the sea wall, by Ramiz Barquet, who has more pieces of public art on display in Puerto Vallarta than any other artist. Other statues include **El Caballito de Mar** (The Seahorse) by Rafael Zamarripa, the first sculpture on the *malecón*, which has stood on this spot for 30 years and is one of Puerto Vallarta's most familiar symbols. You'll also see bronze sculptures of a leaping whale, a mermaid and others. Near the Los Arcos Amphitheater you'll find the **Fuente de los Delfines** (Fountain of the Dolphins) sculpture, also called the Friendship Fountain.

to Hotel Zone and
Nuevo Vallarta ↑

Parque Hidalgo

Downtown Puerto Vallarta

Perú

Argentina

Jesús Langarica

31 de Octubre

Morelos

Juárez

Sánchez

Allende

Pipila

Leona

Vicario

Ortiz de Dominguez

Ordaz

Díaz

Abasolo

Aldama

malecón

playa Camarones

B A N D E R A S   B A Y

0   0.25 mile

0   0.25 kilometer

N

Downtown

Corona

Galeana

Mina

Juárez

Hidalgo

Matamores

Miramar

Iturbide

Cuauhtémoc

Rio Cuale

Plaza de Armas

Indepencia

Zaragoza

Guerrero

Gringo Gulch

Libertad

Rodríguez

Isla Río Cuale

5 de Febrero

Aguiles Serdán

Naranjo

Camichin

Francisco I. Madero

Lázaro Cárdenas

Venustiano Carranza

Basilio Badillo

Encino

Constitución

Ignacio Vallarta

Zona Romántica

200

200

SIGHTS & LODGING

Ⓐ Antiteatro los Arcos
Ⓑ Casa Amorita
Ⓒ Centro Cultural Vallartens
Ⓓ El Caballito del Mar
Ⓔ Fuentes de los Delfines
Ⓕ Hacienda San Angel
Ⓖ Hotel Encino
Ⓗ Hotel Rosita
Ⓘ La Nostalgia
Ⓙ Los Cuatro Vientos
Ⓚ Los Milenios
Ⓛ Mercado Artesanía
Ⓜ Museo Arqueológico
Ⓝ Parroquía de Nuestra
    Señora de Guadalupe
Ⓞ Presidencia Municipal
Ⓟ Primera Iglesia Bautista
Ⓠ Suites Plaza del Río
Ⓡ Villa David

PARROQUÍA DE NUESTRA SEÑORA DE GUADALUPE ✉Hidalgo #370 ☎322-222-1326

A short block uphill from the west side of the plaza stands Puerto Vallarta's main cathedral and most recognizable landmark. Despite its vaguely colonial appearance, the brick and stone church is not very old, having been built from 1929 to 1941. It is dedicated to the Virgin of Guadalupe, and on December 12, the Feast Day of Guadalupe, groups of pilgrims come from all over the states of Jalisco and Nayarit to attend rituals in the church. Amid the hand-carved columns and ornate moldings of the church's interior are works of religious art including the Stations of the Cross carved by renowned Mexico City sculptor Jesús Ramirez. Other artworks in the church include a painting of the Virgin of Guadalupe by Ignacio Ramirez, which the church's priest at the time (1945) carried to Mexico City and back so it could be blessed at the Basilica de Nuestra Señora de Guadalupe there; and a painting of the Holy Trinity, by prominent local artists Daniel and Malena Lechón, on the dome over the altar. The church is open almost all the time, but signs at the entrance warn visitors that proper attire is required, meaning no shorts, sleeveless shirts or just about anything else you'd be likely to wear on a hot afternoon in downtown Puerto Vallarta. If you left your proper attire home, you can see inside from the front steps, where elderly women sit begging for alms. And, of course, you can get a photogenic view of the church tower with its distinctive, ornate crown on top, which is said to be a replica of the one worn by Queen Carlota, wife of Emperor Maximilian, who ruled Mexico on behalf of its European creditor nations from 1864 to 1867. The original crown on the church was made of sculpted brick and was toppled and broken during an earthquake in 1995. The more ornate replacement looks like wrought iron but is actually made of fiberglass.

GRINGO GULCH

✉*Zaragoza* Zaragoza turns into a long, very steep stairway behind the south corner of the cathedral and makes its way uphill to the center of the enclave where movie stars lived during the filming of *The Night of the Iguana* and other early expatriates bought their Puerto Vallarta homes. The houses of Richard Burton and Elizabeth Taylor were at the upper end of the street, above the intersection with Carranza. Taylor's house is at 445 Zaragoza, where she lived part-time for 26 years. After Taylor sold it, it was operated for several years as a private museum and bed and breakfast under the name Casa Kimberley. It's closed and up for sale as this book goes to press. Burton's former house is across the street, connected to Taylor's by an arched pink-and-white *puente de reconciliación* ("love bridge"). The upper end of the street affords a good view of the Río Cuale below.

MERCADO ARTESANÍA ("FLEA MARKET") ✉*Encino del Río* A four-block walk south along Hidalgo (from the church) or Juárez (from the plaza) will bring you to the walkway above the north bank of the Río Cuale, the river that flows out of the mountains through the center of Puerto Vallarta. It was the discovery of gold and silver farther upriver that gave Puerto Vallarta (then called Puerto de Los Arcos) its start in the late 19th century. Proceed upriver along the walkway for a couple of blocks, dodging the time-share touts, and you'll come to the arts-and-crafts market, a two-story building that once housed the town's municipal marketplace. As the fishing town transformed into a world-class tourist resort, the produce and meat stalls gradually gave way to vendors of local handicrafts, and they in turn were displaced by the labyrinth of crowded, open-front shops you find there today selling colorful manufactured—and usually imported—curios. You won't find much in the way of authentic regional arts and crafts. What you will find are lots of souvenir T-shirts and baseball caps, along with coarse yet colorful weavings and hammocks from Guatemala and other low-end Mexican crafts knock-offs from China. Still, it can be fun to poke around in the two-story labyrinth of market stalls while vendors call out, "Hey, amigo, I got what you're looking for. ¡*Pasa adelante*! Almost free—how much you want to pay?" Asking prices start high and are quite negotiable.

PARQUE HIDALGO

✉*Argentina #181* ✆*322-222-1322* If you follow the *malecón* all the way to the north end, you'll reach the southern tip of Playa Los Camarones, the Hotel Zone beach. Across the street from the Hotel Rosita is another public plaza. The park was razed in 2005 to install an underground parking garage, then rebuilt with ramadas for shade and a fountain in the center. As is traditional for Mexican town plazas, a church—the **Parroquía de Nuestra Señora del Refugio**—graces the east side of Parque Hidalgo. Also adjoining the park is a Baptist church, the **Primera Iglesia Bautista**.

TERRA NOBLE SPA, ART & HEALING CENTER ✉*Avenida Tulipanes #595* ✆*322-223-3530* ✐*www.terranoble.com, info@terranoble.com* Many hotels, especially large resorts, have spa facilities, and you'll find professional massage therapists on just about every block downtown and in the Zona Romántica. But nothing else in Puerto Vallarta (or, maybe, anywhere else) can compare with this day spa on a hilltop overlooking Bahía de Banderas. It offers a relaxed atmosphere and relatively moderate prices for broad range of services, including Swedish massage, shiatsu, aromatherapy, cranial-sacral therapy, reflexology, acupressure and seaweed wraps. There's a native-style four-person sweat lodge (*temazcalli*), as well as a picturesque villa inspired by African village architecture where clay and art workshops are given by local artists. The well-marked road to the spa turns west off the Libramiento bypass road above downtown, just before the big tunnel.

LODGING

HOTEL ROSITA

$$ 115 ROOMS ✉*Paseo Díaz Ordaz #901* ✆*322-223-2000, 877-813-6712*
✆*322-223-4393* ✐*www.hotelrosita.com, sales@hotelrosita.com*

One of Puerto Vallarta's first tourist resorts, marking the edge of the old city before the Hotel Zone was conceived, this refurbished hotel strikes a balance between economy and location. The five-story building stands at the north end of the *malecón*, across the street from Parque Hidalgo. All guest rooms have balconies—some overlooking the ocean, others looking out on the swimming pool or the buildings of downtown. The rooms vary in size and amenities; the best, facing the ocean, are two-room units designed to sleep families, with queen-sized beds in the "master bedrooms," which have large double doors opening onto the balconies, and two or three beds in a larger adjoining room. The decor in most rooms is bare-walls simple. Some rooms have television sets. Some are air-conditioned, while others have only ceiling fans.

CASA AMORITA

$$–$$$$ 5 ROOMS ✉*Calle Iturbide #309 at Calle Matamoros*
✆*322-222-4926* 🖱*www.casaamorita.com, ritalove@hotmail.com*

Just behind the Parroquía de Nuestra Señora de Guadalupe, this is a modernistic five-unit B&B in a custom-built two-story home with Moorish and Mediterranean architecture. Viewed from the terrace and any guest room, the landmark fiberglass crown atop the church dominates the view of downtown and the ocean beyond. The guest rooms each have a private bath and balcony, as well as an in-room dining area. There are also fireplaces, sundecks, a solarium and a tropical garden with towering stands of bamboo, a fountain and bird feeders. The downtown location couldn't be more central; the *parque central*, the *malecón* and the Río Cuale are all within a three- or four-block radius.

LOS CUATRO VIENTOS

$$ 14 ROOMS ✉*Matamoros #520* ✆*322-222-0161* 📠*322-222-2831*
🖱*www.chezelena.com, fourwinds@cuatrovientos.com*

This a long-established inn is set against the hillside behind downtown and wrapped in gardens of tropical flora. Guest rooms are simple and cheerful, their walls festooned with folk art and painted with colorful patterns. Hand-painted Mexican ceramics and tilework brighten the bathrooms. There are ceiling fans but no air conditioning, phones or TVs. Some accommodations are multiroom suites that can sleep up to six people. In the evening, guests can sip margaritas on the rooftop terrace with a view of the church, the ocean and the terra-cotta rooftops of town. There's a small swimming pool.

HACIENDA SAN ANGEL

$$$$ 9 UNITS ✉*Miramar #336* ✆*322-222-2692, 877-815-594*
🖱*www.haciendasanangel.com, info@haciendasanangel.com*

Maybe the classiest address in downtown Puerto Vallarta, Hacienda San Angel offers atmospheric luxury, a scenic hillside location in Gringo Gulch and a remarkable history. The main hacienda, with nine suites, was bought as a 1982 Valentine's Day gift by film star Richard Burton for his then-wife, Susan Hunt. Burton devoted much of his last two years of life to redecorating the mansion with sculptures, artwork and antique architectural elements from all over Mexico. Hacienda San Angel has expanded to include three other nearby houses, broken up into three to six suites, each individually decorated with Spanish colonial antiques, handcrafted furniture and contemporary artworks. All suites are air-conditioned, with private baths, DVD players and wireless internet access. There are two heated swimming pools—one overlooking the city and the ocean, the other secluded in a tranquil interior courtyard—as well as a rooftop jacuzzi. A full buffet breakfast is included in the room rate, and other meals are available on request.

VILLA DAVID

$$–$$$ 10 ROOMS   ✉ *Calle Galeana #348*   ☎ *322-223-0315, 877-832-3315*
☎ *724-573-4693 (in the U.S.)*   ⌕ *www.villadavidpv.com, bill@villadavidpv.com*
This Gringo Gulch hostelry is a gay men–only, clothing-optional B&B in a hacienda-style mansion set high on the hillside; its rooftop bar and jacuzzi deck offer a panoramic view of the entire bay and Puerto Vallarta shoreline. The ten guest rooms are impeccably decorated with handmade furnishings (for instance, one has carvings of stallions for headboards; another uses an antique door as a headboard). All rooms have private baths and ceiling fans. The area around the heated pool is one of the most famous party spots in the local gay scene.

HOTEL ENCINO

$$ 75 ROOMS   ✉ *Juárez #122*   ☎ *322-222-0051, 800-326-3600 (within Mexico)*
☎ *322-222-2573*   ⌕ *www.hotelencino.com, info@hotelencino.com*
When Puerto Vallarta's art gallery owners bring artists to town from other parts of Mexico for exhibition openings, they usually put them up here. Along with affordable rates and great views from the upper floors, the hotel is located just a block from the Río Cuale and a block from the malecón, making it convenient to all the downtown galleries as well as the restaurants and clubs of the Zona Romántica. The 75 guest rooms open onto exterior walkways that surround the open central courtyard, with its tropical plants and fountain in the shape of a natural waterfall. All rooms have TVs, ceiling fans and balconies (for the best view, get one that faces south toward the river). Rooms vary in size and decor—some have bright pink walls guaranteed to wake you up in the morning. There is a rooftop swimming pool with a panoramic view.

SUITES PLAZA DEL RÍO

$$–$$$ 24 UNITS   ✉ *Hidalgo #116*   ☎ *322-222-0051, 800-326-3600 (in Mexico)*   ☎ *322-222-2573*   ⌕ *www.hotelencino.com, info@hotelencino.com*
Under the same management as the Hotel Encino and a block down the street, Suites Plaza del Río features 24 light, cheerful guest units ranging from doubles to one- and two-bedroom suites, all with TVs, ceiling fans, kitchenettes and balconies looking out over the river or the ocean—a bargain for families or groups traveling together.

CAFÉ DES ARTISTES

$$$ INTERNATIONAL   ✉Guadalupe Sánchez #740 ✆322-222-3228

Setting the standard for haute cuisine in Puerto Vallarta, Café des Artistes styles itself as a "bistro"—defined by the dictionary as "a small, unpretentious restaurant," which is actually a misleading characterization of this elegant, intimate gourmet restaurant. Owned and operated by world-renowned chef Thierry Blouet, president and founder of the annual Puerto Vallarta Festival Gourmet International, Café des Artistes started in 1990 as a little hole-in-the-wall restaurant that has grown into several adjacent houses in what has become Puerto Vallarta's art gallery district. A variety of dining areas include a courtyard garden and intimate indoor rooms appointed with silk fabrics and gleaming brass fittings as well as fine paintings, sculptures and murals. The bill of fare blends fresh Mexican ingredients with French cooking techniques, resulting in such dishes as octopus fettuccini Provençale; grilled tuna filet served over a stew of broad beans, capers, peas and pecans; or a soft-shell crab and beef tongue fantasy with lentil butter. Also available are tantalizing desserts such as a warm pear, grapefruit and almond tart with merlot sherbet, as well as fine French wines and brandies, designer tequilas that cost as much as US$40 a shot and such unusual specialty drinks as tamarind margaritas. The "formal casual" dress code means that this is one of the few restaurants in town where you'll feel uncomfortable in jeans and a tank top. Reservations are strongly advised. Valet parking is available. Dinner only.

THIERRY BLOUET COCINA DE AUTOR

$$$$ INTERNATIONAL   ✉Guadalupe Sánchez #730 ✆322-222-3228

Next door to the Café des Artistes, under the same ownership, Thierry Blouet Cocina de Autor serves a kaleidoscopically changing array of chef's special dishes from a prix-fixe menu—you mix and match your three-, four- or five-course dinner for a single, astonishingly high price.

LOS XITOMATES

$$$$ GOURMET MEXICAN   ✉Morelos #610 ✆322-222-9434
🖱www.losxitomates.com

A newer contender in the realm of *alta cocina* (Spanish for "haute cuisine") is the award-winning Los Xitomates (Aztec for "tomatoes"), an intimate, candlelit restaurant decorated in earth tones and accented with Mexican artworks. The menu focuses on seafood but also includes beef and vegetarian options; among the house specialties are grilled salmon fillet in a sauce of poblano chiles, squash blossoms and corn, as well as red snapper with a sauce of hearts of palm, ginger and Yucatecan *xcatic* chile. The tortilla soup is incomparable. Reservations are essential.

PAPAYA 3

$ VEGETARIAN ✉*Abasolo #169* ☎*322-222-0303*

If you're vegan, or completely vegetarian in that seafood is on the list of things you don't eat, you may find dining out in downtown Puerto Vallarta to be a real challenge. The solution is this deli-style natural foods restaurant that uses only fresh, organic ingredients and is often packed with foreign visitors. Here, "vegetarian" definitely doesn't mean bland; Mexican and Caribbean herbs and spices add spectacular flavor to rice and veggie dishes. The menu includes a variety of soups and big salads, as well as hot and iced herbal teas and fruit smoothies. Portions are large enough to share, and there's a large lunch buffet. There is a second Papaya location in the Zona Romántica at Olas Altas #465.

THE BLUE SHRIMP

$$ SEAFOOD ✉*Morelos #779* ☎*322-222-4246*

The furniture is blue and the shrimp are huge. In fact, half a dozen of the jumbo shrimp served here will fill up a dinner plate. You order your shrimp by the kilo (2.2 pounds), half kilo or quarter kilo, prepared in your choice of styles, such as *a la diabla* (in a spicy sauce), *al mojo de ajo* (in garlic butter), cooked with coconut, sautéed for fajitas or even flambéed with tequila. The restaurant also serves lobster, dorado and rib-eye beefsteak and offers one of the best salad bars (it's free with all entrées) in the downtown area. The decor is a perplexing mix of undersea and nautical themes, fresh flowers and artificial trees.

TRIO

$$$ CONTINENTAL ✉*Guerrero #264* ☎*322-222-2196*

A favorite of American expatriates and European visitors, Trio epitomizes the wave of fusion cuisine that has swept over the Puerto Vallarta dining scene. Co-owned by German and Swedish chefs, this air-conditioned, stylishly simple little white-tablecloths-and-crystal restaurant in a multilevel townhouse serves fare that the managers characterize as "Continental." True, the menu's European roots show in such selections as roasted rabbit with garlic sauce and Italian vegetables; beef carpaccio with aged balsamic vinegar and shaved parmesan cheese; and even wild boar loin with porcini mushrooms. The cuisine takes some daring international spins, though, with signature dishes such as fried soft-shell crab with cucumber salad and Thai peanut sauce, a Lebanese salad of baked beet slices and marinated goat cheese, and curried shrimp paella with three-chile sauce.

PARADISE BURGER

$–$$ AMERICAN ✉*Paseo Díaz Ordaz #740* ☎*322-223-2328*
🖰*www.paradiseburger.com*

The longtime fast-food favorite across from the *malecón* (returning visitors may remember it as Cheeseburger in Paradise), Paradise Burger serves an array of burgers—try one heaped with bacon or covered with avocado, melted jack and cheddar cheeses and jalapeños—as well as giant burritos, fish tacos, mahimahi sandwiches and french fries smothered in cheese. The upstairs location offers a great view of the promenade and the ocean.

LA DOLCE VITA

$$ ITALIC ✉*Díaz Ordaz #674* ☎*322-222-3852*

This enormously popular, family-run two-story restaurant, with its central *malecón* location, a great view of the bay and a local reputation for high-quality food,presents a range of dishes from many parts of Italy. Favorites include chicken cacciatore, veal cutlets *alla* Milanese and fish filets San Pietro. The menu also features pasta and 18 kinds of wood oven–baked pizzas. Of course, there's also a good selection of Italian, Mexican and Chilean wines, as well as tiramisu and gelato for dessert. There's live jazz on Thursday and Friday evenings.

LAS PALOMAS

$–$$ MEXICAN ✉*Paseo Díaz Ordaz #610* ☎*322-222-3675*

Another long-established local favorite on the *malecón*, Las Palomas offers a mixed menu of seafood, Mexican and American dishes. Hamburgers of ground filet mignon are grilled with cheese inside or topped with ham and pineapple. Mexican specialties include chicken enchiladas in mole sauce and ground beef chiles *rellenos*. This is a great place to come for Mexican-style breakfasts, which feature unusual selections such as scrambled eggs with *machaca* (shredded beef), *entomatadas* (stuffed tortillas smothered in tomato sauce) and, for the truly experimental, an "omelet loco" filled with pork rind and topped with green tomatillo sauce. There's live music every evening and a bigscreen TV that blares sporting events in the afternoon. Check out the big wall mural of customers and staff, painted by local artists who hang out here.

CHEZ ELENA

$$$ INTERNATIONAL ✉*Matamoros #520* ☎*322-222-0161*

Hidden away on a back street behind the cathedral, Chez Elena has been a local secret for more than 50 years, since the dawn of tourism in Puerto Vallarta. The small open-terrace restaurant surrounded by the lush tropical gardens of the Cuatro Vientos B&B inn feels very secluded; dinner guests can also retire to the rooftop El Nido bar for a sunset view overlooking downtown. The short menu of carefully chosen dishes includes Mexican regional fare, seafood and beefsteaks, as well as creative international choices such as the house specialty: Indonesian satays (skewers) of shrimp, pork and beef in a spicy peanut sauce.

PLANETA VEGETARIANO

$ VEGETARIAN ✉*Iturbide #270* ☎*322-222-3073*

Look for vegetarian fare at this mellow little place that offers economical all-you-can-eat buffets for breakfast, lunch and dinner. Buffet items change daily; typical specialties include tofu enchiladas *en mole poblano* and banana lasagna. Closed Sunday.

MERCADO ARTESANÍA COMEDORES

$ MEXICAN ✉*North bank of Río Cuale near Insurgentes bridge*

For a full, hot meal that costs no more than a cup of coffee at most downtown cafés, visit the *comedores* on the upper level of the Mercado Artesanía. You can watch the cooks prepare pork sandwiches, *menudo, birria* and other local favorites while you wait. You eat your meal, which is served in a paper bowl or plate with plasticware, at one of the picnic tables in the center of the food section. Sanitation is no problem, except that there's no place nearby to wash your hands before eating.

LAS CARMELITAS

$$$ MEXICAN ✉*Camino a la Aguacatera, Km. 1.2* ☎*322-223-2104*

This palapa-style restaurant on a steep hillside above the long tunnel on the Libramiento highway between Old Puerto Vallarta and the Hotel Zone offers the best view anywhere of the town and the entire Banderas Bay coastline—not to mention the sunset, which is the main attraction here. Dinner entrées, all grilled over an open wood fire, include filet mignon, Mexican-style *arachera* (marinated skirt steak), shrimp and *huachinango* (red snapper); there's also great guacamole and big, pricey margaritas. Service is leisurely, so plan to make this your main event of the evening; live music adds to the ambience. To get there, take the Par-Vial—the signed route from downtown Puerto Vallarta to the Libramiento—to a small traffic roundabout and go north. On your right you'll see the brick entrance gate, where you will be charged 50 pesos (about $5) entrance fee per person, which will be deducted from your dinner bill (the toll is designed to discourage sunset-gazers who don't eat). From here, follow the bumpy, winding dirt road for 1.2 kilometers up the mountain. You'll reach the restaurant soon after you start thinking you must be lost. Or better yet, take a taxi.

SHOPPING

INSTITUTO DE ARTE JALISCIENSE

✉*Juárez #284* ☎*322-222-1301* Arts and crafts are often subsidized by both Mexican federal and state agencies, which buy folk art from villagers at fair prices to sell later in government stores, thus stabilizing incomes for craftspeople. The only such government store in Puerto Vallarta is the "state art institute," where you'll find beautiful examples of *artesanía* from all over the state, including the Talavera ceramics and other styles of pottery for which the Guadalajara-area towns of Tlaquepaque, Tonalá and Zapopán are famous.

QUERUBINES

✉ *Avenida Juárez #501-A* ☎ *322-223-1727* The owner travels all over Mexico to hand-pick high-quality folk art and handcrafts including embroidered clothing, Panama hats, wool rugs, tinwork and much more. The shop is in a historic building that was once the home of Puerto Vallarta's first mayor.

GALERÍA ARTE POPULAR MEXICANO

✉ *Libertad #285* ☎ *322-222-6960* Bridging the gap between folk art and fine art, exhibiting works from all parts of Mexico. Of special interest is a good selection of La Catrina figures in clay and wood. Though these tall, elegantly dressed, grinning woman skeletons represent Death, they are anything but grim. Their message is to glory in the joy of life even in the face of a grim fate.

GALERÍA DE OLLAS

✉ *Corona #176* ☎ *322-223-1045* This shop showcases Mata Ortiz pottery, unique ceramics that come from a small desert village near the Pueblo Indian ruins of Casas Grandes in northern Chihuahua. Around 1950, a poor woodcutter named Juan Quezada collected ancient pottery shards in the area and began 15 years of experimenting to replicate their strength, lightness and finish, using local materials. Samples of his work made their way across the border to New Mexico, where anthropologist Spencer McCallum saw them, sought out Quezado and financed his pottery work, which ultimately employed hundreds of artisan potters, providing the main source of income for the village. While based on pre-Colombian designs, each artist's pottery is modernized and stylized differently. Since 2005, when Mata Ortiz pottery began to appear in museums around the world, it has become highly collectible and is now sold by a handful of shops around Puerto Vallarta. Galería de Ollas, devoted exclusively to these ceramics, is one of the best.

HUICHOL COLLECTION GALERÍA MUSEO

✉ *Morelos #490* ☎ *322-223-2141* Although today Puerto Vallarta has no indigenous people—the once-large population of the central Pacific coast was completely wiped out by European diseases within a century of their first contact with the Spanish—the city has adopted as its own the art of the Huichol (also called Wixáritari or Watakame) Indians, who live to the north in a vast, inaccessible area of Nayarit. The most familiar Huichol art is the bright-colored yarnwork and beadwork glued with beeswax to carved wood surfaces. This work is nontraditional, though the patterns represent symbols that are part of the Indians' age-old peyote ceremonies. They were originally invented in the 1960s and '70s for sale to folk art galleries, and the proceeds from the sale of these items often goes to support communes of displaced Huichols or to buy offerings given to the sea goddess at annual ceremonies held in San Blas, Nayarit. You will sometimes also find more traditional Huichol items such as masks, musical instruments, votive gourd bowls, decorated arrows, yarn "God's eyes" and shamans' hats adorned with feathers or squirrel tails. On the low end of the price spectrum are beaded eggs and T-shirts printed with Huichol designs. Of the half-dozen fine Huichol galleries downtown and in the Zona Romántica, Huichol Collection stands out because it has a Huichol lifestyle display and because a Huichol artist is often at work in the store's display area.

GALERÍA VALLARTA

✉Juárez #263 ✆322-222-0290 ✎www.galeriavallarta.com A completely different kind of shopping experience awaits in the art galleries of downtown Puerto Vallarta, which have given Puerto Vallarta a well-deserved reputation as the biggest and best fine-arts market in the country. My personal favorite is Galeria Vallarta. Barbara Peters, who established in 1989, exhibits a wide array of original paintings, limited-edition lithographs, sculptures and quality folk art from all over Mexico.

SERGIO BUSTAMANTE ✉Juárez #275 ✆322-223-1405 ✎www.sergio bustamante.com.mx Next door, don't miss the works of the Guadalajaran master who ranks among Mexico's greatest living artists. He doesn't often put in a personal appearance here, of course; he works at his studio in the Guadalajara suburb of Tlaquepaque and sells his limited-edition ceramic, wood and bronze pieces at eight galleries like this one in resort areas throughout Mexico. His art speaks for itself. Bustamante has a second gallery location at Paseo Diaz Ordaz #542; 322-222-5480.

GALERÍA UNO

✉Morelos #561 ✆322-222-0908 A few blocks away, there's another cluster of galleries around the intersection of Morelos and Corona. Among these, the standout is Galería Uno. Though it was one of Puerto Vallarta's first galleries, and the white stucco exhibit areas are done in soft curves reminiscent of the adobe architectural style of Santa Fe, New Mexico, the paintings and sculptures by the roughly 30 regional artists the gallery represents are contemporary and often edgy.

GALERÍA 8 Y MÁS

✉Miramar #237 at Guerrero ✆322-222-7971 ✎www.artismexico.com Three blocks east, this space is a cooperative venture of eight owner/artists, mostly from Guadalajara, who offer quality work—and free lattés—at good prices. Galería 8 also shows work by about 40 rising young Tapatio (Guadalajaran) painters and sculptors. There is a second location at Corona #186; 322-223-9700.

PV ART GALLERY

✉*Corona #160* ✆*322-222-7028* Formerly the studio of renowned painter Judith Ewing Morlan, this new gallery continues to showcase Ms. Morlan's work, as well as that of several other Puerto Vallarta area artists.

GALERIE DES ARTISTES

✉*Avenida Leona Vicario #248* ✆*322-223-0006* This space owned by the Café des Artistes across the street got its start in the early 1990s. Today it is the cornerstone of a concentration of galleries with a distinctly international flavor toward the north end of downtown on and around Leona Vicario, which is now known as the most upscale street in Old Puerto Vallarta. Galerie des Artistes exhibits an eclectic array of objets d'art ranging from prints by famed Mexican artists such as Diego Rivera and José Clemente Orozco to paintings by renowned German-born artist Evelyn Boren, who splits her time between her studios in Sayulita, Nayarit and Santa Fe, New Mexico.

GALERÍA OMAR ALONSO ✉*Avenida Leona Vicario #249* ✆*322-222-5587*
⌨*www.galeriaomaralonso.com* Under the same ownership as the Galerie des Artistes, this was the first Puerto Vallarta gallery to showcase fine-art photography. On display are photo images and some works in other media by prominent artists from throughout Mexico, the United States and South America.

GALERÍA CORSICA

✉*Leona Vicario #230* ✆*322-223-1821* ⌨*www.galeriacorsica.com* In the same block as Galerie des Artistes, this gallery's Italian owners exhibit only works by artists who are also displayed in Mexico City's Museo de Arte Moderno. There's a second location at Guadalupe Sanchez #735.

GALERÍA ARTE LATINOAMERICANO

✉*Avenida Josefa Ortiz Dominguez #155* ✆*322-222-4406* ⌨*www.galeriaal.com* Occupying two stories in a historic building, this gallery was started in 1998 by former employees of Galeria Pacifico to promote the works of promising young local artists. Today, some of the original artists have achieved international fame and still show at this gallery alongside rising stars from throughout Latin America.

CERROBLANCO ✉*Leona Vicario #226* ✆*322-223-3546* One of the first things shoppers notice about Old Puerto Vallarta is that, like other Mexican megaresort towns, it's full of stores that sell mass-produced silver jewelry, as well as street vendors selling "silver" jewelry that is actually *alpaca*, a nickel alloy that contains no silver but may be silver-plated. But if you're looking for fine custom jewelry rather than tourist bling, this is one of the best places to shop for it. Pepe Cerroblanco is a retired bullfighter and third-generation jewelry designer in San Miguel de Allende, where his family has been manufacturing one-of-a-kind custom jewelry for Saks Fifth Avenue and other international retailers for more than 60 years.

DANIEL ESPINOSA ✉*Aldama #114* ✆*22-222-6909* Inventive fantasy and sensuality are the hallmarks of the works in semiprecious stone and silver by this world-renowned designer. A native of the old mining town of Taxco, where most Mexican silver jewelry comes from, Espinoza studied with master jewelers in Italy, the Netherlands and New York and sold his work through fashionable shops in Canada and France for years before returning to Mexico. He boasts a customer list that includes Shakira and Madonna. Espinosa has a second location at Morelos #600; 322-223-0863.

LA CASA DE TEQUILA

✉*Morelos #589* ✆*322-222-2000* In Old Puerto Vallarta, you're never more than half a block from a liquor store, or at least a small grocery store that sells liquor; all of them stock an assortment of tequilas. One of the widest selections in town is found at La Casa de Tequila, across the street from the *malecón*. A specialty is tequilas infused with natural flavors such as vanilla, almond and tamarind. Besides retail sales, the store has a garden bar that serves many brands of tequila by the shot.

LA CASA DEL HABANO ✉*Aldama #174* ✆*322-223-2758* Some visitors from the United States crave Cuban cigars, if only as "forbidden fruit," since an economic embargo has prevented them from being imported into the U.S. for almost half a century. For the most complete selection of Cuban cigars, this is the place to go. It also has a cigar bar on the premises. For visitors who want to (legally) take a souvenir box back to the United States, the shop also carries fine cigars from the Dominican Republic, where they make counterfeit Cuban cigars banded as Cohibas, Romeo y Julietas and such, which look just like the real thing and, according to some connoisseurs, are every bit as high in quality.

SIERRA MADRE ✉*Paseo Díaz Ordaz #732-B* ✆*322-223-0661* Near the north end of the *malecón*, this nonprofit curio shop sells nature-oriented T-shirts, posters and other gift items promoting environmental preservation efforts in Mexico, from rainforest preservation to sea turtle rescue programs.

The *malecón* is party central any evening, but especially Sunday. There's live music, local art and street performers of every description. If it's dance music and alcohol you're after, a four-block stretch across the street from the *malecón* has the highest concentration of bars and nightclubs in town. A cacophony of blaring mixed dance music competes for your attention late into the night.

CARLOS O'BRIAN'S

✉ *Paseo Díaz Ordaz #796* ☎ *322-222-1444* At the center of the action is this chain that has locations in most Mexican beach resort areas and also owns the Carlos & Charlie's and Señor Frog's franchises in the same areas. Though this "restaurante & bar & clothesline" serves food, emphasizing bar fare such as oysters, tequila shrimp and spicy buffalo wings, it hits its stride later in the evening with lots of tequila shooters and beer, a mostly twentysomething crowd and a nonstop, anything-goes party atmosphere that makes every night seem like spring break.

LA BODEGUITA DEL MEDIO ✉ *Paseo Díaz Ordaz #858* ☎ *322-223-1585* A spinoff of the famous Havana, Cuba nightclub that is said to have been among Ernest Hemingway's favorites, La Bodeguita features live, loud Cuban music, with a danceclub on the ground floor and a second-floor restaurant/bar serving pork loin sandwiches, fried *plantanos* and other Cuban fare.

MANDALA ✉ *Morelos #635* ☎ *322-223-0966* Young and loud, this new club is the largest disco in downtown Puerto Vallarta. While it operates as a restaurant and bar during the day, things really get going after 11 at night as techno plays, the ambient lighting goes down to pitch-black and colored floodlights roam at random.

ZOO ✉ *Paseo Díaz Ordaz #630* ☎ *322-222-4945* One of Puerto Vallarta's biggest and most famous danceclubs, where Paris Hilton is said to hang out when she's in town, the Zoo features deejays whose eclectic mixes range from techno to salsa to reggae to hip-hop with an occasional golden oldie thrown in. Cover.

HILO ✉ *Paseo Díaz Ordaz #588* ☎ *322-223-5361* This trendy deejay club with its bizarre artwork mixes every imaginable kind of high-energy music to the delight of the perpetual party crowd in the center of the room. Cover.

TEQUILAS

✉ *Galeana #104* ☎ *322-222-6722* Just around the corner from the *malecón*, a Mexican-style change of pace awaits. A strolling mariachi band entertains nightly and the menu of tequila cocktails is among the largest in town (try a shot *completo* with

4

PUERTO VALLARTA DOWNTOWN PUERTO VALLARTA NIGHTLIFE

a chaser of the bar's signature sangrita verde—citrus juice, mint, cilantro and green chile).

BEACHES

PLAYA CAMARONES

✉*Accessible from the north end of the malecón or from parking spaces along Avenida Paraguaynear the Hotel Buenaventura*

🛶 🛥 ⛵ Named "Shrimp Beach" because fishermen used to drag their pangas up onto the sand here to unload their catch, the northernmost of the city beaches is shared by local people and guests at a handful of nearby resort hotels. Because public access is easier than at the main Hotel Zone beaches, it is also teeming with curio hawkers, hair braiders and the occasional marijuana seller. Still, it's much quieter than the main public beach, Playa Los Muertos.

⚠ Camping is not permitted on city beaches, and would not be safe if it were allowed.

RÍO CUALE

The Río Cuale, a small river with an island in the middle, slices Old Puerto Vallarta in two. In the middle of the river, the Isla Río Cuale, a narrow eight-block-long, mostly paved island, is accessible by stairways down from three traffic bridges across the river. The island is packed with pricy cafés and open-air curio stands, along with a small museum and a cultural center. It's a top point of interest for downtown sightseeing tours that come from the big resort hotels and cruise ships, as you might suspect from the rows of jewelry stores, tacky curio shops and expensive cafés along the central walkway. Men stroll around leading burros with which they'll let you take a photo for a fee of US$10, and boys sometimes hang around with large iguanas, which they'll try to get you to hold and then charge you the same $10 whether you take a photo or not.

SIGHTS

MUSEO ARQUEOLÓGICO
✉*Isla Río Cuale* Toward the western tip of the island, near the Ignacio Vallarta traffic bridge, the museum contains a small but interesting collection of ancient ceramics from around the region, including unusual depictions of shamans and magical beings. It also displays a number of fine examples of "Colima dogs," unique red clay figurines of small dogs called *xoloitz–cuintli* (similar to Chihuahua and Mexican hairless breeds), which were kept as pets and also bred for food. The fanciful statues, which depict the dogs dozing, gorging on corn or even dancing together, were found in 50-foot-deep shafts used as royal tombs around 1400 years ago. Admission.

SUSPENSION FOOTBRIDGES
✉*Río Cuale* A bridge made from wood planks with chain-link

sides to keep pedestrians from falling overboard crosses to the island from the Mercado Artesanía on the downtown side of the river, and another continues over to the south bank. Even if you don't want to cross over into the Zona Romántica, you must give the bridges a try, preferably while sober. They're not only the oldest bridges in town but also the most exciting cheap (in fact, free) thrill.

JOHN HUSTON STATUE

✉ *Isla Río Cuale* In the center of the island, a bronze statue John Huston sitting in a director's chair in a pose not unlike Rodin's *The Thinker* perches on a low stone pedestal. Huston's decision to film *The Night of the Iguana* near Puerto Vallarta touched off the tourism boom that built the village into a major resort city. After completing the movie, the maverick filmmaker, who won an Oscar for *The Treasure of the Sierra Madre* and is remembered for such classics as *The Maltese Falcon*, *The African Queen* and *Prizzi's Honor*, spent the last 23 years of his life in Puerto Vallarta.

CENTRO CULTURAL VALLARTENSE

✉ *Isla Río Cuale* ☎ *322-223-0095* At the east end of the island, the municipal cultural center hosts workshops in drawing, painting, sculpture and music and has a free public gallery showcasing the works of local artists. Classes are nominally priced and open to the public. A schedule of classes is posted beside the entrance to the amphitheater, which seats audiences of about 80 for dance performances and poetry readings.

DINING

LE BISTRO JAZZ CAFÉ

$$$ CONTINENTAL   ✉ *Isla Río Cuale #16-A* ☎ *322-222-0283*
🖅 *www.lebistro.com.mx, lebistro@prodigy.net.mx*

This is one of two Isla Río Cuale fine dining restaurants masquerading as "cafés." located right by the statue of John Huston near the Insurgentes Bridge, strives for a romantic European ambience with stonework, statuary, brass trim, dim lighting, big potted plants and a riverside terrace; a piano player provides contemporary jazz from breakfast time until late into the evening, alternating with recorded picks from what purports to be the largest jazz collection in town. The cuisine is mostly Continental and quite haute, ranging from crêpes to duck magret in blackberry sauce, with a few creative Mexican dishes such as crab chipotle enchiladas; the house specialty is jumbo coconut shrimp. You can enjoy the ambience without busting your vacation budget by stopping in for a sumptuous dessert such as the double-fudge chocolate crêpes with Kahlúa or the house-special coffee with Grand Marnier, brandy and homemade ice cream.

RIVER CAFÉ

$$$ CONTINENTAL   ✉Isla Río Cuale #4   ✆322-223-0788   ⌨www.rivercafe.com

Farther down the island, below the Ignacio L. Vallarta Bridge, the River Café may not be exactly a clone of Le Bistro, but the two restaurants certainly share the same concept—romantic, jazzy and European. Even the menus are strikingly similar, though the River Café offers pasta dishes like lamb and wild mushroom lasagna as well as some tantalizing specialty entrées such as chicken breast stuffed with goat cheese, spinach and piñon nuts with a rosemary red wine sauce. Also like Le Bistro, the River Café serves gourmet breakfasts. The menu includes not only crêpes and American-style egg and meat breakfasts but also traditional Mexican breakfasts such as quesadillas topped with chile strips, huitlacoche and squash blossoms, or *enfrijoladas de chicharrón* (a tortilla filled with pork rind in black bean sauce).

OSCAR'S

hidden

$$ SEAFOOD   ✉Isla Río Cuale #1   ✆322-223-0789

Less pretentious and more secluded than the other Isla Río Cuale restaurants, this palapa situated on the seaward tip of the island affords a fine sunset view. Towering shade trees shelter it from the traffic noise on the Vallarta Bridge overhead, and the big neighboring Molino de Agua condominium complex overshadows it, adding to the hidden feel. The food here focuses on seafood and Mexican regional fare, adapted for health-conscious international patrons with less cheese, less frying, more emphasis on fresh vegetable ingredients, and liberal use of chiles and spices. Among the specialties is red snapper marinated in lime juice and grilled with poblano chile and onions. The atmosphere is quiet (no jazz), and the serving staff is unobtrusively attentive. A second round of drinks comes free with meals.

SHOPPING

MERCADO RÍO CUALE ✉Isla Río Cuale You'll find larger open-air shops selling essentially the same kind of colorful, mostly imported wares as the arts-and-crafts market at the semi-permanent open-air stalls that line most of the length of the Isla Río Cuale. Vendors tend to be more fast-talking and aggressive here, especially in the morning when most souvenir shoppers are out. As the day grows hotter, a sort of lassitude sets in until it's hard to get some sellers to stir themselves enough to tell you the asking price of an item.

ZONA ROMÁNTICA

South of the Río Cuale is a neighborhood officially named Colonia Emiliano Zapata. Until the mid-1990s, it was a dirt-road maze of one- and two-story buildings connected by a tangle of overhead telephone and electrical wires. Many local people who worked in the Hotel Zone lived there, and construction workers who built Marina Vallarta and Nuevo Vallarta by day camped by night in makeshift shelters on Playa del Muerto—a beach that, in those days, was junky but not at all touristy. Except for an occasional old-timer, nobody calls it that anymore; in the 1990s the tourism department dubbed it the "Zona Romántica" in an attempt to overcome the district's low-budget reputation, and it worked.

The municipality tore up the clattery cobblestone streets to bury water mains and sewage pipes that would provide public utilities to all the properties in the district, and investors rushed in to transform parts of the old neighborhood into a hotel and restaurant zone that would also become the closest thing to a historic district on Mexico's west coast— a fascinating mix of restaurants and clubs, traditional *tienditas* (small stores), affordable hotels and local family residences blended into a beachfront neighborhood that feels exotic by day and exciting by night. The Zona Romántica has also emerged in recent years as the heart of Puerto Vallarta's lively yet unobtrusive gay community. (Not to worry— it also remains as "straight-friendly" as ever.)

Because it sits at an angle to the coastline, you can't walk from one end of the Zona Romántica to the other without jogging toward the beach. Otherwise, you'll find yourself in a small but tricky maze of back streets that end abruptly or turn into steep stairways. The main streets, where most of the hotels, restaurants, clubs and shops are to be found, follow a zigzag course through the district: Ignacio L. Vallarta from the bridge over the Río Cuale for five blocks; turn right on Basilio Badillo for two blocks; then turn left on Olas Altas, which continues for another five blocks.

Besides the public beaches—the lively Playa Los Muertos and the calmer beaches beyond it—the Zona Romántica does not have an abundance of sightseeing highlights. But strolling this compact, remarkably varied neighborhood is an adventure in and of itself.

After crossing the Río Cuale on a new, arched footbridge, the downtown *malecón* now extends most of the length of Playa Los Muertos, with palapa restaurants, bars and shops blocking the view of the ocean for much of the way, to the weatherbeaten concrete pier where the water taxis load passengers bound for Yelapa and other South Shore beaches.

SIGHTS

PARQUE LÁZARO CÁRDENAS ⊠*Olas Altas between Cárdenas and Carranza* This pretty, shady plaza just off the beach is tranquil in the morning, hot in the afternoon and full of the joy of life in the evening. Lovers stroll, their arms entwined, and linger on benches nestled in the gardens; children run and rollerskate along the wide concrete walkways; guitar players set their music free on the night breeze; vendors serve up quesadillas and fish tacos hot off the grill, while those in other stalls hawk T-shirts, toys and shiny balloons. Here, as few other places in Puerto Vallarta, you'll experience the sights, sounds and scents of the "real" old town that has managed to welcome international visitors and newcomers without being swallowed up by big tourism.

GALERÍA OLINALÁ
PAGE 134

Two floors filled with quality village and tribal folk art from all over western Mexico

CAFÉ DE OLLA
PAGE 130

Enchiladas, chiles *rellenos*, potent strawberry margaritas and a festive atmosphere at a locally loved, family-run eatery

VILLA MERCEDES
PAGE 128

Elegant, warm rooms and balcony views in a mansion with original architecture—the former retreat of a wealthy Guadalajara family

MUELLE LOS MUERTOS ✉*Francisco Rodríguez at the waterfront* Several blocks down the beach from the park, is Muelle Los Muertos is commonly called the New Pier. (In fact, it's the only municipal pier, the "old pier" having been demolished long since by storms and progress). The New Pier is where water taxis and private *pangas* depart for remote spots such as Quimixto and Yelapa on the rugged south shore of Banderas Bay. It's also where dive boats set off for scuba and snorkeling excursions to nearby Los Arcos. Many of the people on the long pier aren't going anywhere, though. This is the best place in town for fishing from shore or, if you're a kid, leaping off into the water.

LODGING

POSADA DE ROGER
$–$$ 47 ROOMS   ✉*Basilio Badillo #237*   ☎*322-222-0836*   📠*322-223-0482*
🖥*www.hotelposadaderoger.com, posadaroger@yahoo.com*

For affordable accommodations in the heart of the Zona Romántica, the place to go is this three-story, white-and-orange hotel. This no-frills, Mexican-style lodging upstairs from Fredy's Tucán Restaurant and Bar has private rooms with phones, cable TV, private baths and ceiling fans. Some have air conditioning, and a few hostel-like rooms have four beds, ideal for families and groups who don't object to close quarters. There's a small rooftop swimming pool and sundeck. The location is two-and-a-half blocks from Playa Los Muertos.

HOTEL ELOISA
$$ 75 ROOMS   ✉*Lázaro Cárdenas #179*   ☎*322-222-6465*   📠*322-222-6465*
🖥*www.hoteleloisa.com, info@hoteleloisa.com*

The Eloisa has air-conditioned guest accommodations ranging from standard rooms with two double beds to studios with kitchenettes and couches. Many rooms have balconies, some overlooking Parque Lázaro Cárdenas across the street, others on the higher floors looking out over Banderas Bay. Bright bedspreads and curtains and dark wood furniture accent the otherwise stark white walls and white tile floors, both in the rooms and in the small lobby area downstairs. There's a swimming pool in the central courtyard and another shallow one with a sunbathing deck on the rooftop. The north end of Playa Los Muertos, the liveliest beach in town, is half a block away.

CASA ANDREA

$$ 10 ROOMS ✉*Francisca Rodríguez #174* ☎*322-222-1213*
🖥*www.casaandrea.com, casaandrea@aol.com*

Situated just a block from Playa Los Muertos and the New Pier and within a few blocks of all the best restaurants, clubs and shops in the Zona Romántica, this quiet, homelike hideaway has ten imaginatively decorated one- and two-bedroom suites. They open out onto a secluded courtyard landscaped with palms, mangos and hibiscus and a swimming pool and manmade waterfall; some units have kitchenettes. Though the suites have no air conditioning, only ceiling fans, all open toward the west to take maximum advantage of the sea breezes. Amenities include coin-operated washers and dryers, an exercise room with a treadmill, stationary bike and weight machines, a heated whirlpool, and a library with a big-screen TV, as well as free wireless internet access for guests.

PLAYA LOS ARCOS

$$–$$$ 171 ROOMS ✉*Olas Altas #380* ☎*322-222-2583* 📠*322-226-7104*
🖥*www.playalosarcos.com, hoteles@playalosarcos.com*

One of the few comparatively large hotels in the Zona Romántica, the family-oriented Playa Los Arcos stands four stories tall and fronts on the beach. Its guest rooms and suites are arranged in a U-shape around a courtyard with three swimming pools, decorated with statuary that includes whimsical frog fountains. Though on the small side, the rooms have been recently renovated in light, cheerful shades of yellow and beige. You can choose between a king-sized or queen-sized bed or two double beds. All rooms are air-conditioned and have telephones and cable TVs; their balconies overlook the swimming pools, which are colorfully lit after dark. A spa on the premises offers massage, shiatsu, aromatherapy and reflexology services.

LOS ARCOS SUITES

$$–$$$ 44 UNITS ✉*Manuel Dieguez #164* ☎*322-226-7101*
📠*322-226-7104* 🖥*www.playalosarcos.com/losarcossuites,*
hoteles@playalosarcos.com

Tucked away in a narrow, almost-dead-end side street behind the Playa Los Arcos and under the same ownership is a much smaller all-suite hotel where all units have balconies (not much

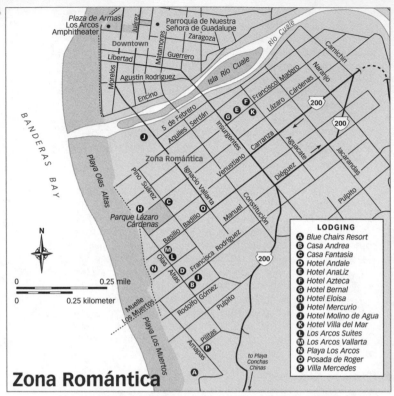

Plaza de Armas
Los Arcos
Amphitheater
Parroquía de Nuestra
Señora de Guadalupe
Zaragoza
Downtown
Libertad
Guerrero
Morelos
Agustín Rodríguez
Encino
Juárez
Matamoros
Río Cuale
Isla Río Cuale
Carnichin
Francisco Madero
Lázaro Cárdenas
Naranjo
200
200
BANDERAS BAY
Playa Olas Altas
5 de Febrero
Aquiles Serdán
Insurgentes
Carranza
Aguacate
Jacarandas
Zona Romántica
Ignacio Vallarta
Venustiano
Diéguez
Pulpito
Pino Suárez
Manuel
Constitución
Parque Lázaro
Cárdenas
Basilio Badillo
Francisca Rodríguez
200
Olas Altas
Rodolfo Gómez
Pulpito
Muelle
Los Muertos
Playa Los Muertos
Pílitas
Amapas
to Playa
Conchas
Chinas
N
0   0.25 mile
0   0.25 kilometer

LODGING
- Ⓐ Blue Chairs Resort
- Ⓑ Casa Andrea
- Ⓒ Casa Fantasia
- Ⓓ Hotel Andale
- Ⓔ Hotel AnaLiz
- Ⓕ Hotel Azteca
- Ⓖ Hotel Bernal
- Ⓗ Hotel Eloisa
- Ⓘ Hotel Mercurio
- Ⓙ Hotel Molino de Agua
- Ⓚ Hotel Villa del Mar
- Ⓛ Los Arcos Suites
- Ⓜ Los Arcos Vallarta
- Ⓝ Playa Los Arcos
- Ⓞ Posada de Roger
- Ⓟ Villa Mercedes

Zona Romántica

in the way of ocean views, though) and kitchenettes. King-sized beds are partly separated by low walls from living areas with two sofas that fold out into additional beds. There's a large, attractive courtyard swimming pool, and guests have the use of the beach facilities, swimming pools and spa at the Playa Los Arcos. There's wireless internet access in the lobby.

CASA DOÑA SUSANA

$$$ 42 ROOMS   ✉ Manuel Dieguez #171   ☎ 332-226-7101
📠 322-226-7104   ✎ www.playalosarcos.com/casadonasusana,
hoteles@playalosarcos.com

In this colonial-elegant, adults-only boutique hotel directly across the narrow side street from Los Arcos Suites, he walls are muraled in bright yellow and the air-conditioned guest rooms and suites feature Spanish colonial reproduction furnishings and balconies, their railings tangled with big yellow copa de oro flowers. There's a rooftop pool and a solarium terrace with a wide-angle view of the city. Guests can also use the beach, pools, spa and other facilities at the Playa Los Arcos. There is wireless internet access in the public areas.

HOTEL ANDALE

$$ 11 ROOMS ✉*Olas Altas #425* ☎*322-223-2622* ✍*www.andales.com,*
info@andale.com

Situated above the popular Italian restaurant of the same name
(which, in turn, is upstairs from the bar of the same name), is con-
sidered "historic" by Puerto Vallarta standards, though it has only
been in operation since 1999. There are standard guest rooms,
one-bedroom suites and two-bedroom luxury suites. All are air-
conditioned and have queen-sized beds and traditional Mexican
decor of bare red-brick walls and Mexican tilework. The suites
have balconies, though only two have kitchen facilities. There's a
small swimming pool, and the beach is just a block away.

CASA FANTASIA

$$$ 6 ROOMS ✉*Pino Suárez #203* ☎*322-223-2444* 📠*322-223-4035*
✍*www.casafantasia.com, information@casafantasia.com*

This six-room bed and breakfast occupies two adjacent villas
with a walled swimming pool and garden area. The decor is lavish with original artwork and antiques. Guest rooms have king-
sized beds with handcarved headboards. Each has a garden or
pool view and a private bath with a large, open shower stall.
There's no air conditioning, but the ceiling fans are high-
powered. A bus stop in front can make it noisy in the early morning. No smoking, no children. This is a couples-oriented establishment, equally gay- and straight-friendly; because of the
valuable artworks, no unregistered overnight guests are permitted. Room rates include a full gourmet breakfast made by one of
the co-owners, who is a former California restaurateur.

HOTEL MERCURIO

$$–$$$ 28 ROOMS ✉*Francisca Rodríguez #168* ☎*322-222-4793,*
866-388-2689 ✍*www.hotel-mercurio.com, reservations@hotel-mercurio.com*

Guest rooms in this chic, gay-owned and gay-friendly lodging
("*Very* gay," the management emphasizes) feature contemporary furnishings including a choice of one or two double beds
or a king-sized bed, with pastel walls and floral-pattern fabrics. All are air-conditioned and have refrigerators, and some
have kitchenettes. Amenities include evening turn-down service, expanded continental breakfast by the swimming pool, a
concierge who is knowledgeable about the Puerto Vallarta gay
scene, and massage services available on the premises. The location is just off Olas Altas, where you'll find many of the Zona
Romántica's best restaurants and clubs, and less than two
blocks from Playa Olas Altas and the dock where boats leave
for Yelapa and other spots that can't be reached by road.
Adults only.

VILLA MERCEDES

$$$ 14 ROOMS   ✉Amapas #175   ✆322-222-2148
🖰www.villamercedes.com.mx, villamercedes@yahoo.com

Half a century ago, the Villa Mercedes was the vacation retreat of a wealthy Guadalajara family. The original architecture of the three-story mansion was preserved during its recent renovation into an elegant small hotel with six studios, five suites, two one-bedroom apartments, and a two-bedroom penthouse. All units have air conditioning and kitchenettes, and are individually decorated in warm hues with colorful contemporary artworks; most have balconies overlooking the bay or the mountains. A continental breakfast is served daily in the garden courtyard. The location is at the southern end of the Zona Romántica, less than a block from Playa Los Muertos.

BLUE CHAIRS RESORT

$–$$$ 40 ROOMS   ✉Almendro #4   ✆322-222-5040, 888-302-3662   📠322-222-2176
🖰www.hotelbluechairs.com, reservations@bluechairsresortbythesea.com

The Blue Chairs Resort bills itself as the world's largest gay beachfront resort. In fact, the blue beach chairs from which the name derives mark the gay-and-lesbian-friendly southern part of Playa Los Muertos that is commonly called Blue Chairs Beach. Until 2001, the "resort" was an aging, rundown six-story family hotel. Since the present management, a male couple from Georgia, acquired the property, they have continuously upgraded the guest units and common areas, and the best suites are as tastefully decorated as one could hope. Room sizes (and rates) vary tremendously. All rooms have partial or full views of the beach, and all have cable TV and aging air conditioners. The rooftop terrace, with its nightly entertainment, bar and small pool, is a popular late-night party place, as is the beach in front of the hotel, so this is not a place for people seeking peace and quiet; if you want to be at the center of the action, though, this is the spot. Adults only; nobody under age 18 is allowed on the premises at any time.

Surprisingly enough, it's still possible to find extremely low-budget lodging in Puerto Vallarta. The place to look is away from the beach in the back streets of the Zona Romántica, along Francisco I. Madero, the street where the bus stations were located before the completion of the new bus terminal in the northern part of the city.

HOTEL ANALIZ

$ 23 ROOMS   ✉Madero #429   ✆322-222-1757   🖰hotelanaliz@hotmail.com

About five blocks from the ocean, the 400 block of Madero is completely lined with small one-star hotels, including the Hotel AnaLiz. It's family run and typically quite clean, though bare light bulbs may dangle from wires and the walls may be in desperate need of paint. Don't expect such amenities as air conditioning, TVs or elevators, though rooms do have ceiling fans. Beds are foam rubber mattresses on concrete block pedestals, and the only other furnishings in the small, spartan rooms are a desk and chair. The main virtue is price—around US$30 a night.

DINING

ÉPOCA

$$ MEXICAN ✉*Aquilas Serdán #174* ✆*322-222-2510* ✑*www.epoca-pv.com*

Fronting on the north end of Playa Los Muertos, Época offers dining on the open-air terrace or indoors under a palapa roof. The clean, minimal red-tile-and-white-stucco decor makes it appear almost a clone of Daiquiri Dick's, the famous, long-established restaurant farther down the beach, whose head chef is also the executive chef and part owner here. Bay views and spectacular sunsets set the ambience. The menu offers both Mexican and American-style options. Breakfasts range from huevos rancheros to eggs Benedict. For other meals, try the tuna tacos or the house specialty, whole grilled red snapper.

LA TÍA

$ MEXICAN ✉*Lázaro Cárdenas #179* ✆*322-222-7545*

This unpretentious longtime local hang–out adjoins the Hotel Eloisa across the street from Parque Lázaro Cárdenas. Pleasingly decorated with framed photos, folk-art paintings and a pottery fountain, it serves standard Mexican dishes such as enchiladas and *pollo en mole* (a half chicken smothered in chocolate-chile sauce), fresh seafood and satisfying breakfasts of *chilaquiles* (strips of day-old tortillas cooked in red chile sauce with ranch cheese) as well as American-style bacon-and-egg breakfasts.

KAISER MAXIMILIAN

$$$ CONTINENTAL ✉*Olas Altas #380-B* ✆*322-223-0760* ✑*www.kaisermaximilian.com*

The labor of love of Austrian chef Andreas Rupprechter has a thoroughly European look inside and out, with its dark interior woodwork, white tablecloths and crystal, and sidewalk tables under a broad magenta awning. The menu features Austrian dishes such as *zweibelrostbraten* (flat-pounded beef loin covered with a heap of onion rings and sautéed potatoes) as well as other European fare. You might start your dinner with an appetizer like sautéed squid and shrimp and finish with crème brûlée. An adjoining espresso bar serves coffee specialties and Austrian pastries.

COCO TROPICAL

$$–$$$ CONTINENTAL ✉*Basilio Badillo #101* ✆*322-222-5485* ✑*www.cocotropical.com*

The chef comes from Switzerland by way of fine restaurants in Germany, Holland, Canada and Curaçao. Before starting his own establishment, he came to Puerto Vallarta to manage the then-German-owned Krystal resort. The cuisine at this stylish open-air eatery has a distinctly European accent, with flavors ranging from French (escargot Bourgogne) to Italian (tagliatele *al frutti di mare*, a seafood pasta dish) to Austrian (breaded, fried wienerschnitzel). Also on the menu are wild salmon from Alaska and rabbit in merlot sauce. Although the restaurant's terrace is right on the beach, the "casual" dress code does not allow guests to dine in beachwear. At the restaurant's adjoining "beach club," however, you can sunbathe all afternoon and admire the sunset from your lounge chair while sipping Coco Tropical cocktails.

LA PALAPA

$$$ INTERNATIONAL   ✉*Pulpito #103*   ✆*322-222-5225*
🖰*www.lapalapapv.com*

This long, narrow, open-air restaurant on Playa Los Muertos has evolved over the years from a typical palm-thatched, sand-floored beachfront eatery into a tropical-motif seafood restaurant that participates in the annual Puerto Vallarta Festival Gourmet Internacional. The ambience is relaxed and comfortable by day, with a front-row view of the beach action. By night, creative lighting and live Latin jazz transform it into one of the most romantic restaurants in the Zona Romántica. Signature entrées include a pepper-crusted tuna steak served with garlic spinach, cranberry corn galette and shiitake mushroom sauce. There are also non-seafood selections such as adobo grilled beef filet served with fresh rosemary, *huitlacoche*, leek mashed potatoes and a mild pasilla chile sauce.

CAFÉ DE OLLA

$–$$ MEXICAN   ✉*Basilo Badillo #168*   ✆*322-223-1626*

A favorite of locals and visitors in the know, this always-crowded restaurant is one of the best places in town for traditional Mexican food. The menu at this down-to-earth family-run restaurant features hearty fare such as enchiladas, carne asada, chiles *rellenos* and good tortilla soup filled with avocado pieces. There's also a heaping fresh seafood platter for two. A living tree in the center of the dining area grows through the ceiling, local artwork adorns the walls and strolling mariachis provide entertainment. The strawberry margaritas are huge and potent.

FAJITA REPUBLIC

$$ MEXICAN   ✉*Pino Suárez #321*   ✆*322-222-3131*

Fajitas, as my Mexican friends often remind me, are not *really* Mexican food (they are said to be the recent invention of a gringo restaurateur from Texas). And despite its festive decor, the Fajita Republic isn't *really* a Mexican-food restaurant (the salsa is disappointingly mild), but that hasn't stopped this place from ranking among Puerto Vallarta's most popular restaurants for more than a decade. Strips of beefsteak are stir-fried with sweet peppers and onions and served with soft flour tortillas and an array of toppings. There are also shrimp and vegetarian fajitas, as well as barbecued ribs and big caesar salads, one of the few genuinely Mexican items on the menu—invented at the old Hotel Caesar in Tijuana. Mango margaritas, served by the pitcher, are a house specialty. Guitarists stroll through the dimly lit palapa-style restaurant nestled in palms and mango trees.

LOS PIBES hidden

$$$ ARGENTINEAN ✉Basilio Badillo #261 ✆322-223-1557

If thick slabs of beef are your passion, this Argentinean restaurant is the place to go in the Zona Romántica. Waiters in gaucho clothing bring you an assortment of raw beefsteaks and other meats to choose from. Then you sip Chilean or Argentine wine, nibble on appetizers such as *aluvias* (spiced white beans) and listen to the Andean musical trio while your meat is cooked to order. Although the cooking and decor are South American, all the beef is imported from the United States, so it's well-marbled, juicy and packed with hormones.

FREDY'S TUCÁN

$–$$ INTERNATIONAL ✉Basilio Badillo #237 ✆322-222-0639

The restaurant below the Posada Roger hotel is one of the most popular breakfast spots in the Zona Romántica. Here you'll find American-style bacon and eggs, waffles with whipped cream and fresh strawberries, or traditional eggs Benedict, as well as Mexican-style huevos rancheros or *chilaquiles* and gourmet options like a Florentine omelet stuffed with spinach and shrimp. There's a wide selection of fruit juices and smoothies. The restaurant also serves lunch and dinner, including Mexican combination plates and thick steaks. But the very inexpensive breakfasts are the real crowd-pleaser here. After dark, the restaurant morphs into a partying sports bar.

ARCHIE'S WOK hidden

$$–$$$ ASIAN ✉Francisco I. Rodríguez #130 ✆322-222-0411

The claim to fame at Archie's Wok is that it was started by filmmaker John Huston's personal chef, Arsenio "Archie" Alpenia, a Filipino American whose imaginative pan-Asian cuisine started the international fusion trend leading to Puerto Vallarta's amazing present-day restaurant scene. (Archie passed away several years ago, and the restaurant is now run by his wife, son and daughter.) Buddha statues and other Asian decorations, along with live music (Wednesday through Saturday) by the resident flute and guitar duo, create a soothing, unpretentious atmosphere in which to savor lumpia (Filipino egg rolls), Thai garlic shrimp, Singapore-style chicken satay with coconut-peanut sauce or Chinese cashew chicken. The catch of the day is grilled in teriyaki sauce. Dishes such as tofu and fresh vegetable stir-fry appeal to vegetarians. The homemade Key lime pie is legendary. Late lunch and dinner. Closed Sunday.

LA PIAZZETTA

$$ ITALIN   ✉ *Rodolfo Gómez #143 at Olas Altas*   ✆ *322-222-0650*

Owned by native Italian chef Dommenico "Mimmo" Iorruso, this local favorite is known for its traditional Napoli-style pizzas baked in wood-fire ovens, offered in 24 ingredient combinations, from classics such as *quattro formaggi* (four-cheese) or prosciutto *e funghi* (thin-sliced ham and mushrooms) to chef's originals like the Don Michele, topped with artichoke hearts, black olives and Roquefort cheese. The menu also includes a long list of pastas such as the spaghetti *cozzolino*, topped with shrimp, squid and clams in a white wine sauce, and beef, chicken and seafood entrées. The decor is cheerful, the Old World background music is bouncy, and Mimmo is effusively gracious.

SHRIMP FACTORY

$$$ SEAFOOD   ✉ *Ignacio L. Vallarta #237*   ✆ *322-222-2365*

Part of a chain that also has restaurants in Mazatlán and Los Cabos, serves huge portions of blue shrimp, priced by the kilo, with garlic butter, hot salsa, cocktail sauce and tartar sauce. Unlike at most restaurants in town, the shrimp does not come from Banderas Bay but is flown in fresh daily from Mazatlán. Lobster and fish are also available, and mango margaritas are a house specialty. The restaurant has big picture windows that look out on one of the liveliest streets in the Zona Romántica, making it a good place for watching people while you dine (and for passersby to watch you eat).

DAIQUIRI DICK'S

$$$ INTERNATIONAL   ✉ *Olas Altas #314*   ✆ *322-222-0566*   🖉 *ddpv.com*

Started in the early 1980s as a typical sand-floor palapa restaurant on Playa Los Muertos, Daiquiri Dick's grew into such a popular hangout that in 1995 the owners replaced it with a more permanent, contemporary building with indoor and outdoor seating but keeping the same great sunset view. The food, too, has evolved from its original, conventional seafood menu into an ambitious fusion of Mexican, American and Continental cuisines with surprising Asian, Indian and North African influences. You might start your dinner here with Cuban black bean soup, shrimp wontons in cucumber salsa or grilled, Serrano ham–wrapped asparagus with romanesco. Entrées range from mahimahi in wasabi butter to barbecued ribs. Reservations are recommended. New additions are made to the menu often, and there are nightly chef's specials. Closed in September and on Tuesdays off-season.

¡ANDALE!

$–$$ MEXICAN/AMERICAN   ✉*Olas Altas #425*   ✆ *322-223-2622*

Long a local favorite, this second-floor restaurant offers dining either indoors or on the balcony with a view of the ocean and the lively street scene below. It's especially popular for breakfast, which boasts Mexican standbys like *machaca*, *chilaquiles* and *huevos motuleños*. Other house specialties include a shrimp and spinach omelette and crêpes filled with fresh tropical fruit. Lunch and dinner feature some Italian dishes such as seafood linguini in garlic sauce and osso buco *milanesa*, as well as Mexican fare, including the unique, traditional chile *en nogada*, a poblano pepper stuffed with beef and fruit, smothered in walnut cream sauce and topped with pomegranate.

LAS CAZUELAS

$$$ MEXICAN   ✉*Basilio Badillo #479*   ✆ *322-222-2498*

Stonework, rough-painted plaster, wrought-iron grillwork, antique chandeliers, stained glass and Talavera ceramics, along with a courtyard fountain, create a Spanish colonial hacienda atmosphere. This intimate, formal restaurant has been run by the same family in the same location since 1968. Although the food is Mexican and traditional, it's not what one usually thinks of as Mexican food. Instead, it's the kind of meal people in the chef's hometown of Puebla would cook at home on very special occasions. The short menu, limited to just seven entrées, features such dishes as lamb *cazuela* (a *cazuela* is a casserole or a type of clay pot used to make casseroles) and roast pork in fruit salsa, and there are daily gourmet specials. You choose an appetizer and a main course for a fixed price. Reservations are essential, since there are only 16 tables. Located near the tunnel, past the end of the Zona Romántica's "restaurant row." Dinner only.

TACO STANDS (COMEDORES)

$ MEXICAN

Away from the main tourist streets, the Zona Romántica has dozens of small, open-air, family-run taco stands. Priced around 5 to 10 pesos per item, they are by far the most affordable places to eat in this part of town, and they present a chance to try the typical day-to-day foods that local Mexican people eat, such as tacos filled with shrimp, smoked marlin or *birria* (goat stew). Sanitation is a concern at some of these places because they have only ice chests for refrigeration and lack running water for washing hands or utensils. To avoid the need for dishwashing, stands use disposable paper or plastic picnic plates; it is common practice to place a plastic bag around the plate so it can be reused.

Watch to see that the person who handles the food is not also handling money or dirty dishes. All these vendors are required to pass periodic health inspections, and most are relatively safe even for sensitive gringo stomachs. Like restaurants, these stands survive on their reputations. Those with the tastiest food and cleanest premises also have the most regular customers and are generally worth waiting in line for. The stands start serving around midmorning and continue until they're sold out, usually after the lunch hour; a few reopen in the evening. Two of my favorites are **Birria Roble** (near the corner of Constitución and Venustiano Carranza) and **El Moreno** (Constitución at Francisco I. Madero). Or you can try **Tacos de Marisco** (Constitución at Aquiles Serdán), **La Horniga** (Lázaro Cárdenas near the corner of Insurgentes) and **Marisma** (Naranjo between Lázaro Cárdenas and Venustiano Carranza).

SHOPPING

HUARACHERIA FABIOLA ⌂*Ignacio L. Vallarta #145* ☎*322-221-4959* The main streets of the Zona Romántica offer an intriguing mix of high-class galleries and local shops that have been around since pre-tourist times. An intriguing example of the latter is *huaracheria*, where shoe-makers will trace your feet and custom-make a pair of fine traditional *huaraches* (Mexican-style half-shoes/half-sandals woven from narrow strips of leather), better for street wear than for the beach. There are also other reasonably priced custom-made shoes and leather goods.

LUCY'S CUCU CABAÑA AND ZOO

⌂*Basilio Badillo #295* ☎*322-222-1220* One of the most unusual places in town to shop for *artesanía*, Lucy's CuCu Cabaña and Zoo specializes in animal motif (especially cats and kittens) folk art from all over Mexico, with lots of original items not sold elsewhere. The shop is small, but the inventory is personally selected with lots of love by the owner and her artist husband. Profits fund the volunteer-run Puerto Vallarta spay-and-neuter program.

GALERÍA OLINALÁ

⌂*Lázaro Cárdenas #274* ☎*322-222-4995* Folk-art buffs will also want to check out this gallery named for the village in Guerrero state that produced most of the *artesanía* that was sold in the store in its early days. The gallery now features two floors filled with a wide variety of quality village and tribal folk art (some of it museum-quality), especially pottery and ceremonial masks, from all over western Mexico. There's a good selection of Huichol art.

TALAVERA ETC.

✉ *Ignacio L. Vallarta #266* ✆ *322-222-4100* This classy shop specializes in colorful, traditional decorative tiles, sinks and ceramics custom-designed by Mexican artists in the city of Puebla. The shop also carries wood carvings from Oaxaca and other handcrafted gift items.

MUNDO DE AZULEJOS

✉ *Venustiano Carranza #374* ✆ *322-222-2675* This is the only factory in Puerto Vallarta producing distinctive, colorful Talavera ceramics—tiles, wall plaques, pottery and sinks in the style that originated in colonial-era Spain and is traditionally associated with the city of Puebla, Mexico. The family-owned enterprise started in the mid-'80s as a store importing the ceramics from central Mexico, but the business soon outstripped its suppliers, and long shipping delays became a problem. So the owners went to established Talvera factories to study the process for two years, then taught craftspeople in nearby Nayarit to make the tiles and pottery from local clay and trained young Puerto Vallarta artists to paint and glaze them.

MOSAIQUE ✉ *Basilio Badillo #277* ✆ *322-223-3146* This charming little boutique sells fashionable clothing made of handmade, hand-dyed fabrics from around the world, as well as jewelry and home decor—a wonderful place to shop for gifts. There's a second location downtown at Avenida Juárez #279; 322-223-3183.

JUNE ROSEN LOPEZ ✉ *Francisca Rodríguez at Pino Suárez* ✆ *322-222-5049* If you're looking for something really unique in the way of jewelry, get in touch with this New York expatriate designer, who showcases her one-of-a-kind silver, turquoise and coral pieces in original styles inspired by traditional native adornments. Open by appointment only.

LA PIEDRA ✉ *Basilio Badillo #216* ✆ *322-223-2242* Another unusual jewelry shop, La Piedra (which means "the stone") makes one-of-a-kind creations in shell, coral, crystal and wood. They also sell beads and other materials and offer individual jewelry-making lessons. There's a second location downtown at Mexico #1087.

MATA ORTIZ ART GALLERY

✉ *Lázaro Cárdenas 268-A* ✆ *322-222-7407* This gallery exhibits ceramic works from Mata Ortiz, a village in northern Chihuahua near the New Mexico border where the revival of ancient Paquime and Mimbres pottery making has evolved into a unique style highly prized by collectors. Besides the work of the Quezeda family and their protégés in Mata Ortiz, the gallery also shows works in clay by other contemporary artists, including Gustavo Pérez, who is widely considered to be Mexico's best living ceramicist.

NIGHTLIFE

MARIACHI LOCO ✉ *Lázaro Cárdenas #254 at Ignacio L. Vallarta* ☎ *322-223-2205* For an authentically Mexican experience, visit this lively club where bands—both local and from Guadalajara, where mariachi music originated—perform dinnertime stage shows at 9 p.m. nightly for a mixed crowd of North American visitors and enthusiastic Mexicans who often sing along. They're followed by Spanish-speaking comedians. Later in the evening, the musicians stroll from table to table performing boleros and ranchero ballads by request. The standard charge for table performances is 100 pesos, a universal rate established by the Guadalajara-based mariachi union (no kidding). Off-season, Mariachi Loco also presents male strip shows on some weekend nights. Curiously enough, in the midst of Mexico's best known gay zone, these shows are for ladies only. Open until 4 a.m.

SEÑOR FROG'S ✉ *Venustiano Carranza #218 at Ignacio L. Vallarta* ☎ *322-222-5177* Owned by Mexico's largest restaurant company, which also owns Carlos O'Brien's and Carlos & Charlie's locations at beach resorts throughout Mexico and the Caribbean, Señor Frog's attracts the same young, boisterous crowd with its party-'til-you-drop philosophy. (If you do drop, chances are you'll notice the glow-in-the-dark murals on the ceiling.) There's live music sometimes, but more often the big dancefloor is the scene of festivities such as foam parties, wet T-shirt contests, wet boxer shorts contests and Girls Gone Wild nights. Open until 6 a.m. The cover charge includes a souvenir Señor Frog's beer mug.

CACTUS SOUTH OF THE BORDER ✉ *Ignacio L. Vallarta #264* ☎ *322-222-4060* The is about the closest thing in the Zona Romántica to a neighborhood pub, where you can converse with fellow visitors and watch all kinds of people make their way along the busy street. There are pool tables and a jukebox, and during the winter there's live rock-and-roll from house band Che Boludos Thursdays through Saturdays starting at 10 p.m. There's no cover, but drink prices are higher when the band is playing.

ROUTE 66 ✉ *Ignacio L. Vallarta #217* ☎ *322-223-2404* This club features live rock, reggae and salsa music nightly from house musicians Pico and Rodrigo. Though it may not look like much from outside, it has a big dancefloor, intimate hideaway nooks and a dim atmosphere befitting the only blues venue in Puerto Vallarta. Featured are top American-style R&B bands from all over western Mexico. Packed on weekends. No cover.

CUATES Y CUETES ✉ *Francisca Rodríguez #163* ☎ *322-223-2724* This early-evening bar, located by the New Pier on Playa Los Muertos, fills up for happy hour and features live music that ranges from reggae and salsa to jazz, starting at sunset and continuing until the 11 p.m. closing hour.

(The name, which you probably won't find in your Spanish-English dictionary, is Mexican slang meaning "friends and drunks"—in other words, drinking buddies.)

CLUB PACO PACO ✉*Ignacio L. Vallarta #278* ✆*322-222-1899* There are no fewer than 16 gay bars in Puerto Vallarta, most of them conveniently located within a few blocks of each other in the Zona Romántica. The discos tend to get going very late—well past midnight—with stage shows earlier in the evening. The largest and one of the oldest, dating back to 1989, the three-story Paco Paco has a large dance floor where drag queens perform Show Travesty on Thursday through Sunday evenings. There's also a country-western area out back called The Ranch, as well as additional performance areas on the second and third floors. More lesbians come here than to most other gay bars in town. Cover.

BAR LOS AMIGOS ✉*Venustiano Carranza #237* ✆*322-222-7802* Next door to Paco's Ranch, this upstairs club bills itself as the friendliest Mexican gay bar in town. It caters to a young, largely local mix of Mexicans and Anglo expatriates and is the closest thing you're likely to find south of the border to a "neighborhood" gay club. There's gay bingo on Wednesday evenings.

ANTROPOLOGY ✉*Morelos #101* ✆*322-223-1159* Another three-story club, Antropology (The Study of Man) has a disco dance floor, the largest male strip show in town—seven to ten dancers—and intimate conversation areas. Cover.

THE PALM ✉*Olas Altas #508* ✆*322-223-4818* This newly remodeled club serves up stage shows featuring female impersonators such as Ida Slapter and Kim Kuzma on Wednesday and Friday nights, and The Palm Pilots male erotic dancers on Sunday nights.

GARBO ✉*Pulpito #142* ✆*322-229-7309* For something mellow and gay-friendly but not exclusively gay, check out Garbo, a dressy ArtDeco piano bar that often presents jazz combos.

APACHES ✉*Olas Altas #439* ✆*322-222-4004* Also on the quiet and romantic side, this is the oldest of the growing number of martini bars, which seem to have a competition running not only on the variety of vodka martinis they offer (mango-tangerine, banana crème, jalapeño...) but also on which one is really the "only" martini bar in Puerto Vallarta.

SUNREST BAR ✉*Pino Suárez #583* ✆*322-222-5229* For a great sunset view combined with gay-friendly ambience, go to the rooftop Sunrest Bar at Descanso del Sol. Closes at 9 p.m.

BLUE SUNSET ROOFTOP BAR ✉*Malecón y Almendro #4* ✆*322-222-5040* Atop the legendary Blue Chairs Resort, long the center of the action in gay Puerto Vallarta, you'll find two separate clubs—the poolside Blue Sunset Rooftop Bar, home of the Dirty Bitches female impersonators, the Blue Hombres male strippers and gay bingo. Also on the roof, Blue Moon offers an intimate atmosphere, piano and vocalist entertainment and gay-theme comedians. Monday is movie night.

BEACHES

PLAYA OLAS ALTAS

✉ *Starts just past the footbridge over the Río Cuale at the south end of the malecón*

"High Waves" is something of a misnomer for this busy city beach lined with seafood vendors and tables under palm-thatch sunshades. The beach is a little steeper than others along the bay, but the surf is minimal. There is a pier from which you can fish, and you'll often find horses for rent by the hour (riding horses in the water is a popular Mexican pastime). Its proximity to Parque Hidalgo, where lovers stroll, lends the beach an air of romance, especially toward sunset.

PLAYA LOS MUERTOS

✉ *South from the pier to the Blue Chairs*

For years, the city's convention and visitors bureau has been trying to change the name of this pretty white-sand beach to Playa del Sol (Beach of the Sun), but locals have refused to relinquish its traditional name, "Beach of the Dead," supposedly named after a 19th-century battle between pirates and miners from the upper Río Cuale that left the sand strewn with corpses. Other old-timers say the original town cemetery was located nearby. Whatever the case, this has been the favorite local beach for as long as anyone can remember. In the 1980s, Playa Los Muertos was polluted and trashy, and tourists avoided it. Today, thanks to the city's aggressive cleanup and public awareness campaign, it is busy but attractive, lined with small palapa restaurants and bars. The beach is walled in by condominiums and hotels against a backdrop of expensive villas climbing up the steep, jungle-covered slopes of the Sierra Madre. On weekends, especially, it is packed shoulder-to-shoulder with sun worshippers, people-watchers, pelican-watchers, volleyball players, parasailers, souvenir sellers, beach food buffs and sunset gazers. The rocks at the south end of the beach are said to be the best place on the bay for fishing from shore. Also at the south end is Puerto Vallarta's gay beach area, referred to as the "blue chairs" (in front of the gay-owned Blue Chairs Resort) and the "green chairs" (in front of the neighboring Beach Café, which broadcasts rock and reggae music along the beach). Nude sunbathing is a no-no, but very revealing men's bathing suits are in vogue.

PLAYA CONCHAS CHINAS

✉ *Past the rock outcropping at the south end of Playa Los Muertos*

To discover a series of small hideaway beaches within walking distance of town, take the narrow trail that leads over the rocks beyond the Blue Chairs. On the other side, you'll descend to a series of sandy coves separated by more rock outcroppings. There are no restaurants or bars, and rarely any souvenir hawkers. In fact, you may find one of the coves where you can enjoy complete privacy—except for the highway on the hillside high above and, beyond it, the many oceanview villas and condo high-rises that make up the PV suburb of Conchas Chinas, the most exclusive residential area in the city. Fortunately, with the splendor of Banderas Bay spread out before you, it's easy to ignore the signs of civilization behind you. (But don't even think of camping or nude sunbathing.)

THE SOUTH SHORE

The Puerto Vallarta tourism department likes to refer to the area along Route 200 south from the Zona Romántica to Mismaloya as the Zona Hotelera Sur—the South Hotel Zone—but in reality it bears little resemblance to the city's north-side big-resort hotel zones. In fact, most of this area is subject to special environmental protection regulations. Except for the blocky high-rises that crowd the beach at Mismaloya itself, most of the lodgings in the area are small inns set on jungle-clad hillsides. There are relatively few restaurants in the area—though among them are some of the best in the city—and nightlife is virtually nonexistent. Fortunately, it's just a short drive or taxi ride to the Zona Romántica and downtown Puerto Vallarta—shorter, actually, than from the Hotel Zone or Marina Vallarta.

Farther south along the bay, the mountains drop steeply to the ocean, making most of the shore impossible to reach, let alone build on. Here and there rivers and creeks empty into the ocean, forming pocket beaches where little villages and rustic resorts have sprung up, including Yelapa, a special spot that manages to be legendary and idyllic at the same time.

SIGHTS

LOS ARCOS ⊠*South of Puerto Vallarta* As you leave old Puerto Vallarta heading south on Route 200, the first eight miles of highway will take you along verdant mountain slopes high above the ocean. You'll get your closest look at "The Arches," the towering offshore rock formations between the Conchas Chinas and Playa Mismaloya. The area of Los Arcos and the waters surrounding them is a federal nature preserve and is the most popular place in the Puerto Vallarta area for both snorkeling and scuba diving.

MISMALOYA

idden

⊠*Route 200, Km. 14.8 south of Puerto Vallarta* Beyond Los Arcos, the highway overlooks Playa Mismaloya, which was the location for the film *The Night of the Iguana*. How times change! Once the epitome of romantic tropical bays, where Richard Burton and Sue Lyon cavorted in the sea, today the beach is a paradise lost, literally overshadowed by ten-story-tall resort hotels and condominium developments. The less noticeable village of Mismaloya is located up the creek from the beach, on the other side of Route 200. Chickens scurry and kids play in the middle of an unpaved road that leads past modest homes, a motel, a cantina and a tortilla factory, and then continues into the jungle along the Ríto Mismaloya.

South Shore

Puerto Vallarta

HOTEL PLAYA CONCHAS CHINAS

PLAYAS LAS ANIMAS

Mismaloya

EL NOGALITO

BOCA DE TOMATLÁN

HOTEL PLAYA CONCHAS CHINAS

PAGE 143

Spacious, modern accommodations with oceanview balconies on a jungle hillside just outside of town

PLAYA LAS ANIMAS

PAGE 150

A seashell-strewn, white-sand beach, sheltered in a notch between steep jungle slopes—excellent for snorkeling

BOCA DE TOMATLÁN

PAGE 141

A short, protected stretch of sands—the closest thing to an unspoiled fishing village in the Puerto Vallarta area

EL NOGALITO

PAGE 147

Fresh lobster, shrimp and other seafood cooked creekside on a lush nature preserve

ZOOLOGICO DE VALLARTA

✉ *Mismaloya* ✆ *322-222-6622* Opened in September 2007, this small zoo was created by the environmentally minded Castañeda-Jiménez family, who moved here from San Antonio, Texas. It now covers just over 12 acres of forested land but, but the family plans to gradually expand it to 208 acres over the next ten years, adding not only more animal exhibits but also a water park, an amusement park and rental cabins. Approximately 100 species kept here include camels, a rare white Bengal tiger and endangered Mexican wolves, as well as animals native to the area such as jaguars, pumas, coyotes, tepezcuintles (large rodents also known as pacas) and guacamayas (scarlet macaws).

EL EDEN

✉ *Ríto Mismaloya Office: Ignacio L. Vallarta #228, Zona Romántica* ✆ *322-222-2516* ✎ *www.canopyeleden.com* This private nature park located on the unpaved road up the Ríto Mismaloya past the village is one of two places in the Puerto Vallarta area offering zipline canopy tours. The tour consists of 12 different zipline cables, totaling two miles in length. Protected by a helmet and safety harness, you hang onto handles on each side of a pulley and fly high above the river. El Eden also has a lovely jungle swimming hole fed by waterfalls, as well as a restaurant and a small shop that offers tastings of tequila and raicilla (a potent agave "moonshine," much stronger than tequila, which used to be made and sold clandestinely in the area but is now distilled legally in Mismaloya). El Eden prides itself on having been used as the location for *Predator*, a 1987 horror/action thriller in which a carnivorous space alien matches wits with Arnold Schwarzenegger. Many tour vans shuttle tourists from Puerto Vallarta to El Eden every day. To go on your own, drive south on Route 200 from old Puerto Vallarta for seven miles, turn left on the unpaved road through Mismaloya village and follow the signs to El Eden.

BOCA DE TOMATLÁN

✉ *Route 200, Km. 18 south of Puerto Vallarta* The closest thing to an authentic, unspoiled fishing village that you can drive or bus to in the Puerto Vallarta area, Boca de Tomatlán is situated at the foot of a steep dirt road that turns off to the right from Route 200 about three miles south of Mismaloya. The name means "Mouth of Tomatlán," referring to the mistaken belief that the Río Tomatlán emptied into the ocean here. Only recently was it discovered that two different rivers originating close together at a high point in the densely wooded Barranca de Tomatlán flowed out opposite ends of the gorge. The real Río Tomatlán reaches the ocean about 55 miles to the south after meandering through a broad agricultural valley. The river at Boca de Tomatlán is now called Río Horcones. By any name, the freshwater flowing out of the jungle meets the saltwater surf of Banderas Bay head-on, piling up a broad sand bar that makes a short, perfect stretch of beach and also protects the cove behind it, where local fishermen keep their boats. The biodiversity that comes from the slow ebbing and flowing action between fresh and salt water attracts an abundance of pelicans, herons, gulls and other birds, who flock to the spot with very little fear of humans. Beyond Boca de Tomatlán, Route 200 turns inland, following the rim of the gorge called Barranca de Tomatlán.

VALLARTA
BOTANICAL GARDENS

✉ *Route 200, Km. 24 south of Puerto Vallarta* ☎ *322-223-6182* ✐ *www.vallartabotanicalgardensac.org* The lush diversity of the tropical forest is shown off in all its glory at this 20-acre nature park set 1300 feet in elevation against the mountainous backdrop of the Sierra Madre. Jungle trails wind among wild palms and orchids, tall cactus and blue agave, a rose garden, a fern grotto and even a carnivorous plant collection. While you are welcome to explore on your own, guided four-hour hiking and birding tours are available for a fee.

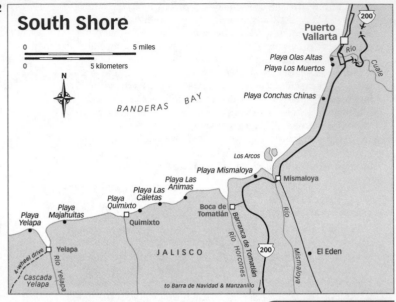

South Shore

0 —————————— 5 miles

0 —————————— 5 kilometers

N

BANDERAS BAY

Puerto Vallarta

RÍO

Cuale

200

Playa Olas Altas
Playa Los Muertos

Playa Conchas Chinas

Los Arcos

Playa Mismaloya

Mismaloya

Playa Las Animas

Playa Las Caletas

Playa Quimixto

Boca de Tomatlán

Barranca de Tomatlán

RÍO

Mismaloya

Playa Majahuitas

Quimixto

Río Horcones

El Eden

Playa Yelapa

4-wheel drive

Yelapa

Río Yelapa

JALISCO

200

Cascada Yelapa

to Barra de Navidad & Manzanillo

YELAPA

hidden

✉ *37 km. southwest of Puerto Vallarta's Los Muertos Beach by boat* ✍*www.yelapa.info* Most of the beaches and coves farther west along the shoreline of Banderas Bay are isolated by steep cliffs and can only be reached by boat. The main village is Yelapa, with a population of about 1000. It's so remote that electricity and telephone service did not reach Yelapa until 2001. Today, public telephones are numerous (prepaid phone cards are required and not always readily available in the village), and there are even a couple of internet cafés. There are no cars, trucks or buses in Yelapa, and most "streets" are cobblestone pathways wide enough for horses but not vehicles. There actually is a road to Yelapa, which ends just outside of town and is used for bringing in construction materials, but it's so steep, narrow and rocky that it can only be driven in a high-clearance, four-wheel-drive vehicle, and only during the dry part of the year. Locals worry that the government may someday pave the road and thus open Yelapa up to bus traffic, but so far this seems unlikely. Still, in the middle of any given day during the winter, tourists are likely to outnumber locals by a wide margin. A handful of palapa restaurants line the beach where the boats land. From the main beach, a trail leads around the cove and over a concrete pedestrian bridge over the Río Yelapa to the village center, where homes and shops rise up the verdant hillside. Besides basking on the beach, the main visitors' activity in Yelapa is to hike or rent a horse and climb the two-mile trail to the Cascada Yelapa waterfall, which drops 150 feet down a sheer cliff. The trail starts near the village center—turn left between Laticia's grocery store and Pedro & Eva's candy and hardware store, toward the pool hall and continue as the trail winds back to the river. Although Yelapa is often characterized as a "fishing village," most local residents make their living by renting horses, running restaurants, renting tourist lodgings or operating water taxis. There are also many artists and musicians and a few yoga instructors. A visit to Yelapa is most rewarding if you can stay overnight there and can experience it without the crowds. While there are many individual palapas and casitas for rent, they tend to book up quickly for peak tourist season, so reservations should be made far in advance. To get to Yelapa from Puerto Vallarta, take one of the regularly scheduled 20-passenger water taxis that leave from the New Pier on Playa del Muerto in the Zona Romántica. Tickets are available at a kiosk at the end of the malecón near the pier. The water taxi operators live in Yelapa, so the last boats of the day do not return to Puerto Vallarta until the next morning. Boat transportation can also be arranged informally from Playa Mismaloya or Boca de Tomatlán.

LODGING

HOTEL PLAYA CONCHAS CHINAS

$$ 19 ROOMS ⊠*Route 200 South, Km. 2.5* ✆*322-221-5763* ☏*322-221-5763* ⌲*www.conchaschinas.com*

A hidden jewel just out of town in one of Puerto Vallarta's most exclusive residential areas, Hotel Playa Conchas Chinas stands on a jungle hillside directly above the secluded beach of the same name. Its spacious, modern, air-conditioned guest rooms have kitchenettes, oceanview balconies and a light, airy feel. The swimming pool overlooks the palm-fringed beach and the ocean. The view alone makes this small hotel a real bargain.

DREAMS PUERTO VALLARTA RESORT & SPA

$$$$ 337 ROOMS ⊠*Playa Las Estacas, Route 200 South, Km. 3.5* ✆*322-226-5000, 866-237-3268* ☏*322-221-6000* ⌲*www.dreamsresorts.com/drepv, info@dreamspuertovallarta.com.mx*

The newest face on the big-hotel scene south of town is secluded (or as secluded as a pair of 11-story arc-shaped high-rise hotel towers like this can be) on its own private cove and small, pristine beach. Its guest rooms and suites are spacious (even the smallest measure 475 square feet) and feature polished marble floors, satellite TVs with DVD players, and bathrooms with tubs. Original prints by prominent Puerto Vallarta artist Manuel Lepe decorate the walls. All units have ocean views, though some lack balconies; king-sized beds are available. The spa offers facials, seaweed wraps and a range of relaxing and therapeutic massage techniques.

PLAYA DEL SOL COSTA SUR

$$$ 208 ROOMS ⊠*Playa Mismaloya, Route 200 South, Km. 4.5* ✆*322-226-8050, 866-921-0126* ☏*322-221-5155* ⌲*www.playadelsolpv.com/costasur, pdsvacations@playadelsolpv.com*

This recently remodeled high-rise located on the oceanfront between

Conchas Chinas and Mismaloya has guest units ranging from studios with a queen-sized bed and a pull-out sofa bed to two-bedroom suites with a king-sized bed, two single beds and a sofa bed. All have fully equipped kitchens, though those in the studio suites have only stoves and microwaves, not ovens. All rooms and suites have balconies, most with ocean views. Down at the beach, there's a manmade saltwater lagoon in front for safe swimming and snorkeling amid tropical fish. There is a swimming pool and a health club on the premises, and guests have privileges at the spa in the Playa del Sol Grand downtown.

PRESIDENTE PUERTO VALLARTA RESORT

$$$$ 120 ROOMS ✉ *Route 200 South, Km. 8.5* ☎ *322-228-0191* 📠 *322-228-0609*
🖰 *www.ichotelsgroup.com, puertovallarta@interconti.com*

As you go farther down the highway from town, the hotels grow larger. The InterContinental hotel group's ten-story resort has recently remodeled, very spacious guest rooms with luxury amenities such as a DVD/CD player, a miniature Zen garden and a minibar stocked with bottled waters from around the world. On the grounds are tennis courts and a swimming pool. Parking is limited. If you're interested, Vallarta Action's 120-foot bungee jump is conveniently located within easy walking distance of the hotel.

BARCELÓ LA JOLLA DE MISMALOYA

$$$$ 317 SUITES ✉ *Route 200 South, Km. 11.5* ☎ *322-226-0660* 📠 *322-228-0500*
🖰 *www.barcelolajollademismaloya.com, sec7@barcelo.com*

A guarded gate admits only guests to the big kahuna on Playa Mismaloya, a pair of nine-story towers right on the sand. If you're wondering how the idyllic beach you saw in the movie that made Puerto Vallarta famous became so uglified with high-rises, this is the place that started it. It offers 317 one- and two-bedroom suites. All are air-conditioned and have two-line phones with modem hookups as well as wireless internet access. All have balconies or patios, though only the premium suites on the sixth through ninth floors have ocean views. Some come with fully equipped kitchens, though you won't need one if you choose the all-inclusive option, which includes three meals a day at any of five restaurants on the premises, from buffets to a dressy, formal Spanish dining room. There are three outdoor pools, a lighted tennis court, a spa and mountain bike and horse rentals. The hotel stands on the spot that was originally occupied by the set of *The Night of the Iguana* and later by director John Huston's home.

CASA IGUANA HOTEL

$$–$$$ 53 ROOMS ✉ *Avenida 5 de Mayo #455, Mismaloya*
☎ *322-228-0186 or 877-893-7654* 📠 *322-228-0087*
🖰 *www.casaiguanahotel.com*

Hidden up a cobblestone road from the main highway, this yellow, four-story hotel is the largest building in the picturesque little village of Mismaloya. The beach is a five- or ten-minute walk away, on the other side of the highway, but you may find that you prefer the peace and quiet of the hotel's two swimming pools, jacuzzi, lush gardens and palm trees. Guest units are air-conditioned two-bedroom and three-bedroom suites designed to accommodate groups traveling together—and fairly afford-able, especially if the rates are divided among several people. Each has a fully equipped kitchenette and a balcony overlooking the gardens and pool area. There is a food store and a 24-hour internet café on the premises, as well as a 60-person meeting room and a presentation theater.

MAR SERENO HOTEL AND SUITES

$$ 30 UNITS   ✉Route 200 South, Km. 15   ☎322-228-0879
📠322-228-0591   ⌨www.marsereno.com, reservaciones@marsereno.com

Midway between Mismaloya and Boca de Tomatlán, sculpted into a hillside high above the ocean and surrounded by jungle, this hotel rises 11 stories (you descend by elevator from the re-ception area at the top) but has just three guest units per floor. All of the one- and two-bedroom air-conditioned suites include kitchenettes and ocean-view balconies, with your choice of a king-sized bed or two doubles. The floors are polished marble, and dark wood furnishings set off the warm golden decor. Besides a conventional swimming pool with a panoramic ocean view, there's a natural saltwater swimming pool by the shore, surrounded by boulders, and a jacuzzi on the upper terrace. A free introductory scuba lesson is included in the room rate.

HOTEL LAGUNITA

$$–$$$ 32 UNITS   ✉Yelapa   ☎322-209-5055
⌨www.hotel-lagunita.com, info@hotel-lagunita.com

In Yelapa, the closest thing to a "real" hotel has thatch-roofed concrete casitas that look more rustic on the outside than in their brightly painted, simply furnished interiors. All have one or two double beds, ceiling fans, electricity private baths with hot water, and individual patios. Scattered among palms and flowering trees along the base of a jungle hillside, the casitas open directly onto a stretch of sand protected from erosion by a stone wall and are a short walk from a very wide natural beach. The hotel also has a swimming pool.

HOTEL BLUE MOON

$–$$ 8 ROOMS   ✉Yelapa   ☎322-209-5062   javier_rodriguez@yahoo.com

The spacious but very basic rooms in this unmarked motel be-hind Chico's restaurant have bare white walls, solar-heated showers and sparsely equipped kitchenettes. Most have a dou-ble bed and a single bed. The main beach, horse rentals and the river trail to the waterfall are all just a few steps away. Javier, the owner, also has five houses for rent nearby.

PALAPA IN YELAPA

$–$$$ ✉ ✆ 322-209-5214 ⬥ www.palapainyelapa.com,
lazy@palapainyelapa.com

Besides the two hotels, there are about 50 guest rentals scattered through all areas of the village of Yelapa for visitors who wish to stay overnight or longer. Many are booked through this central agency located at the south end of the beach. Among them are a small casitas, large old-fashioned palapas, a two-bedroom house on a trail high above the bay and rooftop apartments. Brad at the agency office can usually locate a place to suit your needs on short notice during the off-season, but reservations should be made far in advance during the November-to-April high season. If you arrive in Yelapa without reservations and plan to spend the night, be sure to come on an early boat or you'll most likely find yourself sleeping on the beach with the sand fleas, hermit crabs and scorpions that come out at night. Additional rentals can be located through the directory found at www.yelapa.info, which is not a central reservation service but instead puts you directly in touch with the owners by phone or e-mail.

MAJAHUITAS RESORT

$$$$ 8 UNITS ✉ Playa Majahuitas ✆ 322-293-4506
⬥ www.majahuitas-resort.com

If you really want to get away from it all, consider one of the eight casitas at this primitive but exclusive resort situated on the secluded beach of the same name located midway between Boca de Tomatlán and Yelapa. You can't get there by road. A staff member meets you on your arrival at the Puerto Vallarta airport and takes you to the resort by boat. When you do arrive, you'll find that your lodging is in a large casita nestled into the tropical hillside and fronting on the beach. The casitas vary in configuration from studios to split-level two-bedroom units. They have no windows but are open to the sea breezes. There is no electricity—illumination after dark is provided by oil lamps—and the only telephone at the resort is a radiophone for emergency use only. Kayaks and snorkeling gear are available. Three meals a day are included in the rate. There's a four-day minimum stay during high season; at other times of year, shorter stays may be allowed depending on availability. Closed mid-June through September.

DINING

EL SET

$$$$ STEAK/SEAFOOD ✉ Route 200 South, Km. 2.5 ✆ 322-221-5342

Built into the side of a cliff above Playa Conchas Chinas, next door to some of Puerto Vallarta's most palatial mansions, El Set specializes in steaks, seafood and sunsets. The name derives from Puerto Vallarta's reputation as a movie location, though nothing much has actually been filmed on this site, spectacular as it is. As with other clifftop restaurants south of the city, you pay a premium for the view and the romantic atmosphere. El Set prides itself on its courteous, attentive (though not always fast) waitstaff. Baja lobster is a house specialty. You can also order a two-person combination plate of filet mignon, lobster and shrimp, accompanied by a bottle of fine—and quite expensive—French wine.

EL NOGALITO

$$$ SEAFOOD   ✉ *Calzada del Cedro, off Route 200 South, Km. 8*
✆ *322-221-5225*

Situated on a ranch and nature preserve in lush jungle surroundings teeming with birds, this luxurious restaurant serves lunch and stays open until 5:30 p.m. Lobster, shrimp, red snapper and beef shish kebabs are cooked over an outdoor charcoal grill while you relax on the terrace beside a gently murmuring creek. A visit to El Nogalito is meant to be an all-afternoon experience. Several hiking trails meander through the forest, and you can hire a guide at the restaurant to take you around and tell you about the native flora and fauna.

EL EDEN RESTAURANT AND BAR

$$–$$$ STEAK/SEAFOOD   ✉ *Ríto Mismaloya* ✆ *322-222-2516*

Located in a private nature preserve with zipline canopy tours and hiking trails through some of the lushest tropical forest in the region to picturesque waterfalls, El Eden is a destination for bus and van tours carrying cruise ship passengers and big-resort guests, and its prices reflect the steady flow of "captive" tourists. Still, the steak-and-seafood fare is quite good (especially if you've worked up a fierce appetite riding the park's canopy ziplines), and the restaurant's setting, above the bank of a picture-perfect jungle pool fed by waterfalls, is hard to beat. To get there without taking a tour, drive south on Route 200 from old Puerto Vallarta for seven miles; turn left on the cobblestone road through the village of Mismaloya and continue on the unpaved road, following the signs, to El Eden.

CHINO'S PARADISE

$$ SEAFOOD   ✉ *Rito Mismaloya, Km. 2* ✆ *322-225-5271*

Also on the road to El Eden is this large palapa restaurant perched above the creek beside a shallow natural pool surrounded by jungle. You can order your afternoon meal (the restaurant is only open from 11 a.m. to 5 p.m.), take a half-hour hike in the jungle or swim in the river below a small waterfall, and find your meal ready when you return. The menu is very short, consisting of just four selections: jumbo shrimp wrapped in cheese and bacon, butterfly shrimp, a dorado (mahimahi) filet, and shrimp in garlic butter; you can order a seafood platter with small portions of all of the above.

LE KLIFF

$$$ SEAFOOD   ✉Route 200 South, Km. 17.5   ☎322-228-0666
✍www.lekliff.com, reserva@lekliff.com

Superlatives abound at this eatery, an upscale seafood establishment that has ranked among the Puerto Vallarta area's top restaurants since 1983. The huge palm-thatched roof shelters four levels of open-air dining terraces perched on the edge of a rock cliff that plunges straight down into the crashing surf below. Especially at sunset, the magnificent 180-degree panoramic ocean view justifies the steep prices for dishes such as flounder with goat cheese and honey or yellow curry shrimp satay with saffron couscous. Located just north of the turnoff to Boca de Tomatlán.

CAFÉ PRIMITIVO

$ MEXICAN   ✉Boca de Tomatlán

Like most of the restaurants south of Puerto Vallarta, the most special thing about this laid-back palapa restaurant is its location. Unlike most of the others, the prices don't reflect the view. The fare at this small open-air eatery in Boca de Tomatlán is predominantly Mexican, with fish tacos and fish filets *al mojo de ajo* (in garlic sauce) among the top picks. Or you might just want to sip a Corona while watching the birds and the beach and thinking about what you could tell the people back at the office to make them envious . . . if only Boca de Tomatlán had cell phone reception.

PLANTATION HOUSE

$$ PIZZA   ✉Vallarta Botanical Gardens, Route 200, Km. 24 south of Puerto Vallarta   ☎322-223-6182

Located in the botanical gardens visitor center, this small restaurant commands a lovely view of the surrounding jungle and the mountains beyond. Pizzas cooked in oak-fired brick ovens include the house specialty, a Mexican pizza topped with pork carnitas, caramelized onions and a chipotle cream sauce. There are also soups, salads and shrimp cocktails, as well as beer and wine.

CHICO'S RESTAURANT

$$ MEXICAN/SEAFOOD   ✉Playa Yelapa   ☎322-209-5058

For a small village, Yelapa has a surprising number of restaurants. If you visit during the summer, you'll see why. Chico's is typical of about eight palapa eateries with outdoor tables on the sand that line the beach near where the water taxis land. All of them have about the same menu selection and prices, and most of them are only open from breakfast time until late afternoon when the last tourist boats leave. (Most of the little restaurants across the cove in the village serve dinner, as does the dining room at the Hotel Lagunita.) Chico's *sopa de camarón*, a mildly spicy soup chock full of large shrimp, is a bargain at a fraction of the price you'd pay for locally caught shrimp at most Puerto Vallarta restaurants.

BISTRO SELVÁTICO

$$$ SEAFOOD   ✉ *Yelapa* ⌂ *www.galeriayelapa.com*

The finest dining in Yelapa is at this open-air restaurant and art gallery set among mango trees and passion fruit vines on a hillside above the cobblestone path leading from the main beach to the village. Mexico City-trained chef Tatiana Moreno prepares freshly caught fish using creative recipes she collects while traveling the world during the off-season, when the restaurant is closed. Seating is quite limited, so you need to book table space ahead of time. But as of this writing there is no phone at the restaurant, so you must climb the steep stairway twice—once to make reservations when you first arrive in Yelapa and again for dinner. The gallery, run by Tatiana's husband, Yelapa native Jeff Elles, exhibits paintings, wood carvings, jewelry and other works by several local artists. Dinner only.

NIGHTLIFE

YELAPA YACHT CLUB

✉ *Village playita by the pier, Yelapa* The hottest spot on the isolated south shore is this beachfront bar, which used to serve as a gathering spot for private boaters. Now it has a bare concrete dance floor and is referred to locally as "the disco." There's dancing on Wednesday and Saturday nights during the winter, from around 10 p.m. to 2 a.m., with music that ranges from big-band swing to hip-hop. You can meet most of the local expatriates here on disco nights, since it's pretty much the only nighttime excitement in town. (Well, almost. Locals also get together for big bonfire parties on the beach on full-moon nights during the winter. And on Monday evenings at 6 p.m. a little restaurant called the Passion Flower Garden, located between the pedestrian bridge and the village, shows American movies.)

BEACHES

PLAYA MISMALOYA
✉ *12 kilometers south of Puerto Vallarta off Route 200 South*

This once-lovely crescent of sand was so picture-perfect that director John Huston chose it as the shooting location for the film that made Puerto Vallarta famous. Since then, it has been engulfed by high-rise beach resorts and condos that restrict beach access, making it all but impossible to leave footprints in the sand unless you're a guest.

BOCA DE TOMATLÁN
✉ *18 kilometers south of Puerto Vallarta off Route 200 South*

The interplay of river currents and ocean surf has formed a golden sand bar that's like a beach with water on both sides. There are several small palapa restaurants and bars nearby on the river bank. Variations in the river's flow from year to year mean that the sand bar changes in size and can gain or lose more than half its length and breadth seasonally. A local fishing fleet harbors in the shallow water inside the bar. If you ask around you can often charter a *panga* to take you out to Quimixto, Yelapa or other spots along the south coast of Banderas Bay. Parking is extremely limited. Boca de Tomatlán is also accessible by public bus or sometimes by water taxi from the New Pier at Playa Los Muertos in old Puerto Vallarta.

PLAYA LAS ANIMAS
✉ *3.5 kilometers southwest of Boca de Tomatlán*

Accessible only by boat or hiking trail, Playa Las Animas is a short, wide, seashell-strewn white-sand beach sheltered in a notch between steep jungle-clad slopes and isolated by rocky promontories at both ends. It enjoys a reputation as an excellent spot for snorkeling. It can be very crowded with locals on weekends, and some excursion boats make short stops there on the way to Yelapa. The rest of the time, it's idyllic. Unlike other well-known south coast beaches, Playa Las Animas has no overnight accommodations, though it does have a handful of palapa restaurant/bars and wandering food vendors, as well as beach chairs for rent; Wave Runners and parasailing are available. Playa Las Animas is about 20 minutes south of Boca de Tomatlán by boat or two hours' fantastically scenic hike on a trail along the hillsides above the coast (see Outdoor Adventures: Hiking), which leads to two the small, usually deserted **Playa Los Caballos** along the way. Water taxis from Puerto Vallarta will drop you at Playa Las Animas on request, and you can often hire a boat at Boca de Tomatlán to take you there and pick you up later.

PLAYA QUIMIXTO

✉ *6 kilometers southwest of Boca de Tomatlán*

🚶🏇🏊🚣⛵ Water taxis from the New Pier at Playa Los Muertos en route to Yelapa stop on request at this small, somewhat rocky beach in front of a village of about 250 families' small, thatch-roofed homes. Like Yelapa, Quimixto is not readily accessible by land. Though it fits the description "unspoiled fishing village" better than any other settlement on Banderas Bay, the reality is that the majority of Quimixto residents derive most of their income from renting horses to visitors, who ride up a canyon behind the village to two pretty waterfalls. Green parrots and iguanas are abundant. Playa Quimixto has the only surf break on the south side of the bay. There are no overnight accommodations.

PLAYA LAS CALETAS

✉ *West of Quimixto*

🚶🏊🚣 Farther along the coast, this secluded beach was filmmaker John Huston's personal hideaway for many years. Today it's a wildlife preserve where Vallarta Adventures takes boat excursions for the day. There are a beachfront bar and kayak rentals, as well as nature trails, an orchidarium, a deer sanctuary, an aviary and a day spa. A natural reef close to shore makes it one of the best scuba sites on the bay. To go there, take a Vallarta Adventures excursion, which costs about US$80 per adult and $40 for kids 12 and under. It's also possible to get there by continuing beyond Las Animas or Quimixto on the coastal trail, which becomes overgrown and indistinct in places, but all the facilities there belong to the tour company and are included in the tour prices. Both daytime (9 a.m. to 4 p.m. or 11:30 a.m. to 6 p.m.) and evening (6:30 to 11 p.m.) trips depart from the Maritime Terminal at Marina Vallarta. Contact: Vallarta Adventures (Edificio Marina Golf, local 13-C, Calle Mástil, Marina Vallarta; 322-297-1212, 888-303-2653; www.vallarta-adventures.com, info@vallarta-adventures.com).

MAJAHUITAS

✉ *Midway between Boca de Tomatlán and Yelapa*

🏊🚣 This fair-sized beach, secluded midway between Boca de Tomatlán and Yelapa, feels like the private domain of the small, rustic resort set along its foreshore. A few tour boats put in here, usually for a picnic-and-snorkeling stop around 11 a.m. to 1 p.m. Facilities on the beach are minimal, and the resort is inhospitable about letting boat tourists use the restrooms or otherwise leave the beach. They also ask that nonguests confine their visit to the far end of the beach. Ask at Boca de Tomatlán or at the new Playa Los Muertos pier in old Puerto Vallarta for excursion boats that stop at Majahuitas.

PLAYA YELAPA

✉ *23 kilometers southwest of Boca de Tomatlán by boat; To get there, take a water taxi from the New Pier at Playa Los Muertos in old Puerto Vallarta or from Boca de Tomatlán.*

🚶 🐎 🏊 🛶 ⛵ This crescent beach—which traces a sheltered cove backed by a freshwater lagoon at the mouths of the Río Yelapa and Río Tuito—is adjacent to a village of about 1000 people, many of them expatriate *gringos*, that rises up steep green hills overhead. There are no roads (or cars), and access to hillside houses is by stairways and trails. There are plenty of tourists on the beach from late morning to late afternoon, though, and much of Yelapa's economy depends on the many little palapa restaurants that line the beach. (The Sights section contains more information on Yelapa.)

OUTDOOR ADVENTURES

BIKING

Several companies operate mountain bike tours into the Sierra along the Río Cuale for riders of various skill levels. The downhill ride back to town makes for a thrilling climax to any of the trips.

The most popular bike trip is an "all levels" ride that follows the Río Cuale for three miles to a small village at a river junction. It then follows the Río Vallejo for another three miles through increasingly dense foliage to a dramatic waterfall with a deep pool at its foot where riders cool off before the return trip.

A more advanced bike tour follows the same three-mile route to the first village but then climbs for another eleven miles to an elevation of over 3000 feet. It takes in panoramic views of the Sierra and the bay and passes through several rustic *rancherías* along the way to the secluded village of San Pedro. The return portion of this five-hour trip is the most exciting downhill bike ride in the region.

An even more challenging all-day technical ride turns off the dirt road a short distance beyond the first village and follows a single-track trail up and down hills, over roots and rocks, into the depths of the forest to the Cascada El Salto waterfall, where there's a large swimming hole.

Several unpaved roads that are good for mountain biking wind through the foothills on the Cabo Corrientes cape on the south side of Banderas Bay. They are accessible from the town of El Tuito, 30 miles south of Puerto Vallarta via Route 200. One goes to the fishing village of El Chimo. Another goes to the tiny settlement of Cabo Corrientes (population 85) on the tip of the cape.

ECO RIDE ✉ *Miramar #382* ☎ *322-222-7912* 🖥 *www.ecoridemex.com, ecoridemex@yahoo.com* This young company, which has its bike shop in the hilly back streets of downtown, offers guided tours of various lengths for all skill levels. They also rent mountain bikes and provide maps for self-guided trips.

BIKEMEX ADVENTURES ✉ *Guerrero #361* ✆ *322-223-1680* ✐ *bikemex@zonavirtual.com.mx* BikeMex offers easy to moderate rides along the Río Cuale as well as more challenging mountain rides, including one that climbs 2000 feet on the aptly named Mataburros (Donkey Killer) Trail, and four- to seven-day tours of the Sierra Madre.

BUNGEE JUMPING

VALLARTA ACTION ✉ *Route 200 South, Km. 9.2* ✆ *322-228-0670* If you've ever felt a secret yen to go cliff diving, here's your chance. It's hard to miss the permanent bungee jumping structure mounted from a sheer cliff just south of the Presidente Puerto Vallarta Resort, between old Puerto Vallarta and Mismaloya. It's a 120-foot drop to the ocean below. You can choose to wear a full-body or ankle harness. The company boasts an unblemished safety record since it opened the jump operation in 1993. No reservations required.

CANOPY TOURS

The area south of Puerto Vallarta has canopy tours in which participants careen from one tree platform to the next, dangling by harnesses from steel cables and controlling their speed with handbrakes. The tours provide a heady combination of nature appreciation (a guide tells about the trees, orchids and other flora of the tropical forest canopy at each platform) with a series of pure adrenaline thrills. The tours are offered year-round and depart at various times throughout the day. Participants must be at least eight years old and four feet tall and must weigh less than 250 pounds.

EL EDEN ✉ *Rito Mismaloya; Ignacio L. Vallarta #228 (office), Zona Romántica* ✆ *322-222-2516* ✐ *www.canopyeleden.com* This nature preserve/theme park near the village of Mismaloya has 14 observation platforms, 11 horizontal traverses, a Tarzan swing, two hanging bridges and the steepest descent of any of the tours, reaching speeds of up to 50 miles per hour. To get there without taking a tour, drive south on Route 200 from old Puerto Vallarta for seven miles, turn left on the cobblestone road through the village of Mismaloya and continue, following the signs, to El Eden.

LOS VERANOS ✉ *Las Juntas; Calle Francisca Rodriguez #336 (office)* ✆ *322-223-0504* Farther south, Los Veranos is billed as the highest and longest canopy tour in Mexico, with 1.8 miles of cable in 14 ziplines. There are also waterslides and river pools for swimming, as well as tequila tasting.

FISHING

Muelle Los Muertos (aka the New Pier) on Playa Los Muertos offers good fishing from shore for bonita, jacks, mackerel, corvina, snook, snapper and occasionally large roosterfish.

Many, though by no means all, sportfishing charters operate out of Marina Vallarta. The best months for big-game fishing are when the water near the surface is warmest—which is from April through November, outside of peak tourist season. Charter operators will provide a one-day fishing license and all tackle.

MASTER BAITER'S SPORTFISHING AND TACKLE ⊠*Paseo Diaz Ordaz #915* ✆*322-222-4043* ✐*www.masterbaitersfishing.com, info@masterbaiters fishing.com* This downtown shop sells gear for bait fishing and flyfishing. They also arrange sportfishing charters and freshwater bass fishing trips.

CHARTER DREAMS ⊠*Marina Las Palmas #11–12, Marina Vallarta* ✆*322-221-0690* ✐*www.charterdreams.com, info@charterdreams.com* Try your luck at battling and landing a marlin, a sailfish or a giant tuna. In business since 1998, Ed and Kim Moore operate two boats, one of them air-conditioned.

MR. MARLIN SPORTFISHING CENTER ⊠*Condominiums Puesta del Sol #16, Marina Vallarta* ✆*322-222-0809* ✐*www.mrmarlin.com, info@mrmarlin.com* Legendary billfish tournament champion Juan Moll, the owner of Mr. Marlin, operates three boats ranging in size from 35 to 50 feet.

PUERTO VALLARTA SPORTFISHING ⊠*Marina Vallarta* ✆*322-222-4935, 866-217-9704* ✐*www.puertovallartafishing.net, info@puertovallartafishing.net* This charter company operates seven boats and arranges for big game fishermen to share charters to minimize expense.

GOLF

VISTA VALLARTA I AND II ⊠*Circuito Universidad #653* ✆*322-290-0030* ✐*www.vistavallartagolf.com* Two 18-hole, par-72 championship courses, designed by Jack Nicklaus and Tom Weiskopf respectively, sprawl across 478 acres well inland and due east of the airport. Both were built simultaneously in 2001 and are quite different from one another. The Nicklaus course, the longer of the two at 7073 yards, is located at a high elevation with panoramic views of Banderas Bay. Dense stands of palm trees flank the hilly fairways. The 6976-yard Weiskopf course presents a variety of extreme natural terrain features, including creeks, arroyos and jungle. A gated development, including condominiums, villas and two resort hotels, is planned for the land surrounding the courses, but in the meantime they feel far away from the busy city.

MARINA VALLARTA GOLF CLUB ⊠*Paseo de la Marina #430* ✆*322-221-0073* ✐*www.marinavallartagolf.com, info@marinavallartagolf.com* A longer-established course designed by Joe Finger and under the same ownership as Vista Vallarta, this 18-hole, 670-yard, par-71 course is located near the ocean, just south of the airport and across the boulevard from the bull ring. Besides a clubhouse and pro shop with club and cart rentals, it has practice facilities including a driving range and putting greens. Ponds, lagoons and lakes not only pose water hazards but also invite such wildlife distractions as cranes, herons, iguanas and even an occasional crocodile. Several hotels around Marina Vallarta offer guests privileges at the Marina Vallarta Golf Club, including Velas Vallarta, the

Westin Resort, the Regent Resort, the Golden Crown Paradise, the Sheraton Buganvilias Resort and the Quinta Real.

155

HIKING

If you look east from any of the bridges that span the Río Cuale, you can see that the same river that divides the old part of the city also carves a V through the otherwise formidable wall of jungle-clad mountains. You'd expect to find a trail following the river into the high country. It's actually a rugged, seasonal dirt road, which was used in past centuries to haul supplies up to silver mining towns like Mascota and Talpa de Allende, though today it is used mainly by people who live in a handful of tiny villages along the river. The only challenge in following the river up from town is getting across the fast, busy Libramiento highway that runs around the east side of old Puerto Vallarta. With a car, it's easier. Take the Libramiento through the first tunnel and, after crossing the Río Cuale, turn right onto the unpaved river road and continue along the river bank until you reach another bridge. Then continue for another half-mile and park along the roadside. From here, you can walk on a gentle upgrade through the riparian forest as far as you wish.

MISMALOYA   People visiting the village of Mismaloya will find that the road from the village up Ríto Mismaloya to the nature theme park El Eden lets them experience the jungle up close. For a fee, you can also use the hiking trails within El Eden.

From Boca de Tomatlán, it's possible to follow the river on a foot trail past villagers' houses and continue for quite a way into the deep Barranca de Tomatlán, choked with tall tropical forest. The trail ultimately becomes overgrown and indistinct, so how far you can hike depends on the season of the year and when someone last came through clearing the trail with a machete.

The more popular hike from Boca de Tomatlán, though, is west along the shoreline to the tiny settlement of Las Animas. In fact, this may be the most popular hike in the Puerto Vallarta area. The 3.5-kilometer trail—allow at least two hours one-way—begins as a continuation of the footpath in front of the villagers' houses on the west bank of the river in Boca de Tomatlán; walk downriver, toward the bay, and follow it as it swings to the left and houses become more sparse. The well-defined trail involves many short but sometimes steep ascents and descents, winding through the jungle to circumvent the steep cliffs along parts of the shoreline, and leads to one fantastic viewpoint after another. There are occasional clusters of small houses along the route, where hikers can find themselves trying to follow the path almost through people's yards, and in a couple of spots local dogs can cause scary moments, but for most of the way it is a beautiful and memorable hiking experience. About two kilometers along the trail, nearly uninhabited Playa Los Caballos is an ideal spot for a rest and a swim. By the time you reach Playa Las Animas, the cluster of palapa bars and restaurants will seem almost like civilization, and you'll find that a chilled *cerveza* never tasted so good. You can usually catch a water taxi back to

Boca de Tomatlán—ask about times at one of the restaurants as soon as you get there.

RIDING STABLES

In Yelapa, horses are available at the corral behind the palapa restaurants on the main beach. During the day, while the cruise boats are in, the horses are only used for guided rides to the waterfall. Visitors who spend the night in Yelapa can rent horses early or late, when the crowds are gone, and ride on their own. Horseback tours are also available in Quimixto, where locals say horse rentals are the main industry.

SCUBA DIVING & SNORKELING

LOS ARCOS MARINE RESERVE   The most popular site for snorkeling and scuba trips from Puerto Vallarta is Los Arcos Marine Reserve, located just south of town. Here, ocean currents collide with a sheer and seemingly bottomless underwater cliff called Quijada del Diablo (the Devil's Jawbone), bringing surges of plankton from the depths of the bay to the surface; the rich food source attracts myriad colorful tropical fish including angelfish, parrot fish, damsels, puffer fish and sometimes even mantas and stingrays. The presence of glow-in-the-dark creatures from the bay's deep waters makes Los Arcos the most popular area for night diving.

ISLAS MARIETAS NATIONAL PARK   Longer scuba and snorkeling daytrips go to Islas Marietas National Park, a group of three islands off the north tip of Banderas Bay surrounded by extensive coral reefs at a depth of ten meters. Dolphins, manta rays and sea turtles, as well as an abundance of fish such as Cortez chubs, Panamic sergeant majors and king angelfish, are often spotted in the waters around Islas Marietas.

Other, less crowded scuba sites around Banderas Bay include El Morro, a group of rock pinnacles west of Islas Marietas, where experienced divers can explore a 50-foot underwater tunnel and sea caves frequented by lobsters, sea turtles, octopus, sharks, sea horses and moray eels. Corbeteña is a tiny, remote island where the few experienced divers who go there can expect to encounter large fish including sharks, sailfish and schools of jack tuna.

EL CHIMO   One of the most unusual and little-known scuba dive sites in Banderas Bay, El Chimo lies out beyond Yelapa on the south coast of Banderas Bay. Its uniqueness comes from its undersea rock formations—a mesa about a quarter of a mile in diameter from which tall pinnacles and columns rise like the ruins of some ancient sunken city. Human visitors are uncommon enough so that colorful tropical fish live here in great profusion, dancing colorfully among the rock spires. Snorkeling is prohibited, and access is limited to fully certified scuba divers. While the small fishing settlement at El Chimo can be reached in dry weather via a long, rough unpaved road that turns off from the village of El Tuito, 30 miles south of Puerto Vallarta via Route 200, and takes most of the day to get there, it's much easier to take one of the small group dive excursions offered by the tour operators listed below.

Dive trips can be arranged through the activities desks at most large resort hotels, whether or not you're a guest there. The hotels act as agents for independent dive companies and receive the same commission whether they set up trips for guests or the general public. Snorkeling equipment is usually reserved for guests' use since snorkeling is included among the free activities in most all-inclusive plans.

VALLARTA ADVENTURES ✉*Edificio Marina Golf, local 13-C, Calle Mástil Marina Vallarta* 📞*322-297-1212, 888-303-2653* 🖥*www.vallarta-adventures.com, info@ vallarta-adventures.com* Scuba and snorkeling excursions and dive certification (along with many other outdoor adventures) are available from Puerto Vallarta's largest ecotour company. They also offer three- and four-day dive packages covering most of the major dive sites in Banderas Bay.

PACIFIC SCUBA ✉*Francisco Medina Ascencio #2486* 📞*322-209-0364* 🖥*www. pacificscuba.com.mx, godive@vallartaundersea.com* This PADI dive center takes small-group trips to six local dive and snorkeling sites; top-of-the-line gear and lunch and drinks included. Emphasizing environmental awareness, this dive shop's owner was the founder of Puerto Vallarta's Beach and Bay Underwater Cleanup Group. Night dives are available.

CHICO'S DIVE SHOP ✉*Díaz Ordaz #772* 📞*322-222-1895* 🖥*www.chicos-dive shop.com* Operating in Puerto Vallarta for 40 years, Chico's offers scuba and snorkeling tours to Los Arcos, Las Marietas, Majahuitas and several other dive sites. They also offer beginner and advanced scuba courses.

DISCOVERY VALLARTA ✉*Isla Iguana #17, Marina Vallarta* 📞*322-221-1652* 📞*322-221-1652* 🖥*www.discovery-vallarta.com, info1@discoveryvallarta.com* This company offers supervised snorkeling excursions to Los Arcos and the Islas Marietas. All equipment is provided.

WILDLIFE WATCHING

Dolphins and sea turtles are abundant in Banderas Bay, and it's not unusual to spot them from the water taxis between Puerto Vallarta and Yelapa. In season, hikers sometimes get a look at whales near the shore from the trail between Boca de Tomatlán and Playa Las Animas (see Hiking). But for the best adventure in nature, go with a local guide who knows where to look and how to spot wildlife. A tour is also the easiest way to get transportation to wild areas on land or sea.

For whale watching, the most popular nature-oriented pastime around Puerto Vallarta in the winter, tours usually take place in the morning, departing around 8 a.m. and returning at noon or so. Wear a swimsuit, a hat and sunglasses and bring a windbreaker and plenty of sunscreen. Children under age six are usually not allowed on whale-watching trips. Whale-watching tours are offered from mid-December through the end of March. Off-season, April through early December, some whale-watching tour operators conduct wild dolphin-watching tours. Puerto Vallarta also has captive swim-with-dolphins programs.

Birding tours usually begin in the early morning, around 7 a.m. and return in the early afternoon. There are two types of tours—coastal and marshland (best for beginners because birds are easier to spot in the open), and mountain slope or tropical forest. Some trips include stops in both areas. You'll want to bring all-terrain shoes, a sweater or light jacket, hat, sunglasses and insect repellent. Tour operators usually provide field reference guides and bird checklists and may also have binoculars available. Birding expeditions are available year-round.

For seabird watching, about nine miles out to sea from the tip of the Punta de Mita peninsula north of Puerto Vallarta, Islas Marietas National Park includes three islands that are actually the exposed tips of peaks in the underwater mountain range that marks the western extent of Banderas Bay. As tall as the rock formations of Los Arcos but much more massive, the islands rise out of the sea as sheer cliffs bleached snow-white with many years' accumulation of bird guano. While Islas Marietas are a popular scuba destination, the reason they're under federal protection is their bird life. The islands are home to thousands of seabirds and wading birds, including magnificent frigates, motmots, seagulls, pelicans and the rare blue-footed boobie. The islands have been designated as a UNESCO Biosphere Reserve.

"Turtle camp" tours, which allow visitors to watch and sometimes participate in sea turtle protection activities, take place in the evening hours. They usually begin with a video about worldwide sea turtle conservation efforts. Then the tours go to one of the protected nesting areas, where you can see turtle nests and, if you're lucky, a female laying her eggs or a nest in the process of hatching. Bring a camera with flash, a light jacket, walking shoes and a *natural* insect repellent (*do not* bring repellent containing DEET, which can be harmful to newborn turtles). Turtle camp tours are offered from July through November. They are limited to small groups, so reservations should be made early.

Nature tour operators in Puerto Vallarta include:

THE WHALE WATCHING CENTER/ OPEN AIR EXPEDITIONS

✉ *Guerrero #339* ✆ *322-222-3310, 866-422-9972* ✍ *www.vallartawhales. com, openair@vallartawhales.com* Four-hour morning or afternoon whale watching tours in season, Dolphins in the Wild excursions at other times of year, departing from the Maritime Terminal at Marina Vallarta.

VALLARTA ADVENTURES

✉ *Edificio Marina Golf, local 13-C, Calle Mástil Marina Vallarta* ✆ *322-297-1212, 888-303-2653* ✍ *www.vallarta-adventures.com, info@vallarta-adventures.com* Puerto Vallarta's oldest and largest tour company offers whale watching excursions, turtle camp, and captive dolphin and sea lion encounters.

OCEAN FRIENDLY WHALE WATCHING ADVENTURES

✉ *Paseo del Marlin 510–103, Colonia Aralias* 📞 *322-225-3774* 📠 *322-225-3774* 🖥 *www. oceanfriendly.com, ofrey@oceanfriendly.com* Oceanographer and marine photographer Oscar Frey, who has been doing whale and dolphin research on Banderas Bay since 1994, guides small-group tours.

WILDLIFE CONNECTION

✉ *Francia #140, Departamento 7, Colonia Versalles* 📞 *322-225-3621* 🖥 *www. wildlifeconnection.com, info@wildlifeconnection.com* Marine biologist Maru Rodriguez and wildlife photographer Eduardo Lugo organize whale watching, wild dolphin watching and birding excursions and turtle camps.

DISCOVER PACIFIC TOURS

📞 *322-205-0320* 🖥 *www.discoverpacific tours. com, info@discoverpacifictours.com* Owner Alfredo Herrera has a reputation as Puerto Vallarta's best birding guide. His company also offers whale and wild dolphin watching expeditions.

ECOTOURS DE MEXICO

✉ *Ignacio I. Vallarta #243* 📞 *322-222-6606* 🖥 *www. ecotoursvallarta.com* This agency offers whale watching, wild dolphin watching, crocodile watching, turtle camp and birding trips.

BIRDING MEXICO

✉ *Lázaro Cárdenas #268-A* 📞 *322-222-7407* 🖥 *www.birding inmexico.com, info@birdinginmexico.com* This group guides birding excursions to the Valle de Banderas and Islas Marietas, as well as longer trips into the Sierra Madre and to San Blas. Owner and guide Alejandro Martinez also heads Guacamayas por Siempre, a volunteer organization dedicated to saving the rare green (military) macaw; the Banderas Bay area is one of the few places in the world where these beautiful birds still survive.

WATER SPORTS

Most of the beach resorts listed in this chapter have a wide assortment of water sports equipment available for guests' use. A few also rent equipment to nonguests. If you're staying in an all-inclusive resort, the use of nonmotorized water sports equipment such as sea kayaks, boogieboards and sailboards (often called windsurfers) is included in the package price. You'll still pay a rental fee for jet skis and waverunners, Hobie Cat sailboats and parasails.

For the benefit of condominium and time-share residents, there are also independent equipment-rental operations on most beaches as well as at Marina Vallarta.

MT SAILING CLUB

✉ *Holiday Inn, Boulevard Francisco Medina Ascencio, Km. 3.5* 📞 *322-293-6227* In the Hotel Zone, Hobie Cats, kayaks, boogieboards and sailboards are for rent to the public by the hour or day at the MT Sailing Club.

IGUANA WATER SPORTS

✉ *On the beach* 📞 *322-226-6770* In Nuevo Vallarta, contact Iguana Water Sports.

TRANSPORTATION

BUS

City buses run the length of Boulevard Francisco Medina Ascensio between Nuevo Vallarta, Marina Vallarta, the Hotel Zone and downtown. The one-way fare is a mere 5.5 pesos. Look for the blue-and-white bus stop signs, and be sure to check the sign on the front of the bus saying where it's going before boarding. More buses go to and from the working-class suburb of El Pitillal than between the tourist zones.

TAXI

Taxi fares are regulated, though drivers often try to charge tourists more, and taxis that wait in front of the major hotels typically charge more than those at public *sitios* (cab stands). Ask before you get into the cab. Instead of being metered, fares are set by zone. It costs the same to go anywhere within Zone 1A (Marina Vallarta), Zone 1 (Hotel Zone and downtown), Zone 2 (Zona Romántica) or Zone 3 (Mismaloya), and significantly more to travel between zones. Taxi fares took a big jump in 2008; expect to pay approximately $US6–$7 within a zone and up to $17 between zones in Puerto Vallarta, except for cabs that serve the airport, which must have an expensive special permit and thus charge much more. Cab drivers do not expect to be tipped unless they help you with luggage or packages.

CAR

Visitors staying in Puerto Vallarta, especially in the downtown and Zona Romántica areas, generally find that a rental car is less a help than a hindrance until they decide to take a road trip out of town. You can take a lot of taxi rides for the price of a car rental.

BOAT

Public water taxis operate from Muelle Los Muertos (the New Pier), with departures in the morning to points south including Quimixto (on request) and Yelapa, returning in late afternoon. There is also an afternoon water taxi for people planning to stay the night in Yelapa and return the next day. The round-trip fare to any destination on the south side of the bay is around 220 pesos. Water taxis leave the New Pier at 10 a.m. (except Sunday), 11:30 a.m., 12 p.m. and 12:30 p.m. (except Sunday), with return trips leaving Yelapa at 4 (except Sunday), 4:30 and 5:30 (except Sunday). You are expected to return on the same boat you departed on. There is an extra charge if you have more luggage than you can carry in your arms. Visitors who are staying in Yelapa for a month or more can get a resident card entitling them to a 20 percent discount on water taxi fares. At the New Pier, as well as in Boca de Tomatlán, you can usually also find people who will take you anywhere on the bay in their *pangas* (motorized open fishing boats) for a negotiable price.

ADDRESSES & PHONE NUMBERS

PUERTO VALLARTA MUNICIPAL TOURISM OFFICE ✉*Juárez at Independencia* ☎*322-223-2500*

TOURIST PROTECTION ☎*322-223-2500*

JALISCO STATE TOURISM OFFICE ✉*Plaza Marina #L-144* ☎*322-221-2676*

U.S. CONSULATE ✉*Edificio Consular, Plaza Central* ☎*322-222-0069*

CANADIAN CONSULATE ✉*Edificio Consular, Plaza Central* ☎*322-293-0098*

EMERGENCY NUMBER ☎*060*

POLICE ☎*322-290-0507*

CRUZ ROJA (RED CROSS) ☎*322-222-1533*

Ambulance Service (ground and air)
GLOBAL LIFE AMBULANCE ☎*322-226-1014*

Hospitals
AMERI-MED URGENT CARE ✉*Plaza Neptuno #D-1, Avenida Francisco Medina Ascencio, Marina Vallarta* ☎*322-226-2080*

SAN JAVIER MARINA HOSPITAL ✉*Avenida Francisco Medina Ascencio #2760, Zona Hotelera* ☎*322-226-1010*

THE RIVIERA NAYARIT

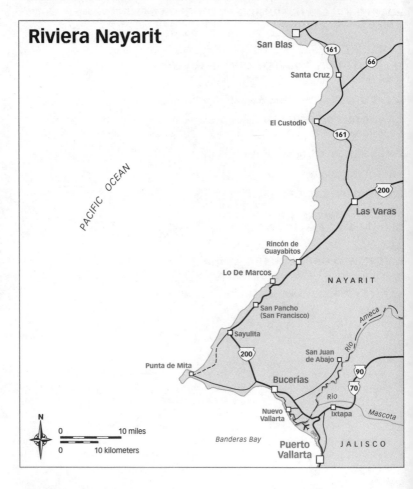

Riviera Nayarit

San Blas
161
66
Santa Cruz
El Custodio
161
PACIFIC OCEAN
200
Las Varas
Rincón de Guayabitos
Lo De Marcos
NAYARIT
San Pancho (San Francisco)
Ameca
Sayulita
Río
200
San Juan de Abajo
90
Punta de Mita
Bucerías
70
Río
Nuevo Vallarta
Ixtapa
Mascota
N
0   10 miles
Banderas Bay
Puerto Vallarta
JALISCO
0   10 kilometers

Just north of the Puerto Vallarta airport, the largest river in the area, the Río Ameca, meanders through the patchwork farmlands of the Valle de Banderas. The river marks the boundary between the Mexican states of Jalisco, which includes Puerto Vallarta, and Nayarit. The state line is significant partly because the time changes there. Jalisco is in the central time zone, and Nayarit is on mountain time. In other words, *it's an hour earlier in Nuevo Vallarta, Bucerías and other*

north coast destinations than in Puerto Vallarta (including the airport). This is a **163**
perpetual source of confusion when it comes to dinner reservations, tour departures, airline flights and so on. Some, but not all, north coast resorts try to deal
with this anomaly by keeping their clocks on Puerto Vallarta time; be sure to ask.
The most workable solution is to keep your wristwatch set to Puerto Vallarta time,
even if you're staying in Nuevo Vallarta, and make mental adjustments as needed.

Large-scale development on the Nayarit side of Banderas Bay is a relatively new
phenomenon. On the Jalisco side, Puerto Vallarta has reached the limit of its
growth, blocked by near-vertical mountain slopes. Progress, which is to say resort
and big-scale real estate development, is galloping quickly toward the north shore
of Banderas Bay, but with a few ambitious and ultra-luxurious exceptions, it hasn't quite gotten there yet. You can strike a comfortable balance between resort
conveniences and traditional Mexican small-town life by staying in the close-together north-shore towns of Bucerías and La Cruz de Huanacaxtle, which still
carry some reminiscence of Puerto Vallarta in an earlier, simpler era. Or you can
continue a few miles farther north and discover the "hidden" villages of Sayulita
and San Pancho, with their endless, almost empty beaches and their mix of
surfers, artists and wealthy villa owners, all blending into the tranquil rhythms of
traditional Mexican small-town life.

Recently, the Mexican government made US$1.5 billion available for infrastructure improvements along the Nayarit coast, including a wide new highway and
improved public utility service. The state government responded in early 2007 by
dubbing the coastal communities north of the state line the "Riviera Nayarit,
Mexico's newest travel destination." The new name not only applies to Nueva
Vallarta, the north shore towns and the villages just north of the bay but also to
about 100 kilometers of mostly undeveloped beaches and wetlands anchored on
the north by San Blas, the old Spanish seaport from which Puerto Vallarta was
originally colonized. San Blas was all but erased from the map by a hurricane in
2002, and much of the government grant money was directed at restoring the historic town.

The Riviera Nayarit promotion did much more than attract tourists' attention,
though; it elevated the interest of international real estate developers. Within
three months after the new name was announced, more private investment
money poured into the area than in the entire previous year. At least 19 new resorts with more than 4000 guest rooms are scheduled to open by 2011. Once-
obscure villages such as Sayulita now rank among the fastest-growing communities in Mexico. Hand-lettered signs offering vacant land for sale line the highway
that makes its way north through jungle and tobacco fields. There's no doubt that
the greater Puerto Vallarta area is poised to become a lot bigger, and one reason to
explore this still mostly pristine area is so that you, like Puerto Vallarta old-timers,
can some day shake your head and say, "I can remember this beach when there
wasn't a single high-rise on it."

5 THE RIVIERA NAYARIT NUEVO VALLARTA

NUEVO VALLARTA

You can't spend much time in Puerto Vallarta without discovering that
condominiums are very big business. In fact, you may not even get out
of the airport before someone presents you with an opportunity to buy

one. Time-shares, part-time and full-time residences—the demand for a place on the shore of Banderas Bay is so overheated that many condo developments sell out before construction even begins. (By the way, if you let yourself get roped into one of the time-share sales presentations that hucksters pitch all over town, make sure it's in Nuevo Vallarta. The state of Nayarit limits such presentations by law to 90 minutes, while Jalisco has no such law and the hard-sell ordeal can last four hours or more.)

The epicenter of all this real estate activity, Nuevo Vallarta ("New Vallarta") first began to sprout in the late 1980s and since then has been springing up at breakneck speed. At first impression, Nuevo Vallarta appears to be a look-alike sprawl of condominium complexes, resort hotels and not much else. In reality, it is centered around Paradise Village, a planned development similar in concept to Marina Vallarta, with a marina, shopping zone, water park, golf course and even its own private zoo.

For many visitors, the drawback to staying in Nuevo Vallarta is that it's a long trip from downtown Puerto Vallarta (or even Wal-Mart). Sure, the brochures all claim that this area is only 15 or 20 minutes from the city center, and by distance alone this might be true, but the reality is that during the busy winter season, it takes an hour or more by taxi or rental car to make the journey through heavy traffic, and cab fares are much higher than from other hotel areas—generally US$15 or more one way. Many people who live in Nuevo Vallarta will tell you that they never go downtown at all. That's why most of the hotels out here are all-inclusive destination resorts designed so that guests rarely, if ever, have to leave the grounds. On the plus side, the beach is the longest, most peaceful and natural-feeling stretch of sand on the populated part of the bay.

SIGHTS

SPLASH WATER PARK ✉Route 200, Km. 155 ✆322-297-0708 ⌇www. splashvallarta.com, info@splashvallarta.com If you're traveling with kids, you won't want to miss the largest water playground in the Puerto Vallarta area, located at the entrance to Nuevo Vallarta. The main attraction here is an assortment of water slides, tubing half-pipes and a body-coasting bowl, all of which plunge, spiral and splash into swimming pools from as much as 60 feet up. If watching your teens beat the heat makes you wish for the same, yet you're feeling too mellow for high-speed thrills, there's also a Lazy River ride where you can float on a gentle current on a long course around the perimeter of the Kids Zone, an area with safe-and-easy action for toddlers and young children. Admission.

THE DOLPHIN CENTER

✉Nuevo Vallarta ✆322-297-1212 ⌇www.vallarta-adventures.com/dolphins, info@vallarta-adventures.com The first captive dolphin facility to train Pacific bottlenose dolphins to interact with humans in the water, the Dolphin Center is owned and operated by Vallarta

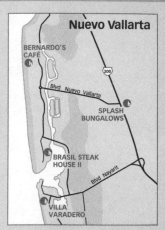

Nuevo Vallarta

BERNARDO'S CAFÉ

PAGE 171

A unique seafood menu ranging from Bahamian conch fritters to lobster stew Creole

SPLASH BUNGALOWS

PAGE 165

Lively, contemporary accommodations—waterslides included—at a family-friendly water park

BRASIL STEAK HOUSE II

PAGE 170

A fixed-price haven for meat-lovers—brisket, rib-eye, chorizo and linguica sausage

VILLA VARADERO

PAGE 167

Brightly decorated rooms and oceanview balconies in an intimate hotel steps from the beach

Adventures, the outfit responsible for most of the nature and outdoor adventure tours in the Puerto Vallarta area. The center presently has 20 dolphins in two manmade lagoons, each of which holds two million gallons of salt water. It also has educational pools, an underwater viewing area and a maternity pool for pregnant and newborn dolphins. Swimming with the dolphins costs from US$79 to $149, depending on the duration of the swim and the size of the group. Special dolphin encounter programs for kids ages four to eight cost $75.

LODGING

With only a couple of exceptions, lodgings in Nuevo Vallarta are in high-rise resort hotels that are way too big to hide. Still, I've chosen to include the main ones in Hidden Puerto Vallarta because they are the key landmarks in town, and people tend to give you directions in terms of which hotel is near the spot you're looking for.

SPLASH BUNGALOWS

$$ 8 ROOMS ✉ *Route 200, Km. 155* ☎ *322-297-0708*
🖰 *www.splashvallarta.com, info@splashvallarta.com.*

Splash Water Park has bright, new bungalows along the side of the main swimming pool. You can't use the waterslides or other

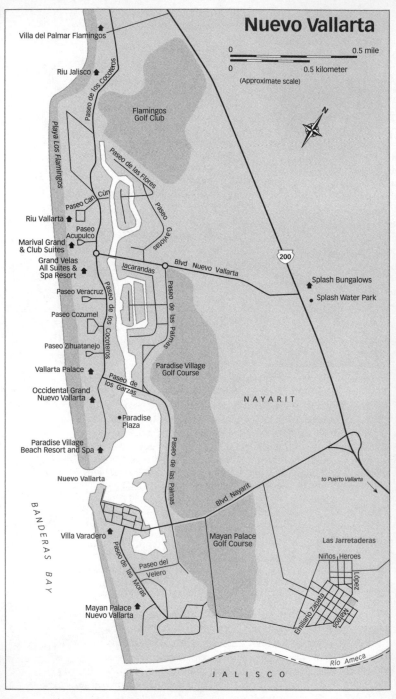

Nuevo Vallarta

0   0.5 mile
0   0.5 kilometer
(Approximate scale)

N

Villa del Palmar Flamingos

Riu Jalisco

Playa Los Flamingos

Paseo de los Cocoteros

Flamingos Golf Club

Paseo de las Flores

Paseo Can Cún

Riu Vallarta

Paseo Acapulco

Marival Grand & Club Suites

Grand Velas All Suites & Spa Resort

Jacarandas

Paseo Gaviotas

Blvd Nuevo Vallarta

200

Splash Bungalows

Splash Water Park

Paseo Veracruz

Paseo de los Cocoteros

Paseo de las Palmas

Paseo Cozumel

Paseo Zihuatanejo

Vallarta Palace

Paradise Village Golf Course

Occidental Grand Nuevo Vallarta

Paseo de los Garzas

Paradise Plaza

NAYARIT

Paradise Village Beach Resort and Spa

Nuevo Vallarta

Paseo de las Palmas

Villa Varadero

Paseo de las Moras

Blvd Nayarit

to Puerto Vallarta

BANDERAS BAY

Mayan Palace Golf Course

Las Jarretaderas

Niños Heroes

López

Paseo del Velero

Emiliano Zapata

Mateos

Mayan Palace Nuevo Vallarta

Río Ameca

JALISCO

rides when the park is closed (7 p.m. to 10 a.m.), and getting the watchman's attention to let you in and out of the park after hours is not always easy. But these are some of the quietest accommodations around after dark, and if your family includes water park fanatics, what could be more cool? The rooms are simple and contemporary, with two king-sized beds, a TV and a refrigerator. Use of all water park facilities is free for guests.

MAYAN PALACE NUEVO VALLARTA

$$$ 523 ROOMS   ✉ *Paseo de las Moras s/n* ☎ *322-226-4003* 📠 *322-226-4006*
🖰 *www.grupomayan.com/mayan-palace/nuevo-vallarta/index.html*,
concierge@grandmayan.com.mx

Everything about this resort seems to be on a grand scale. The hotel has standard rooms and one- and two-bedroom suites with sofas, upholstered chairs, armoires and dark wood trim, in three massive seven-story buildings surrounded by manmade canals and a lagoon. Guests are transported to their rooms by water taxi or small train. The resort has its own 18-hole golf course and a mile of undeveloped beach—no palapa restaurants or curio vendors, though the hotel's common areas seem to have more than their share of time-share hucksters. Miles of walking trails meander through the 250 acres of landscaped grounds, and there's a huge swimming pool—actually several interconnected pool areas, including one with a waterfall. There's a three-night minimum stay, one-week minimum during peak season.

VILLA VARADERO

$$ 56 ROOMS   ✉ *Retorno Nayarit, Lote 83/84* ☎ *322-297-0430*,
800-238-9996 📠 *322-297-0506* 🖰 *www.hotelvillavaradero.com*,
reservaciones@hotelvillavaradero.com

Next up the beach from the huge Mayan Palace, this small, intimate hotel makes for a striking contrast. With just 56 rooms and suites in a four-story building, every guest unit is just a few steps from the beach, where sailboats and other water sports equipment are available. All rooms and suites have two full-sized beds. Standard rooms have small refrigerators and dining areas, with windows looking out on the ocean or the mountains, while the one-bedroom suites, which comprise half the units in the hotel, have fully equipped kitchens and large balconies with ocean views. Rooms and suites are adjacent to each other so that a standard room can be combined with a one-bedroom suite to accommodate a larger family. Walls are painted in bright colors. Although there is only one swimming pool, one restaurant and one bar, the charge for an all-inclusive plan is only slightly higher than for the room alone.

PARADISE VILLAGE BEACH RESORT AND SPA

$$$–$$$$ 490 UNITS   ✉ *Paseo de los Cocoteros #1* ☎ *322-226-6770, 800-995-5714*
📠 *322-226-6752* 🖰 *www.paradisevillage.com, rescenter@paradisevillagegroup.com*

On the north side of Nuevo Vallarta boat channel, this pyramid-shaped hotel is part of the huge Paradise Village development, which also includes a marina, a neighborhood of villas and condominiums, a shopping center, the El Tigre Paradise Village Golf Club and even a zoo and wildlife sanctuary where many of the animals are allowed to roam free. All guest suites in the hotel, from junior suites to three-bedroom units, are extraordinarily spacious and have separate full kitchens, dining and living areas, bathtubs and queen-sized or king-sized beds; all have private patios or balconies. The two large outdoor pool areas are decorated in faux natural style with rock diving cliffs, waterfalls, underwater grottos, Mayan temple replicas and crocodile-shaped water slides. Other facilities include four lighted tennis courts, land and water sports equipment, basketball and bocce ball courts, outdoor barbecues, a playground and a wide expanse of beach with lounge chairs and palapas reserved for guests' use. Guests also have access to the golf club and spa, which are shared with residents of the development.

VALLARTA PALACE

$$$$ 348 ROOMS ✉ *Paseo de los Cocoteros #19* ☎ *322-226-8470* 📠 *322-297-0266*
🖳 *www.palaceresorts.com/resorts/vallartapalace/index.asp*

In a higher price range, this all-inclusive resort has spacious, all-white guest rooms—among the nicest in Nuevo Vallarta, refurbished in 2005—with dark wood and earth tones accenting king-sized beds, marble double jacuzzi tubs and narrow ocean-view balconies. The strikingly monochromatic, angular architecture of the lobby and common areas creates a contemporary, elegant ambience with fountains and reflecting pools. The room rate includes the use of bicycles, the fitness center, the sauna and steam bath, basketball and tennis courts and the seven-hole pitch-and-putt golf course, as well as two free-form swimming pools surrounded by palm trees. Rates include all meals at the Mexican and Italian buffets as well as the Brazilian and Asian à la carte restaurants.

MARIVAL GRAND & CLUB SUITES

$$$$ 650 ROOMS ✉ *Paseo de los Cocoteros s/n* ☎ *322-226-8200* 📠 *322-297-0160*
🖳 *www.gomarival.com, reservaciones@marival.com.mx*

The air-conditioned guest units at this all-inclusive resort include standard rooms in bright gold and blue hues and newly remodeled suites with more subdued color schemes. Suites have balconies or terraces with pool and partial ocean views. There are four separate swimming pools, including one for adults only and another with constant upbeat music where water aerobic classes are held. The exceptionally wide selection of activities includes tennis, yoga, Pilates, snorkeling and water polo, among many others, and lessons in Spanish, cooking, bartending and Latin dance. The daily rate includes meals at any of six restaurants and drinks at all seven bars. The kids' club, for ages four through twelve, features miniature golf, mini-rappeling and movies, while the teen club offers archery, soccer and a game room equipped with Nintendo, Playstation and X-Box. The resort is located behind the Flamingos Golf Club.

GRAND VELAS ALL SUITES & SPA RESORT

$$$$ 267 UNITS ✉ *Paseo de los Cocoteros Sur #98* ☎ *322-226-8000, 866-358-4415*
📠 *322-297-2005* 🖳 *www.grandvelas.com, contactcenter@grandvelas.com*

This all-inclusive resort occupies a ten-acre plot of land—rather small for hotels in this area—but packs a lot of one- and two-bedroom suites into its semicircular complex. Wherever your suite is in the resort, when you step out onto the private balcony you'll feel like you're poolside and just steps from the beach. The spacious accommodations are decorated in soft beige and rust tones accented with teak wood trim imported from Bali. All have one king-sized or two queen-sized beds, with down comforters and pillows, per bedroom and large flat-screen TVs. Although it does have a children's pool and activity program, the hotel seems geared mainly toward active, fitness-minded adult couples. All-inclusive rates include a guided hydrotherapy circuit at their extensive spa facilities, as well as workout programs with personal trainers and exercise classes in yoga, Pilates, capoeira, tai chi and meditation. There are lighted tennis courts and an adults-only jacuzzi. Dinner at any of the hotel's specialty restaurants, which are among the finest in Nuevo Vallarta (make reservations as soon as you check in) is included in the daily rate, as are domestic and international premium wines and liquors.

VILLA DEL PALMAR FLAMINGOS

$$$$ 246 UNITS   ✉ *Paseo de los Cocoteros Sur #750* ✆ *322-226-8100, 877-845-5247*
✑ *www.villadelpalmarflamingos.com*

One of the newest hotels to open in Nuevo Vallarta has guest units, ranging from 570-square-foot studios to 2360-square-foot three-bedroom suites that can sleep up to ten people. All units have ocean views, balconies, digital flat-screen TVs, travertine marble bathrooms and kitchens or kitchenettes. The studios have two queen-size beds, while larger suites offer kings, queens and queen-size Murphy beds in the living rooms. All-inclusive resort activities range from beach volleyball and water aerobics to pottery classes and bingo and there's a full fitness center and European-style spa. The unique swimming pool features water-jet fountains. There is a cyber-café/deli and a convenience store on the premises.

RIU JALISCO

$$$ 700 ROOMS   ✉ *Paseo de los Cocoteros s/n* ✆ *322-226-6600* ✎ *322-226-6610*
✑ *www.riu.com, clubhotel.jalisco@riu.com*

The biggest hotel on the beach, this all-inclusive resort is not nearly as tall as some of the other hotels and condos nearby, but it's massively grandiose. Vaguely Moorish architecture incorporating gleaming silver turrets, gazebos, courtyard fountains, hundreds of archways and a giant, ornate crown over the center of the building creates the impression of a fantasy palace. The ostentatious lobby features gleaming marble floors, polished wood trim, mosaics, frescoes and hand-painted floral ceilings. The guest rooms and suites glow with rich gold tones. Bathrooms have full-size tubs and bidets. There are two large swimming pools—one for families and the other adults-only, as well as a gym, a sauna and air gun shooting. Windsurfing, sailing, kayaking and snorkeling equipment and introductory scuba lessons are complimentary. While the resort has play areas and activity programs for kids, its key selling points—apparently aimed at adults—include unlimited free domestic and imported alcoholic beverages as well as free mini-bars and liquor dispensers in every room. Breakfast, lunch and dinner are served buffet-style, and snacks are available 24 hours a day. There are live music shows nightly and an open-bar disco with no cover charge for guests.

RIU VALLARTA

$$$ 550 ROOMS ✉Paseo de los Cocoteros s/n ✆322-226-7250 📠322-226-7255

🖳www.riu.com, clubhotel.vallarta.@riu.com

The new sister hotel to the Riu Jalisco has two elaborate pool areas and a spa, plus four restaurants, five bars and a disco. Otherwise, the accommodations and all-inclusive activities are the same as at the other Riu property. As this book goes to press, the hotel chain is about to open a third all-inclusive resort, the 445-suite Hotel Riu Palace Pacifico, a short distance away on Playa Los Flamingos.

DINING

LA PORTEÑA

$$$ ARGENTINEAN ✉Boulevard Nayarit #250 ✆322-297-4950

This rustic log restaurant looks out on a hillside covered with neatly trimmed grass, two fountains and a creek that tumbles into a fish pond. Soft Latin music accompanies traditional dishes such as appetizers of *proveleta* (grilled provolone cheese with tomatoes and herbs) and *chistorra* (a chorizo-like sausage), followed by rib-eye, New York or arrachera steak entrées barbecued in a wood shed outside behind the kitchen. Also on the menu are fish, chicken and pasta dishes; a barbecue sampler offers a little bit of everything.

BRASIL STEAK HOUSE II

$$ BRAZILIAN ✉Paradise Plaza, local K-10-11 ✆322-297-1164

Brasil II in Paradise Village is a second location of the Zona Romántica restaurant that goes by the same name, but out here in the suburbs it faces less competition from other fine-dining establishments. This is the place to come if you *really* crave meat—and lots of it. Waiters roam the restaurant with large chunks of 12 different kinds of meats, including sirloin, rib-eye and New York steaks, barbecued ribs, turkey, chicken, chorizo sausage, linguica sausage, *arrachera* (marinated beef brisket) and pork loin, skewered on swords, from which they carve off slices onto your plate. Come hungry—a very reasonable fixed price covers all you can eat. Late lunch and dinner.

FRIDA

$$$$ GOURMET MEXICAN ✉Paseo de los Cocoteros Sur #98 ✆322-226-8000

The Grand Velas Resort names all its restaurants for international celebrities, such as Lucca (Italian cuisine) and Piaf (classic French). The hotel bills Frida as its Mexican specialty restaurant, but the creative cuisine here bears little resemblance to the country's traditional foods. You might start your dinner with bean and oyster soup, then move on to a main course of roasted pork filet with eucalyptus honey on green applesauce or a salmon roulade on lobster tail with chile cascabel salsa, and finish it with a chilled watermelon soup. The international wine collection here is said to be the largest in Puerto Vallarta. The restaurant is situated on the second floor above the lobby, with a lovely ocean view, and a guitarist plays romantic background music while you eat. There is an outdoor terrace, but it's only opened when the air-conditioned indoor dining room is full. Reservations required. Dinner only.

LA BELLA ITALIA

$$$$ ITALIAN ✉*Playa del Sol Grand, Boulevard Costero Sur #800, Nuevo Vallarta* ☎*322-226-1050*

Of the many Italian restaurants in the greater Puerto Vallarta area, none surpasses this specialty restaurant in the Playa del Sol Grand resort, in terms of romantic atmosphere, attentive service and fine Old World cuisine. The air-conditioned indoor dining area has floor-to-ceiling glass walls for a fantastic view of Banderas Bay, a view shared by the outdoor terrace with its stone fountains and surrounding gardens. Italian love songs play in the background as waiters present culinary masterpieces such as prosciutto-wrapped shrimp and Milanese veal served on arugula with fennel selected from a prix-fixe menu. Dinner only.

MARLIN DE TEPIC

$$ SEAFOOD ✉*Avenida Tepic #100* ☎*322-297-2409*

This large seafood restaurant, situated at the north entrance to Nuevo Vallarta, is designed to keep children occupied in its special play area while you wait for your meal. When available, it's a good place to try *pescado sarandeado*, a local specialty consisting of fish marinated in a garlic-and-green-chile rub, then grilled over a wood fire and served smothered with onions and other vegetables.

BERNARDO'S CAFÉ

$$–$$$ SEAFOOD ✉*Paseo de los Cocoteros #29, villa 8* ☎*322-297-0401*

With its palm-frond roof and sandy steps, the café looks just like a typical beer-and-snacks-on-the-beach palapa, with the added feature of a swimming pool where you can hang out all day for a fee. It's the cook that makes this place special. A native of Lorraine, France, chef Bernardo worked at resorts in New Orleans and the Caribbean before opening his own place in Puerto Vallarta. His unique, eclectic seafood menu ranges from Bahamian conch fritters and dorado *citron vert* (mahi mahi in lime sauce) to lobster stew Creole and *pescado del sol* (fish filet in cilantro tequila sauce, served on a grilled nopal cactus paddle).

LA LAGUNA TINO'S

$$ SEAFOOD ✉*North entrance to Nuevo Vallarta* ☎*322-297-0221*

This small family-style restaurant, just off the south entrance road to Marina Vallarta, is a casual favorite among condo dwellers in the area. The fare is fresh seafood prepared

Mexican-style, featuring such specialties as *mariscos al ajillo* (mixed seafood sautéed with garlic). The restaurant got its name because it's set on the shore of a small lake whose surface is completely covered with water plants, attracting whistling ducks as well as many other species of water birds and making the spot a popular haunt of serious birders.

LOS ALMENDRITOS

$ MEXICAN   ✉*Route 200, Km. 155* ✆*322-297-1140*

Last but not least, for a very affordable local seafood treat, order a shrimp burger at this family-run fast-food restaurant just off the Splash Water Park exit from the main highway. Other specialties here include chicken parmesan and fish tacos. Closed Saturday.

SHOPPING

PARADISE PLAZA MALL ✉*Paseo de los Cocoteros Sur #85* ✆*322-226-6770*
Although the retail scene is bound to develop in the future, right now Nuevo Vallarta is not a great place for shopping. The sole major shopping area is this mall with 110 stores next to the Paradise Village hotel. You can go half-blind window-shopping there and come away with recollections of nothing but T-shirts and Taxco silver jewelry. In reality, though, the mall offers a full range of shops and services including a bank, a beauty parlor, a dental clinic, a deli, a coffee shop, sportswear stores, a supermarket and a video arcade.

NIGHTLIFE

THE JUNGLE AND XCARET SPORTS BAR ✉*Paseo de los Cocoteros #1* ✆*322-226-6770* The Paradise Village Beach Resort is *the* place to seek out after-dark fun in Nuevo Vallarta. The Jungle has drinks, wild games and dancing to live music from 11 p.m. until dawn. The decor is like a Rainforest Café knockoff, complete with artificial gorillas and leopards and real potted palms. Also in the resort, Xcaret Sports Bar serves drinks to the accompaniment of blaring big-screen TV sports until 2 a.m. (For some reason, Paradise Village has chosen to name most of its restaurants and lounges after famous Mayan sites in and around the Yucatán; besides Xcaret, there are the Faro de Tulum Cafe, the Kabah Lounge, the Tikal Lobby Bar, the Mayapan Garden Restaurant and the Palenque Natural Snack Bar.)

BEACHES

PLAYA LOS FLAMINGOS
✉*Extends for four miles, from the Mayan Palace resort north to the Flamingos Beach and Golf Club condominium complex*
Though fronted by a near-solid wall of hotels and condominium complexes, this sugary-white beach is practically undeveloped, without the obstacles that impede long walks on the other resort beaches to the north—just miles of sand. There is a bird and sea turtle

sanctuary at the south end of the Mayan Palace's stretch of beach. Access is difficult unless you're staying at one of the hotels or condos along the beach.

THE NORTH SHORE

The north shore of Banderas Bay is a long, narrow, hilly peninsula, whose interior is scattered with pastures and farm fields in the lowland, rising to rugged, scrub-and jungle-covered, roadless hills at its center. The peninsula's shore is lined with picture-perfect beaches and a series of small towns—Bucerías, La Cruz de Huanacaxtle and Punta Mita— from which the view of Puerto Vallarta across the water makes the city appear small and distant. The first of these towns you come to, Bucerías, lies close enough to Nuevo Vallarta that it's unquestionably next in line for big condo and resort development—a fact not lost on gringo expatriates seeking to get in on something close to the ground floor of the real estate boom that is already driving property values sky-high. The imminent development of new luxury hotels and golf courses near the end of the peninsula, and the recent improvement of roads and utilities, make it obvious that the day is not far off when the entire north side of the bay will be built up.

Unlike the south shore of Banderas Bay, which is best explored by boat, visitors can see the north shore by rental car or public bus. The main roads were repaved and widened into four-lane thoroughfares in 2006, anticipating major resort construction in the Punta Mita area.

SIGHTS

BUCERÍAS ⊠*Route 200, 12 miles (20 kilometers) north of the Puerto Vallarta airport* Bucerías ("Dive Sites") takes its name from the fact that in earlier times the shallow waters offshore concealed beds of huge oysters, which were the village's main source of income. It's not that the oyster beds are played out today. Some snorkelers still dive for oysters just offshore from the town square. It's just that most of the old-time residents, finding that there's a lot more money in real estate than oysters, have sold their properties to outsiders as the town has boomed to its present population of over 6000. The almost-nine-mile-long beach between Bucerías and La Cruz de Huanacaxtle is a favorite of local Mexican families and is very crowded on Sundays; during the week it's often almost empty. The town proper consists of four residential streets that run parallel to the beach, along with a fast-growing residential neighborhood on the other side of the highway. At the north end is the pretty town plaza. Most small businesses are along Route 200, a busy four-lane highway flanked on both sides by rocky, sometimes muddy *laterales*.

LA CRUZ DE HUANACAXTLE ⊠*Caraterra a Punta Mita, 20 miles (33 kilometers) northwest of the Puerto Vallarta airport* About three miles past Bucerías, the highway splits. If you exit Route 200, you'll find yourself on the Punta Mita highway, which follows the north coast of the bay. You'll soon reach the turnoff for this town, which is considerably smaller than Bucerías but also overrun by gringo expatriates who moved here a

decade or so ago when it was far from the tourist zone and property values were still low. The name means "the cross of guanacaste," an endangered tropical hardwood tree prized by furniture makers because of its resistance to insects. One local legend says the name derives from a cross that was carved into the trunk of a guanacaste tree to mark the grave of an Indian woman whose identity is no longer remembered. If true, the tree has been cut down long since. A different legend holds that a cross made of guanacaste wood washed up on the beach many years ago, the only surviving trace of a shipwreck. Lending credence to this story, a wooden cross that purports to be the same one stands in the enthusiastically decorated traffic roundabout on Calle Langosta. The whole village celebrates for nine days leading up to the annual Fiesta de Santa Cruz, or Feast of the Holy Cross, on May 3. Because Huanacaxtle is quite a mouthful for such a small village, most residents simply call it "La Cruz."

PUNTA DE MITA ⊠ *Caraterra a Punta Mita, 26 miles (42 kilometers) northwest of the Puerto Vallarta airport* Seven miles farther along the coast, you'll reach this village, which is sometimes called Punta Mita; both are correct. It's really two small, new communities called Emiliano Zapata and Nuevo Corral de Riscos, which have run together and have a joint population of around 3000. It does not stand on the point of land, also called Punta de Mita, at the tip of the peninsula. In the early 1990s, a Japanese development company envisioned the resort that eventually became the Four Seasons, leased the land on the point, fenced it off and evicted the people of the fishing *ejido*, or commune, who had lived in shacks there. Outside the perimeter, the government built new lodging for them, naming it after the original Corral de Riscos *ejido*. With its raw cinderblock architecture and paucity of vegetation, this fishing village is still not particularly attractive. As the planned resort moved toward becoming a reality, bringing construction work and later service jobs to the area, more people moved in and formed the non-*ejido* town of Emiliano Zapata. But as the boundaries of the two villages blurred, it became a single haphazard community called Punta de Mita. At present, the route through town to and from the resort beyond seems to have been laid out with an eye toward confounding outsiders, because the streets of the two villages don't align very well. As development continues, the main road is bound to bypass this town as it has Bucerías and La Cruz de Huanacaxtle. A short distance beyond the town, you'll come to the guarded entrance gate to the Four Seasons Punta Mita, described in Lodging below. This area—and the entire north coast of Banderas Bay—will be transformed over the next several years by the construction of five more major resort hotels and two new golf courses besides the one already in operation at the Four Seasons.

LODGING

ROYAL DECAMERON COSTA FLAMINGOS

$$$ 509 ROOMS   ✉*Lázaro Cárdenas #150, Bucerías*   ☎*329-298-0226*
www.decameron.com.mx, ventas@decameron.com.mx

The largest beach resort to spring up in Bucerías so far, the all-inclusive Royal Decameron Hotel is part of a Colombian chain with oceanfront properties from Jamaica to Colombia. The guest rooms are decorated in the same bright hues as the exterior—gold, orange, umber and blue—and offer your choice of one king or two double beds. All are air-conditioned and have telephones and satellite TVs, as well as balconies overlooking the pool, the ocean or the grounds landscaped with neat lawns and rows of palm trees. The food leaves something to be desired at the three separate buffet-style restaurants. If after a few days it seems to have as much allure as college cafeteria cuisine, there are also four specialty restaurants (steak, Italian, Thai and Japanese) on the premises, and the restaurants of central Bucerías are within easy beach-walking distance. The rate, which is quite modest for an all-inclusive resort, includes nonmotorized water sports—boogieboards, kayaks and catamarans), introductory scuba lessons, and the use of tennis, basketball and beach volleyball courts, as well as nightly stage shows by the staff, admission and drinks at the disco on the premises, and free house-brand drinks round-the-clock. Uniquely enough, the all-inclusive rate includes all the cigarettes you can smoke.

CASA LOMA BONITA BED & BREAKFAST

$$$–$$$$ 4 ROOMS   ✉*Nicolas Bravo #26, Bucerías*   ☎*329-298-1565*
www.casalomabonita.com, info@casalomabonita.com

Although it's of recent vintage, this B&B evokes the feel of an old Spanish colonial mansion with wrought-iron chandeliers, dark

North Shore

18th-century-style furniture, and interior and exterior columns. A wide, tiled verandah runs the length of the second floor, affording a fine view of the swimming pool, the beach and lights of Puerto Vallarta across the bay. Accommodations are in two standard guest rooms with shared bath and two large suites with king- or queen-sized beds and private baths, all with polished marble floors and luxury furnishings.

HOTEL PALMERAS

$$ 21 UNITS ✉*Lázaro Cárdenas #35, Bucerías* ✆*329-298-1288*
⌨*www.hotelpalmeras.com, hotelpalmeras35@hotmail.com, hotelpalmeras35@yahoo.ca*
Centrally located in Bucerías, half a block from the beach, this recently renovated small hotel with air-conditioned suites surrounding a large courtyard pool and patio with lush gardens and hammocks. Suites have king-sized and double beds and full kitchens (you may have to provide your own cookware, china and silverware, though). Ten new suites have cable TV and balconies overlooking the bay. There are no phones or TVs in the older guest suites; there is a TV lounge in the lobby, though since this hotel caters to a mostly Mexican clientele, the TV is usually tuned to Spanish-language stations. There's wireless internet access. No smoking.

VILLA BELLA BED & BREAKFAST INN

$$$ 6 ROOMS ✉Calle de Monte Calvario #12, La Cruz de Huanacaxtle
☎329-295-5161 ☏329-295-5305 ✐www.villabella-lacruz.com,
info@villabella-lacruz.com

Perched atop the only hill in La Cruz de Huanacaxtle, this wonderful B&B consists of a multilevel thatch-roofed main house with two suites and two one-room guest units, along with two individual casitas, all overlooking the bay. All are decorated with selected works by craftspeople from the famous artisans' towns of Tonalá, Tlaquepaque and Patzcuaro. There's a swimming pool, a lovely garden, a neatly manicured lawn and an aviary of tropical birds. Rates include a full breakfast with fresh-from-the-oven baked goods. Guests enjoy the use of a private beach club on a small cove two minutes' drive away on the other side of the highway. Hostess Elsa Alba, a veteran of big Puerto Vallarta resorts who built this inn as a labor of love, is also an experienced wedding planner, and it's hard to imagine a better spot for a wedding with a view, not to mention a honeymoon.

FOUR SEASONS PUNTA MITA

$$$$ 173 ROOMS ✉Punta de Mita ☎329-391-6000 ☏329-291-6060
✐www.fourseasons.com/puntamita

With nightly room rates in the $500-and-up range, the has the distinction of being the most expensive resort on Banderas Bay. (It should be noted, though, that there are extremely secluded resorts with similar facilities farther down the coast between Puerto Vallarta and Manzanillo that charge twice as much.) You get what you pay for here, and a lot of what you pay for is privacy. Set on the bulbous tip of the peninsula, the Four Seasons is entirely surrounded by water except for the imposing, well-guarded front entrance gate. It's like being on a small, well-groomed island, with tennis courts, hiking trails, gourmet restaurants and a 19-hole golf course designed by Jack Nicklaus. The lodge-style central lobby area features tall contemporary sculptures and a conical palapa roof that may well be the largest on Banderas Bay. The guest rooms and suites, in two-story, tile-roofed four-plex casitas, stimulate the senses with fresh flowers, rich fabrics, handmade ceramics, marble floors and polished wood louvered doors opening onto ocean-view balconies that are themselves as large as many resort hotel rooms. And, needless to say, king-size beds. Although the decor includes a lot of breakables, childproofed rooms are available by advance arrangement. Amenities include CD/DVD players, down pillows, oversize bath towels, terrycloth robes, fully stocked bars and twice-daily housekeeping service with evening ice delivery. Also, recognizing that some guests may need to be in touch with the real world 24/7 to afford a stay here, each room has multiline speaker phones, separate fax lines, high-speed internet access and in-house voicemail. Off the lobby, a presentation space called the Cultural Center hosts programs on such topics as the Huichol Indians, whales, tequila and the history of Banderas Bay, as well as introductory Spanish lessons and exhibitions sponsored by

Puerto Vallarta art galleries. The spa offers a full line of beauty and therapeutic treatments, including the Four Seasons' special Punta Mita Massage, using local sage oil and (what else?) tequila.

DINING

ROGA'S RESTAURANT

$$–$$$ SEAFOOD ✉ *Nicolas Bravo #26, Bucerías* ✆ *329-298-1565*

On the terrace of the Casa Loma Bonita Bed & Breakfast, Roga's is the best place in Bucerías to sample the crustacean specialty that put the town on the map. The oysters come by the dozen, doused in a spicy sauce, barbecued and arranged on a large platter. Also on the menu are shrimp fajitas, steak and *pollo al jerez* (chicken in sherry sauce). The decor is simple—faux granite tabletops bedecked with hibiscus flowers and surrounded by comfortable pig's-hide *equipal* chairs. The broad view of the beach and bay below creates all the atmosphere you could want.

KAREN'S PLACE

$$ INTERNATIONAL ✉ *Lázaro Cárdenas #77, Bucerías* ✆ *329-298-1499*

A favorite hangout of "local" condo residents and snowbirds, this palapa restaurant fronts on the beach on one side and adjoins the swimming pool of the Costa Dorada condominium complex on the other side. You can dine indoors under the shady thatch roof or outside on the terrace looking out on the bay. The menu features a full range of seafood dishes—try the outstanding coconut shrimp or the parmesan herb-crusted fish filet—as well as Mexican food, filet mignon with béarnaise sauce. The owner is British, and this is probably the only place in the Banderas Bay area where you can order a trifle (a parfait of sponge cake layered with pastry cream and fruit) for dessert. Karen's also has a sushi menu and a popular Sunday brunch. There's live guitar music on Tuesday and Thursday nights.

MARK'S BAR & GRILL

$$–$$$ MEDITERRANEAN ✉ *Lázaro Cárdenas #56, Bucerías* ✆ *329-298-0303*

A block up the street, this establishment has evolved over the years from a typical beach-town bar into a fine dining restaurant in a candlelit, white-tablecloth atmosphere on a garden patio with archways that look out on the beach and ocean. The menu showcases seafood, including house specialties such as herb-crusted mahimahi, lobster ravioli or grilled catch of the day with mussels and mussel-infused saffron sauce. Mark's also makes vegetarian brick-oven pizzas, and on Thursdays serves sirloin cheeseburgers. The bar, which is separate from the main dining area, is a sports bar with nonstop games on TV. Dinner only.

ÉCOLE DE CUISINE LE FORT

$$$$ FRENCH ✉*Lázaro Cárdenas #71, Bucerías* ☎*329-298-1532*
✎*www.lefort.com.mx, mlefort@pvnet.com.mx*

One of the most memorable dining experiences to be had in the north bay area is at this cooking school owned and operated by award-winning chef Gilles Le Fort. Le Fort trained in his native France and worked in prestigious restaurants there for more than a decade, built a pâté manufacturing and exporting company in North Africa and then sold it to buy a 50-foot ketch and sail the world. In 1983 he landed in Ensenada, where he resumed his career as a chef. In 2000, he and his Mexican wife moved to Bucerías to realize his newest dream, a cooking school and gourmet mini-restaurant. The open kitchen, surrounded by a U-shaped counter where guests sit, is the center of attention. Cooking classes are offered daily from 10 a.m. to 1 p.m., and dinner sittings start at 8 p.m. Each sitting is limited to six people, and the first group of six gets to select the bill of fare for the evening. Le Fort entertains his guests as he prepares each plate of the three-course dinner before their eyes. Along with the courses come three kinds of wine from Le Fort's cellar, one of the largest in the Puerto Vallarta area. Dinner finishes with cognac and, if you wish, a fine Cuban cigar—all for US$45 per person including tax and tip. Reservations are essential.

TAPAS DEL MUNDO

$$ SPANISH ✉*Hidalgo at Avenida Mexico, Bucerías* ☎*329-298-1194*

While Bucerías, like most Puerto Vallarta-area communities, has more than its share of international restaurants, you won't find a wider array of cuisine under one roof than at this upstairs dining room on the edge of the town's main residential area. Tapas—small appetizer-like plates that are usually ordered for the whole table and shared—are the Iberian answer to dim sum: you order several of them, ranging from items such as a whole large roasted garlic head (about US$1) to grilled oriental beef strips (about $4) or brie-stuffed chicken breast (about $5), until you've eaten your fill, and the cost comes out about the same as if you'd ordered à la carte at a more conventional restaurant. This is a great option for vegetarians, since about two-thirds of the menu items contain no meat or seafood and almost half are vegan.

BLACK FOREST

$$ GERMAN ✉*Marlin #16, La Cruz de Huanacaxtle* ☎*329-295-5203*
✎*www.blackforestpv.com*

This favorite in La Cruz de Huanacaxtle got its start as a family fast-food restaurant selling pizza by the slice under the name Restaurant Papacito's. When chef Winfried Küffner, who had trained and worked at top restaurants in Germany and Switzerland, became a partner in the enterprise several years ago, it turned into a gourmet pan-European restaurant that is now considered one of the best in the north bay area. Besides fare from Germany's Black Forest region such as schnitzel Baden-Baden (breaded pork loin with red wine gravy, served with spätzle and red cabbage), there are non-German offerings including chicken poblano and tuna a la Provence. Dinner only. Closed Saturday.

FRASCATI RISTORANTE

$$ ITALIAN ✉*Avenida de la Langosta #10, La Cruz de Huanacaxtle*
📞*329-295-6185* ✐*www.frascatilacruz.com, info@frascatilacruz.com*

This rather elegant pizzeria, which shares its premises with an art gallery, also features steaks, homemade pasta dishes and other Italian specialties such as ossobuco in red wine sauce. Given its location near Banderas Bay's main fishing port, it's not surprising that the menu emphasizes fresh seafood, with appetizers like sashimi di tonno (tuna sashimi), a catch-of-the-day fish entrée and a frutti di mare pizza heaped with shrimp, calamari, octopus and mussels.

COLUMBA

$–$$ SEAFOOD ✉*Marlin #14, La Cruz de Huanacaxtle* 📞*329-295-5055*

This down-home, family-run seafood eatery aimed at the tastebuds of locals and long-term residents instead of tourists is one of the longest-established restaurants on the north coast of the bay. It's on the road to the area where the fishermen beach their *pangas*, so the fish here is as fresh as you can get. (You may even see fishermen stopping in to sell their catch while you're eating.) Specialties include spicy fish cakes and an unusual type of machaca made not from meat but from shredded ray flesh, which is rolled into tacos. The hours are meant to serve fishermen as they finish their workday, so it opens at noon and closes at 7 p.m.

SHOPPING

TIANGUIS BUCERÍAS

✉*"Up the arroyo"* Bucerías has a *tianguis*—an open-air public market, the only one in the Banderas Bay area—every Sunday. It's a flea market-like affair, with fewer handicrafts than cheap plastic housewares and toys from China, but it is colorful and one of the best places on this side of the bay to watch and photograph the local people. Many locals do their grocery shopping for the week here, at booths that sell fresh local seafood, fruits and vegetables, salsas, beans and curiosities such as dried hibiscus flowers, used to make a tangy red tea called *jamaica*. To get there, follow the usually-dry riverbed that bisects the town just north of Calle Morelos. You can't miss it.

NIGHTLIFE

MARK'S BAR & GRILL ✉ *Lázaro Cárdenas #56, Bucerías* ✆ *329-298-0303* The 3-D Jazz Trio performs live in the bar here on Tuesday evenings. (The rest of the week, it's a sports bar.)

PHILO'S BAR ✉ *Delfín #15, La Cruz de Huanacaxtle* ✆ *329-295-5068* Parrothead singer-songwriter Philo Hayward sold his California recording studio to open this restaurant, bar and recording studio complex, which has become the music center of the north bay. There's live music Tuesday through Saturday year-round, including open-mic nights on Tuesdays and Thursdays and rock or folk on other nights. For gringo musicians, famous and unknown alike, a pilgrimage to Philo's to jam with the house band is a must when visiting Puerto Vallarta.

BLACK FOREST ✉ *Marlin #16, La Cruz de Huanacaxtle* ✆ *329-295-5203* Latcho and Andrea, the Blond Gypsies, play flamenco music on Wednesday nights. The German-born duo learned their spirited flamenco music while traveling around Europe with Gypsy musicians, including relatives of the Gipsy Kings. They have been playing in the Bucerías-La Cruz area for more than a decade (except when they're "on tour" to California, Guadalajara or downtown Puerto Vallarta).

BEACHES

PLAYA BUCERÍAS
✉ *From Bucerías to La Cruz de Huanacaxtle*

🏇 ⛱ 🏄 The longest and widest stretch of sand on Banderas Bay. Lined with palapa restaurants and bars along its north end, the palm-fringed expanse of white sand extends 8.5 miles, all the way to the marina at La Cruz de Huanacaxtle. Many vacationers use this beach, but most areas remain uncrowded. The slope into the water is gradual, making this a good place to swim with kids.

PLAYA LA MANZANILLA, PLAYA PIEDRAS BLANCAS AND PLAYA ANCLOTE

✉ *South of La Cruz de Huanacaxtle's Marina Riviera Nayarit*

🏇 ⛱ 🏄 A series of short beaches between La Cruz and Punta de Mita are very popular weekend playgrounds for Mexicans from the Puerto Vallarta area. Especially on Sundays, the area is packed with local families, including large numbers of small children along with beach balls and other floating toys and soft drink coolers big enough to sit on. Palapa restaurants along the periphery blare popular *narcocorridos*. All in all, it's such a cultural experience it may give you a headache. On weekdays, though, the beaches are all but deserted.

PLAYA DESTILADERAS
⊠*Punta de Mita*

Most beaches around Punta de Mita have been closed to the public, except for guests at the Four Seasons, in anticipation of planned resort development. An especially sore point is Playa Destiladeras, which was very popular with Mexican beachgoers from Puerto Vallarta. When a large part of it was fenced off in late 2005, it touched off protest demonstrations in the streets of downtown Puerto Vallarta—to no avail.

SAYULITA/ SAN PANCHO AREA

Stay on Route 200 where the road splits three miles past Bucerías, and it will take you to the other side of the peninsula. Often clogged with truck traffic, the highway veers away from the shoreline for a few miles and takes you through green rural countryside and woodlands, nearing the ocean again beyond the north shore of the Punta Mita peninsula, though you'll only catch glimpses of the water in the distance. Miles of secluded beach lie just a short distance away, but locals, surfers and homeowners have banded together to keep tourists from finding it. Here, a pair of very different villages—Sayulita and San Pancho—qualify as the most "hidden" communities in the Puerto Vallarta area—though perhaps not for long. Rough, nameless back roads lead to secluded custom homes overlooking the open ocean and nearly empty beaches that are famed for some of the best surfing in Mexico. Big tourism development has not started galloping in that direction (yet). In fact, just about every time I tell someone I'm writing a book on hidden Puerto Vallarta, their response is, "Oh, you mean San Pancho?" Yet discovering these two towns became a lot easier in 2005, when the government erected towering 20-foot-tall blue "Sayulita" and "San Pancho" signs marking the narrow, unpaved roads into the two towns.

SIGHTS

SAYULITA — ⓗidden
⊠*Route 200, 21 miles (35 kilometers) north of the Puerto Vallarta airport*

Most visitors and many locals in Sayulita are young gringos with blonde dreadlocks, surfboards and bright baggy swimwear. That's because the waves that roll into the beach just two blocks from the town center offer some of the best surfing on North America's Pacific coast. Surfers started coming in the early '70s, when the village was not much more than a cluster of huts housing coconut and mango harvesters, and Sayulita quickly gained a reputation as the most laid-back place on Mexico's west coast. The mellow atmosphere and off-the-beaten-path location, in turn, attracted American and Mexican artists, many of whom live here and exhibit their work elsewhere. Because wooded hills rise from the foreshore north of the village, allowing several tiers of homes to be built with ocean views, a construction boom has lined much of the coast between Sayulita and San Pancho with expensive villas owned by gringo expatriates and wealthy Mexicans. In spite of all that, Sayulita remains a secret, and there isn't a big resort hotel in sight (though some are in the planning stages).

SAN PANCHO

✉Route 200, 4 miles (7 kilometers) north of Sayulita The "real" name of the village is San Francisco, but locals prefer San Pancho (Pancho is the Spanish nickname for Francisco, as in Francisco "Pancho" Villa, the famed Mexican revolutionary). The new, official highway sign says San Pancho, so San Pancho it is—a relatively new village with a unique background. Only four extended families of farmers and fishermen, totaling around 100 people, lived in the San Pancho area in 1975, when Mexican Presidente Luís Echeverría's helicopter set down on the beach and the president declared that it was the spot where he would build his retirement palace. Outside the walls that would surround the vast grounds of his 88,000-square-foot palace, Echeverría imagined, would lie a community that was a model of self-sufficiency and an inspiration to others throughout the Third World. There would be cobblestone streets, plumbing and electricity, public schools and a teaching hospital that would serve all the surrounding villages. There would be orchards of fruit trees complete with state-of-the-art processing plants, as well as a fish processing center and an agricultural university. The broad main street of town would be named Avenida Tercer Mundo—"Third World Avenue." Echeverría offered land grants to workers who would join in making his vision a reality. Ultimately, everything in Echeverría's grand plan for the town materialized except for the university, which was never completed. The processing factories are still there but no longer in use. The land grants turned into extended family compounds where today three generations of houses stand side-by-side. As for Echeverría himself, he had hoped that his experiment in socioeconomic engineering at San Pancho would land him an important position with the United Nations. But he was also known for handling social unrest with an iron fist—ordering police to open fire during two separate demonstrations, resulting in the deaths of at least 330 people— and it caught up with him. When his term of office expired, he was forced to choose between leaving the country and becoming the first Mexican official ever to stand trial for genocide. He fled without ever having occupied his San Pancho estate, which

PLAYA CHACALA
PAGE 191

Nearly untouched, thatched-roof fishing village set at the base of an extinct volcano

PILA DEL REY NATIONAL SACRED SITE
PAGE 185

Ancient petroglyphs on volcanic boulders telling the story of native heritage and religious rites

CASA OBELISCO
PAGE 187

A panoramic rooftop terrace and a hibiscus blossom–draped swimming pool in a charming B&B just off the beach

SI HAY OLITAS
PAGE 188

Old-fashioned Mexican eatery with local-style seafood and tequila from a wooden keg

stood vacant for 20 years before an American developer bought it and turned it into Las Olas, an exclusive gated community with a private golf course.

LO DE MARCOS

✉ *Off Route 200, 11 miles (19 km) north of San Pancho* Referring to resort and beach house development, it's often said that "San Pancho is the next Sayulita." If so, then Lo de Marcos is the next San Pancho—an almost unbelievably quiet little village of 3000 people surrounding a pretty plaza with big trees and a bandstand. While the economy depends increasingly on tourism, most visitors are Mexican nationals. Riders on horseback clop along the cobblestones, men in straw cowboy hats play dominos in the plaza, and dogs lie napping in the middle of the street.

RINCÓN DE GUAYABITOS

✉ *Off Route 200, 7 miles (11 kilometers) north of Lo De Marcos* If you want to see what Puerto Vallarta must have looked like the day before John Huston, Richard Burton and the *Night of the Iguana* crew arrived, this beach village on a picture-perfect crescent beach on

Bahía Jaltemba is pretty much it. Rincón de Guayabitos shares the bay with the somewhat larger village of **La Peñita de Jaltemba**, separated by a river and linked by a local shuttle system. The two towns and the other residential clusters along the bay have a combined population of about 18,000, including a growing number of American and Canadian snowbirds. The economy of Rincón de Guayabitos turns on small-scale tourism, with a row of little resort hotels along the beach and numerous restaurants around the town plaza, while in La Peñita, where people from both villages do their banking and everyday shopping, the main industry is brick-making. The Riviera Nayarit economic development plan envisions a large, Puerto Vallarta-style resort hotel being built on the beach in Rincón de Guayabitos by the year 2011.

PILA DEL REY
NATIONAL SACRED SITE

✉ *Off Route 200, 5 miles (8 kilometers) northeast of Rincón de Guayabitos*
Travelers who are seriously interested in native culture may also want to plan a detour from Route 161 toward the small farming town of Alta Vista, where after eight miles the increasingly rough road ends at a parking area and you can take a half-mile hike to the Pila del Rey National Sacred Site, where 2000-year-old petroglyphs cover at least 90 volcanic boulders. The rock art was the work of the Tecoxquin people, whose trade empire extended along the coast from southern Sinaloa south to Manzanillo Bay. Spanish conquistadors, seeing in the rock art what the believed to be undecipherable writing, numerous crosses (representing the "tree of life," a sacred symbol throughout much of ancient Mexico) and human figures they saw as representing Christ, gave rise to the legend, which still persists today, that Saint Matthew the Apostle traveled to the New World after writing his gospel and ministered to the Indians on this spot. Huichol people come to hold ceremonies and leave offerings of arrows, god's eyes and arrangements of sticks and flowers. Respect this important area while visiting; even one incident of offensive conduct could mean closing the site to outsiders forever.

LODGING

HOTEL LAS GRADITAS

$–$$ 21 ROOMS   ✉ *Sayulita*   ☎ *329-291-3519*
While Sayulita is no longer the cheap hotel heaven it once was, many of the older, funkier surfer lodgings have been nicely renovated and still charge rates that are real bargains compared to almost anywhere closer in to Puerto Vallarta. Accommodations across a wide price range are available at this centrally located,

family-run hotel between the plaza and the beach. There's everything from very low-priced, claustrophobic rooms with single beds starting at US$30 a night to large, air-conditioned rooms that can sleep eight and have ocean views and TVs. There is also a three-room suite on top of the hotel that rents at the top end of the moderate price range. The owners speak little English.

VILLAS SAYULITA

$$ 15 UNITS   ✉*Calle Rosalio Tapia s/n, Sayulita*   📞*329-291-3065*
📠*329-291-3063*   *villasayulita@hotmail.com*

The white stucco hotel stands semi-secluded on a hillside two blocks from the beach. Guest accommodations are in spacious, air-conditioned suites with Mexican tile floors, kitchenettes and dining terraces. The hotel has a large pool surrounded by palm trees and shade palapas, and there's a rooftop sun deck, all for around US$65 a night.

VILLA AMOR

$$$ 33 UNITS   ✉*Sayulita*   📞*329-291-3010*   🖱*www.villaamor.com,*
info@villaamor.com

This cluster of romantic one- and two-bedroom casitas across the road from the beach surrounds a freeform palapa and kidney-shaped swimming pool. Some units have decks and private plunge pools. One is built around a huge tree, and another offers a spectacular 360-degree view from its hilltop location. All accommodations feature handmade furnishings and intriguing folk art decor, as well as coffeemakers and refrigerators; some have kitchens. The surprisingly reasonable rates include the free use of kayaks, snorkeling and fishing gear, boogieboards, surfboards and bicycles. While the management is now trying to sell individual units as full-ownership condominiums, they continue to offer nightly rentals.

COSTA AZUL
ADVENTURE RESORT

$$–$$$$ 27 ROOMS   ✉*San Pancho*   📞*800-365-7613*
🖱*www.costaazul.com, reservations@costaazul.com*

An all-inclusive resort for the kind of vacationer who reads *Outside* magazine, Costa Azul was started in 1991 by a group of surfing enthusiasts from California State University, Chico, whose vision encompassed ecological awareness and local economic development. The resort is a model of water and land resource conservation, including a sanctuary for wildlife, and contributes to programs for the local schools while providing employment and opportunities for advancement to many San Pancho residents. Accommodations are in spacious, modern suites and hillside casitas situated between the surfing beach and the jungle. Individually built over the years, the lodgings differ widely in decor and configuration, and all emphasize comfort and privacy. There are no in-room phones or TVs, though there is wireless internet access in the restaurant and bar area. Otherwise, Costa Azul has all the amenities you'd expect of a Puerto Vallarta all-inclusive resort (but on a much more human scale), including a swimming pool and beach club as well as a restaurant on the premises and a soon-to-open spa. The focus is on outdoor adventures for all levels of ability. Besides surfing, activities include horseback riding, scuba diving, sea kayaking, wildlife watching and hiking on jungle trails in the San Pancho area. There are also field trips for hikes and birdwatching in other areas to the north, including the archaeological site at Alta Vista and the birdwatchers' paradise around San Blas. A full schedule of kids' activities is offered, along with after-dinner entertainment that is different each night of the week, ranging from beach bonfires and salsa lessons to Friday-night excursions to downtown Puerto Vallarta. Besides the all-inclusive option, room-only rates are available.

HOTEL CIELO ROJO

$$ 8 ROOMS   ✉*Calle Asia #6, San Pancho*   ✆*311-258-4155*
✐*www.hotelcielorojo.com, hotelcielorojo@yahoo.com*

Recently renovated, this small three-story hotel just off San Pancho's main "boulevard" has clean, simple guest rooms and suites with queen-size beds, white walls and Mexican tile floors. There are ceiling fans but no air-conditioning. All cleaning products used are biodegradable and environment-friendly. The room rate includes continental breakfast at the hotel's small organic restaurant, which also serves lunch and dinner. Acupressure, reflexology and Swedish massage treatments are offered on the large patio. The decor in the common areas features antique doors and sometimes whimsical works of art, including a life-sized headless priest.

CASA OBELISCO

$$$$ 4 ROOMS   ✉*San Pancho*   ✆*311-258-4315, 415-233-4252 (from the U.S. and Canada)*   ✐*www.casaobelixco.com, reservations@casaobelisco.com*

Set at the end of a nameless back road that parallels the beach, this wonderful Mediterranean-style B&B offers a taste of life in one of the magnificent homes that line the foreshore in the San Pancho area. It stands side-by-side with private villas overlooking the uncrowded sugar-white beach, which is reached by a block-long footpath. The four extraordinarily spacious guest rooms and the central great room, where the hosts serve a gourmet breakfast daily, open out onto a walled swimming pool area ablaze with bright red hibiscus blossoms (*obelisco* is the Spanish word for hibiscus). Decor throughout the casa reflects a sense of quality and warmth, from the doors and trim handmade of perrota (a rare Mexican hardwood tree similar to mahogany) and the cool-hued tilework to the paintings by leading area artists. Guest rooms are individually air-conditioned, and the house has no fewer than 28 ceiling fans to supplement the sea breezes on even the steamiest days of summer. A rooftop terrace provides an incomparable panoramic view, ideal for whalewatching during the winter months.

SUITES MARGARITA

$$ 9 ROOMS ✉ *Lo de Marcos* 📞 *327-275-0452* 🖥 *www.bungalowsmargarita.com,*
admin@bungalowsmargarita.com

The guest rooms and suites in this small beachfront resort are individually decorated in bright colors and have ceiling fans, as well as air-conditioning during the summer months only. Some rooms have refrigerators. There's a restaurant and bar on the premises.

TORREBLANCA SUITES

$$$ 48 UNITS ✉ *Retorno Laureles #11, Rincón de Guayabitos* 📞 *327-274-1263,*
800-696-5765 📠 *327-274-1267* 🖥 *www.torreblancasuites.com,*
torreblanca@guayabitos.com.mx

One of several small (by Puerto Vallarta standards) hotels that line the foreshore at Rincón de Guayabitos, this new boutique resort stands five stories high and is one of the tallest things in the village. Its main virtues are a mile-long beach on one side and an enchanting little village on the other. Guest units are one- and two-bedroom suites with air-conditioning, cable TV and ocean view balconies. The larger units have full kitchen facilities. High-speed wireless internet access in the lobby seems incredible way out here. The hotel's restaurant is open for all meals during the tourist season but serves only breakfast and lunch off-season; the bar is open year-round. The big temperature-controlled swimming pool has separate children's and adults' sections.

DINING

DON PEDRO'S RESTAURANT & BAR

$$-$$$ SEAFOOD ✉ *Marlin #2, Sayulita* 📞 *329-291-3090* 🖥 *www.donpedros.com*

Beachfront palapa restaurants abound in Sayulita, but none can rival this steep-roofed two-story establishment, which started out as a basic fish-on-the-beach food stand but has grown into an elegant restaurant where diners enjoy a front-row view of the best surfing area. The fare is seafood with Mediterranean influences. You might start your dinner with steamed mussels à la Provencale or a Greek salad, followed by the fish of the day grilled with lemon, garlic, olive oil and herbs and served with baby vegetables.

SI HAY OLITAS

$ MEXICAN ✉ *Sayulita* 📞 *329-291-3203*

One of the oldest and friendliest restaurants in Sayulita (the name translates as "If There Are Small Waves") is located just over the village bridge on your left and is so brightly painted with multicolored flowers that you can't miss it. Big, traditional Mexican meals include burritos, quesadillas, enchiladas and huevos rancheros, as well as fish tacos and homestyle seafood dishes. There's also a bar where they pour tequila from a wooden keg.

LA OLA RICA

$$ MEXICAN ✉ *Avenida Tercer Mundo s/n, San Pancho* ☎ *311-258-4123*

In San Pancho, restaurants come and go, but the local favorite is La Ola Rica, which started in 1996 as a *comedor* with one plastic table and four chairs and has evolved into what many call the heart of the village. Local residents insist that it's the best restaurant in the Puerto Vallarta area (and they may be right). The brightly painted walls are covered with fabulous folk art collected from many parts of Mexico, and the food is out of this world—barbecued ribs, coconut shrimp, *carne asada* (strips of beef marinated in red chile and grilled) and the house specialty, *molcajete de res* (steak served with cheese, onions and salsa in a stone bowl). There are also pastas, pizzas and creative daily seafood specials. There's live Cuban music on Tuesday nights and jazz on Thursday nights. Dinner only. Closed in summer.

MAR PLATA

$$–$$$ INTERNATIONAL ✉ *Calle de Palmas #130, San Pancho* ☎ *311-258-4424* ✐ *www.marplata.com.mx*

European, Mexican and Argentinean influences mingle on the menu here. You might start with an appetizer of baked camembert cheese with honey and mustard, followed by a *dorado* (mahimahi) steak grilled with white wine and tarragon. The chef's Belgian roots show in desserts such as chocolate fondue with seasonal fruits. The brick-red interior walls are festooned with lots of Mexican art and artifacts, and flowers and palms in huge handmade pots complete the decor.

SHOPPING

LA HAMACA GALLERY

✉ *Sayulita* ☎ *322-227-5817* In Sayulita, a fortunate combination of local artists, low-rent storefronts and upscale resident homeowners has produced a handful of first-rate galleries and shops. Facing the village plaza, La Hamaca sells unique folk art collected from indigenous villages around Mexico, from hammocks and textiles to jewelry and wooden dance masks. The sand-floored shop has an exceptional collection of Catrina figures, traditional Day of the Dead skeleton dolls in fashionable dress, originally popularized in the art of Diego Rivera.

GALERÍA TANANA

✉*Sauylita* 📞*329-291-3889* One of the best Huichol Indian galleries in the Puerto Vallarta area, Tanana is operated by anthropologist and jewelry designer Susana Valadez. The proceeds of purchases help fund the nonprofit Huichol Center for Cultural Survival and Traditional Arts, which operates a school for native children in the Sierra Huichol.

BEACHES

PLAYA DE LOS MUERTOS

✉*South of Sayulita*

🏃 🏊 🎣 This is the most popular of the public beaches on a series of small coves along the north side of the Punta de Mita peninsula, which can be reached by the rough unpaved road (not the main highway) that connects Sayulita with the town of Punta de Mita. Protected by natural piles of boulders on both sides, Playa de Los Muertos (not to be confused with Playa Los Muertos in Puerto Vallarta's Zona Romántica district) is reached on foot by following a trail along the river from the Sayulita cemetery.

PLAYA CUEVAS

✉*South of Sayulita*

🏃 🏊 🎣 Another beach worth searching for south of Sayulita is the secluded Playa Cuevas, protected by a series of natural stone arches past the south end of Sayulita's Playa Centro and cradled by cliffs that make it one of the most secluded and romantic spots near the coast. Use caution when the tide is rising, as the shape of the cove is such that waves funnel into it and can sweep people out to sea.

PLAYA CENTRO

✉*Sayulita*

🏃 🏊 🎣 The six-mile beach between Sayulita and San Pancho is unbroken enough so that ambitious hikers can walk the whole distance without leaving the sand. Just two blocks from the village plaza in Sayulita is the main surfing beach. It's also where village fishermen pull their boats ashore. The part of the beach in front of Don Pedro's restaurant has calmer water, with a gradual slope and a sandy bottom, and is good for swimming as well as snorkeling for oysters.

✉ *Between Sayulita and San Pancho*

🚶 🏊 🎣 Although the sand is continuous north of the Río Sayulita, locals refer to areas by different names based on their character and access. Except for the main beaches a Sayulita, it can be difficult to reach the beaches by land because property owners who control the foreshore rights try to keep "their" stretches of sand undiscovered. The Río Sayulita flows into the ocean at Playa Pilitas, where herons and egrets gather to feed. Past the river, Playa Questos is another surfing beach, where the waves are best when those on Playa Centro are too powerful for some surfers. The sand continues along the long, broad Playa Litibu, where public access from inland is especially tricky and most of the beachgoers are residents of the villas on the hillside above. If you walk far enough, you'll come to Costa Azul Adventure Resort on Playa Malpasos, then reach the barrier where the real estate magnate who is redeveloping the former estate of President Luís Echeverría has erected barriers to block all public access.

⛺ There are two camping parks at Playa Questos, just north of the village of Sayulita. The better of the two is the **Sayulita RV and Camping Park** (329-291-3126). RV spaces with electric hookups rent for US$15 to $18 a night. Tent spaces run $3 to $4.

PLAYA CHACALA

✉ *5.5 miles (9 kilometers) off Route 200 from the turnoff just before Las Varas*

🚶 🐎 🏊 🎣 Set at the base of an extinct volcano, the 19th-century commercial seaport of Chacala has all but vanished, leaving a thatch-roofed fishing village of about 300 people scattered along the wide, golden crescent—possibly the most "undiscovered" beach hideaway on the Nayarit coast and certainly one of the most beautiful. See it quick, before it's gone. As part of the Riviera Nayarit project, the government recently paved the road into Chacala, and construction has begun on a gated resort community, which will eventually have a hotel, marina and golf course, a few miles away in Chacalilla.

SAN BLAS AREA

From where the highway splits between Bucerías and La Cruz de Huanacaxtle, the Riviera Nayarit continues north for 88 miles (146 kilometers) to the historic seaport of San Blas, where the original settlers of Puerto Vallarta came from. The main attraction of San Blas is not history but nature. The abundance of insects that breed in the wetlands on the outskirts of town provides the food supply for an astonishing array of bird life. Tour operators from Puerto Vallarta take regularly scheduled birding tours to San Blas, and just about every hotel and restaurant in town sells birders' checklists.

The drive to San Blas, on good two-lane blacktop roads, can be done in three hours from four hours from Puerto Vallarta. While it's possible to do this excursion as a day trip if you get an early start, it's better to plan it as an overnight. Follow Route 200 north past Sayulita, San Pancho, Lo de Marco and Rincón de Guayabitos, then turn left onto Route 161 at the stoplight in the middle of the town of Las Varas. Watch carefully—it's hard to spot the sign marking the turnoff until it's almost too late to pull over onto the *lateral* to the right of the highway, where you need to be in order to make a left turn. From there, most of the route runs at a distance from the seashore, past Mexican towns where tourists are rarely seen, among fields of tobacco and between dramatic mountain ridges. It's 54 miles (88 kilometers) from Las Varas to San Blas.

San Blas was the first major shipping port on Mexico's west coast. Established in 1768, it was the staging area for expeditions up the Pacific coast. Father Junipero Serra set sail from San Blas in 1769 to take control of the missions in Baja California and establish the missions that would form the nucleus of California cities and towns including San Diego, San Luis Obispo, Monterrey and San Francisco. As San Blas became a key link in the Spanish shipping trade with Asia, it grew into a city of about 30,000 people—roughly four times its present-day population. In the 1850s, traders from San Blas who carried supplies to the mining towns of the Sierra Madre set up an outpost on Banderas Bay that would eventually become Puerto Vallarta. In 1873, San Blas was decommissioned as a maritime port and began a decline from which it has never fully recovered. Today, the old port facilities have been upgraded to serve as a Mexican naval base.

Back in the 1970s, when it was a favorite hangout of American hippies and low-budget snowbirds, optimistic locals enthusiastically predicted that San Blas would be "the next Puerto Vallarta." They failed to take a few things, such as the lack of an airport, into account. And the fact that the town electricity generator rarely worked for more than a few hours at a time. And the abundance of insects. There were giant, four-inch-long rhinoceros beetles strolling across the town plaza, and other round beetles that had a knack for landing on their backs and wriggling on the sidewalks by the hundreds trying to turn over. But far more annoying were the *jejenes* (no-see-ums), tiny biting gnats that descended in swarms from the nearby wetlands. Not to mention the large crocodiles that would occasionally show up on the beach. A 150-room resort hotel was built on the beach east of town, and the president of Mexico came to the grand opening to proclaim San Blas a prime candidate for a new megaresort. Unfortunately, according to legend, swarms of gnats descended from the nearby swamps to drive the revelers away, and the hotel never opened for business. It has since fallen into ruins, and no other resort nearly its size has ever been built in the San Blas area.

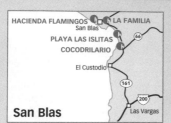

HACIENDA FLAMINGOS · LA FAMILIA
San Blas
PLAYA LAS ISLITAS
COCODRILARIO
El Custodio
San Blas   Las Vargas

HACIENDA FLAMINGOS

PAGE 195

Comfortable guest rooms with courtyard gardens in a restored 125-year-old mansion

LA FAMILIA

PAGE 197

Grilled red snapper and other local-style Mexican dishes in a traditional, open-air garden setting

PLAYA LAS ISLITAS

PAGE 197

Home to the "longest wave on earth"—old-timers claim waves can reach 20 feet high

COCODRILARIO

PAGE 193

A reserve for injured crocodiles that allows a safe, up-close peek at the fascinating creatures

Reality struck home in October 2002 in the form of Hurricane Kenna, which destroyed 85 percent of San Blas. It had been crumbling already, of course. From the late 18th and early 19th centuries, when San Blas was the largest shipping port on North America's Pacific coast, the town had dwindled to a small fraction of its past population, leaving only toppling red brick columns to mark what had once been its huge customs house. After the hurricane, relief aid financed the rebuilding of the customs house into a new cultural center and paid for many other once-proud buildings to be restored to their past grandeur. The electrical system was replaced and now works most of the time.

SIGHTS

COCODRILARIO

✉*Off Route 161, 4.5 miles (7 kilometers) southeast of San Blas* On a side road south of town is a fascinating *cocodrilario*, or crocodile reserve, where injured or toothless reptiles up to 15 feet long are rescued and bred and their offspring are returned to the river. After climbing an unpaved road to the parking area, you hike down a steep path to where the largest crocs are held in chainlink pens. They don't do much—one of the things crocodiles excel at is remaining absolutely motionless, not even blinking, for hours on end—but seeing these primeval monsters close up is a visceral thrill. If you'll be taking a boat tour up the Río Tovara during your visit to San Blas, a visit to the cocodrilario adds to the experience by showing you what's likely lurking in the mangroves.

RÍO TOVARA

✉ *San Blas* A popular nature tour takes visitors by small boat up the Río Tovara along tangled channels through mangrove jungles rich with wildlife. You'll see turtles, herons and many other bird species, iguanas and possibly river crocodiles. The boats stop at a cool freshwater spring for swimming (an underwater fence keeps the crocodiles out) and refreshments. For an extra fee, the tour can be extended to include the crocodile reserve. The tour can be arranged at the front desk of your hotel, or you can book a trip at a booth near the bridge into town where the boats depart.

PLAZA PRINCIPAL ✉ *San Blas Centro* The main plaza in the center of San Blas has undergone a recent renovation, repairing the near-total destruction from Hurricane Kenna, planting new trees, lawns and gardens, installing a new lighting system and making it once more the town's social hub. Two churches stand side-by-side facing the plaza, though only the newer one is in use. The original 18th-century church has been restored, with a plaque on the facade quoting part of the poem "The Bells of San Blas," Henry Wadsworth Longfellow's last work, written just nine days before he died.

CENTRO CULTURAL DE SAN BLAS ✉ *Calle Juarez, three blocks southwest of the plaza* The old aduana, or customs house—the first one on Mexico's west coast when it was built in the late 1700s, was already a roofless ruin of crumbling red-brick pillars and archways long before Hurricane Kenna struck. It's sheer size provides some idea of San Blas's importance as a seaport in centuries past. Now it has been fully restored and houses the town cultural center. Visitors see historic photos and exhibits of work by local artists. It also hosts concerts and stage plays, as well as aerobics, yoga and karate classes.

TEMPLO DE LA VIRGEN DEL ROSARIO

✉ *Cerro de San Basilio* The bells that Longfellow must have heard as his ship sailed past were from another church, whose ruins stand on Cerro de San Basilio, a hill on the outskirts of town. Built in 1769, it was used for more than a century but has since fallen into ruin. The remains of a *contadura*, or counting house, uphill from the church, also date from Spanish colonial times when San Blas was a major seaport. Destruction of both buildings was completed by Hurricane Kenna, and what had been known to locals as "las ruinas" became "las ruinas de las ruinas." The church is now being restored, and the hilltop still offers the best view of San Blas. The trail to the ruins starts near the cemetery beside the docks where the La Tovara tour boats launch, at the bridge on the road into town.

ISLA DEL REY

The "island" where the town lighthouse is located, actually a peninsula surrounded by an estuary and lagoon but linked to the mainland by a narrow natural bridge, lies directly west of San Blas, across the estuary from the Centro Cultural. A Huichol pilgrimage trail leads to an altar called Tatei Aramara, dedicated to the goddess of the sea and corn. Native people have come to this spot to make offerings to Aramara in a colorful annual pilgrimage that begins about two weeks before Easter. While the ceremonial site has been used for countless centuries, it was only deeded to the Huichol people a few years ago to quell protests after the government inadvertently destroyed a sacred cave nearby while quarrying stone.

LODGING

HACIENDA FLAMINGOS

$$ 21 ROOMS ✉ Juárez #105 ☎ 669-985-5252 📠 669-985-1185
🖥 www.sanblas.com.mx, reservaciones@sanblas.com.mx

There are a half-dozen good hotels in and around San Blas, but the best by far is this 125-year-old mansion, built by a wealthy German plantation owner. He was also an honorary German consul, so it is often (though inaccurately) said to have been the German Embassy during San Blas's heyday. It had deteriorated to near collapse before the 2002 hurricane but has now been beautifully restored, with courtyard gardens and fountain, a large swimming pool and 21 comfortable air-conditioned rooms. The location is two blocks from the town plaza.

CASA ROXANNA BUNGALOWS

$–$$ 8 ROOMS ✉ Callejon El Rey #1 ☎ 323-285-0573
🖥 casaroxanna@yahoo.com

Set amid palm trees and gardens in a residential area close to the center of San Blas, this affordable hideaway, a birder's favorite, has air-conditioned rooms with Mexican tile floors and kitchen facilities. Interiors and exteriors are white, emphasizing the spick-and-span cleanliness, accented by local artwork. Bungalows come in two sizes—large ones that sleep five, and smaller ones that sleep three. There's a swimming pool, off-street parking and wireless internet access.

HOTEL GARZA CANELA

$$-$$$ 50 ROOMS ✉*Paredes #106 Sur* ☎*323-385-0112* ✐*www.garzacanela.com*

This relatively large hotel on the east side of town dates back to 1970 and has been owned and operated for more than 20 years by the same Mexican family. Their enthusiasm for birdwatching is reflected in the new name they gave the hotel when they acquired it: *garza canela* means "cinnamon heron," a rare local species. Today, the hotel caters principally to birding tour groups. The spacious, colonial-style rooms are air-conditioned and decorated in warm hues, and most (except for a half-dozen luxury suites) have small balconies, two full-sized beds and satellite TV, though no in-room phones. El Delfín, one of the best restaurants in town, is on the premises.

CASA DE VALORIEN

$$ 3 ROOMS ✉*Tio Pancho #9, Playa Los Cocos* ☎*713-870-7088*
✐*casa-de-valorien.com, haysred@sbcglobal.net*

Set on a cliff overlooking Los Cocos Beach, about five miles (8 kilometers) south of San Blas on Matachén Bay, this small bed and breakfast has two main-floor guest rooms and a second-floor suite that can sleep up to six people; all units are air-conditioned. A bottle of wine awaits guests on their arrival, and the hostess, Janice, a Culinary Arts graduate of the Art Institute of Houston, prepares breakfast, lunch and dinner. There's a three-day minimum stay. No smoking.

DINING

MCDONALD'S

$–$$ MEXICAN ✉*Juárez #35*

A good place to eat (and no relation to the golden arches), this classic hippie hangout from the 1970s has been upgraded since the hurricane and is now an attractive Mexican restaurant serving such local specialties as *sopa marinera*, fresh grilled fish . . . oh, and hamburgers.

CASA DEL CANIBAL

$–$$ INTERNATIONAL ✉*Juárez 53* ☎*323-285-1412*

This is the place to come when you're homesick. American comfort food like grilled chicken breasts with mashed potatoes shares the menu with other standbys like spaghetti with meat sauce, beef stroganoff and New York strip steak. There are also good local shrimp dishes like lime habanero prawns and shrimp cocktails. For dessert, would you believe flaming bananas Foster? You're likely to find more *norteamericano* expats and snowbirds than Mexicans dining at this long-established restaurant.

EL DELFÍN

$$ INTERNATIONAL ✉*Paredes #106 Sur* ☎*323-385-0112*

Betty Vasquez, owner and operator of the Hotel Garza Canela, is also the chef at the hotel's restaurant. Before coming to San Blas, she studied the culinary arts at Le Cordon Bleu and worked under legendary chef José Mari Arzak at his namesake restaurant in San Sebastián, Spain. The fare, which focuses on seafood but also includes beef and chicken entrées, uses the freshest local ingredients in classic continental and fusion recipes.

LA FAMILIA

$–$$ MEXICAN   ✉ *Batallon #18*   ✆ *323-385-0258*

In a lovely, traditional open-air garden setting, this friendly, homelike restaurant serves a full range of Mexican dishes with emphasis on seafood. The house specialty is grilled *huachinango* (red snapper), served whole.

NIGHTLIFE

SAN BLAS SOCIAL CLUB ✉ *Juárez #6* The closest thing to a nightclub in San Blas is this ultra-casual little jazz bar just off the main plaza. They serve beer and cocktails in the evening and "real" coffee in the morning. Besides live music, they show movies some evenings and display works by local artists. Besides this place, the only after-dark action is on the plaza itself, where local musicians often get together and San Blas residents linger and socialize almost every evening.

BEACHES

PLAYA LAS COCOS

✉ *6 miles (10 kilometers) south of San Blas near the south end of Matachen Bay*

🏃 🏊 🎣 This beautiful beach used to be surfers' heaven, but changes in the sea floor have seemingly calmed the once-formidable waves. Today the scattered palapa restaurants and bars are only open on weekends. The rest of the time, the only footprints you're likely to see in the sand are left by seclusion-loving American and Canadian expats who have built homes in the area.

PLAYA LAS ISLITAS

✉ *4 miles (6 kilometers) south of San Blas*

🏃 🏊 🎣 This gently curving beach is known in surfing circles for what the *Guinness Book of World Records* has certified as the longest wave on earth, which it's said a good surfer can ride for a full mile. Old-timers claim waves here can reach 20 feet high. However, big surfing waves rarely happen, and only in the summer. The rest of the time, Las Islitas is better suited to boogieboarding.

PLAYA BORREGO

✉1 mile (1.6 kilometers) southeast of the San Blas plaza—follow Calle Batallón de San Blas

🏃 ⛵ 🏄 The main beach at San Blas is packed on Sundays and blissfully quiet the rest of the week. The long, wide stretch of brownish sand is festooned with many small, colorful seashells. While it's not a major surfing destination, there is a decent shore break, and you'll often find surfers nursing Coronas at the palapa bars along the north end of the beach while watching for the possibility of big waves.

OUTDOOR ADVENTURES

DIVING

Bucerías, the "Place of the Divers," got its name long before scuba gear was invented. Today the waters offshore are popular for snorkeling but rather tame as a scuba destination.

DOS GRINGOS DIVERS ✉*Bucerías* 📞*392-298-0941* This is the place where scuba enthusiasts staying in Bucerías can arrange dive trips out to the Marieta Islands.

GOLF

FLAMINGOS GOLF CLUB ✉*Carretera a Bucerías, Km. 145* 📞*329-296-5006* 🌐*www.flamingosgolf.com.mx, reservations@flamingosgolf.com.mx* The first golf course in the Puerto Vallarta area (built in 1978), the Flamingos has 18 holes, 6982 yards and par 71. Laid out by legendary British designer Percy Clifford, who created more top-ranked courses in Mexico than any other golf designer, the Flamingos is lined with citrus and mango trees, as well as more than 1800 mature palm trees. The fairways slope gently among natural lagoons, estuaries and marshlands that are home to hundreds of bird species, not to mention turtles, armadillos, deer and crocodiles. Shared carts are included in the green fees, which are the most reasonable in the Puerto Vallarta area. A caddy is required. Wilson, Mitsushiba and Callaway clubs are available for rent.

MAYAN PALACE GOLF CLUB ✉*Avenida Paseo de las Moras s/n, Nuevo Vallarta* 📞*322-297-0773* 🌐*www.mayanpalace.com.mx* This 18-hole, 6446-yard, par-71 course was designed by Jim Lipe of the Jack Nicklaus & Associates firm. Opened in 2003, it is part of the Mayan Palace Resort but is open to the public, with green fees somewhat lower than most Puerto Vallarta golf courses. The first nine holes, with one ocean-flanked fairway, encircle the hotel's spacious grounds, while the back nine, on the other side of the highway, follow the Río Ameca. Water hazards also include seven lakes.

EL TIGRE PARADISE VILLAGE GOLF CLUB ✉*Avenida Paraiso #800, Nuevo Vallarta* 📞*322-297-0733* 🌐*www.paradisemexico.com* A huge replica of a Mayan stone gateway marks the entrance to this golf course designed by Robert Van Hagge and built in 2002. Although the 7239-yard, par-72 course has few trees, it has plenty of tricky bunkers, swales, lakes and creeks to challenge golfers of all skill levels. Golf carts are included in the green fee, and Callaway clubs can be rented. Caddies are not available. There's a snack bar on the ninth hole. The clubhouse, the largest and most lavish in the Puerto Vallarta area, features a complete spa with masseurs, jacuzzis and steam baths.

PUNTA MITA FOUR SEASONS GOLF CLUB ✉*Punta de Mita* ✆*329-291-6000* Designed by Jack Nicklaus, this 19-hole signature par-72 course (or par 75, if you play the extra hole, known as the Tail of the Whale, with its green on a natural island about 175 yards offshore (which you reach on a stone pathway at low tide or by a boat that resembles an amphibious golf cart when the water rises) has eight holes bordering Banderas Bay or the Pacific Ocean. The course length is an impressive 7014 yards, though five different sets of tee boxes allow less seasoned golfers to play shorter lengths, down to 5037 yards. A shared golf cart is included in the green fee, and club rentals are available. There are no caddies. While this semiprivate course is now open to nonmembers, club members and guests at the Four Seasons hotel have priority for tee times.

SURFING

Sayulita enjoys an international reputation for great surfing. It has often been selected as the site of major surfing competitions, including Mexico's National Surf Selective Championship and three annual regional championships. The village sits at the back of a protected cove where waves break consistently along a reef. There are two popular areas—a longboard right break in front of the village, just two blocks from the plaza, and a faster left break in front of the campgrounds farther down the beach. Surfboards, as well as sea kayaks, can be rented at **Papas Palapas** on the beach. **Santa Crucita** in the center of town also rents surfboards, as well as wet suits and boogieboards. Several surf camps operate in Sayulita:

SAFARIMEX ✉*Sayulita* ✆*322-118-2416* ✐*www.safarimex.com, info@safarimex. com* Safarimex offers six-day surf camps for both beginners and experienced surfers. While surfing in Sayulita is the primary activity, the program also includes canopy ziplining, horseback riding and snorkeling, as well as a surfari to a remote break.

LAS OLAS SURF SAFARIS ✉*Sayulita; contact Las Olas Surf Safaris, P.O. Box 4669, Carmel, CA 93921* ✆*831-625-5748* ✉*831-625-4267* ✐*www.surflasolas.com, info@surflasolas.com* The world's first all-women surf camps when they started in 1997, Las Olas continues to offer camps for women only with an all-woman staff. Rates are higher than some competitors' camps because lodging is in luxury villas.

SAYULITA SURF AND SPANISH SCHOOL ✉*Sayulita* ✆*329-291-2027* ✉*603-388-1383* ✐*www.surfnspanish.com, surfnspanish@yahoo.com* Weeklong programs that combine 1.5 hours of surfing classes and 2.5 hours of one-on-one Spanish language classes per day, along with other activities such as a canopy tour, horseback riding, a salsa dancing lesson or a boat tour to the Marieta Islands. Yoga and Spanish School programs are also available.

Playa Islitas and Playa Los Cocos, south of San Blas, also attract surfers during the summer months. These beaches on Matachen Bay boast the longest surf waves in the world, according to the Guinness Book of World Records, but great waves have become rare, apparently because of shifts in the ocean floor offshore.

WILDLIFE WATCHING

The top area for birding around Puerto Vallarta is the **Valle de Banderas**, which follows the Río Ameca and Río Mascota east of Nuevo Vallarta. The river, the riparian deciduous forest around it and the mangrove estuary where it flows into the bay are home to more than 300 bird species. For Puerto Vallarta area birding guides, see Outdoor Adventures in Chapter 4.

The San Blas area is internationally known as a top birding area. Birding trips can be as simple as taking one of the daily "jungle tours" up the **Río Tovara**, which can be combined with a visit to the nearby crocodile reserve, or as ambitious as a customized expedition deep into the **Marisma Nacional de México** (the National Swamp). Trips can also be arranged to inland areas such as the forest around the village of **La Bajada**, home to birds like the elegant trogon and the orange-fronted parakeet, or **Mirador del Aguila** near Tepic, where rare macaws can be seen. **Singayta**, a 40-family *ejido* five miles outside of San Blas, is becoming a favorite area for birding tours of the mangrove estuaries as well as horseback riding; the village used to depend for its subsistence on harvesting palm fronds for palapa roofs, but after Hurricane Kenna destroyed the palm trees, it obtained an environmental protection green grant to help develop ecotourism.

SAN BLAS BIRDING AND NATURE TOURS

✉ *San Blas* ☎ *323-285-0558* ✐ *sanblasbirdingtours.com* Manuel the Jungle Man has been guiding birding enthusiasts in the San Blas area for more than 30 years. He guides four-hour to all-day tours on the Río Tovara and the Río San Cristobal, as well as excursions into mountain forests and walking tours of historic San Blas.

TRANSPORTATION

TAXI

Taxis to north shore destinations and beyond can be quite expensive—US$65 by airport taxi or $40 for other taxis to Sayulita (about $5 less to Bucerías or $5 more to San Pancho).

AUTOTRANSPORTES MEDINA Autotransportes Medina buses run regularly between the terminal near Puerto Vallarta's sports stadium and all north shore communities, costing about US$1.20 one-way to Bucerías and US$2 to more distant destinations such as Punta de Mita, Sayulita and San Pancho. The trip to any of these destinations takes at least an hour from Marina Vallarta or about two hours from downtown Puerto Vallarta. Buses run about once every half-hour.

TRANSPORTES NORTE DE SONORA ✆ *323-285-0043* Transportes Norte de Sonora runs four nonstop buses daily from the Puerto Vallarta bus terminal to San Blas for about $30 one-way. Once in San Blas, brightly painted, aging local buses run about every half-hour to outlying villages and beaches.

ADDRESSES
& PHONE NUMBERS

EMERGENCY NUMBER ✆ *066*

POLICE ✉ *Bucerías/La Cruz* ✆ *329-2980-1020*

POLICE ✉ *San Blas* ✆ *323-285-0615*

THE SIERRA MADRE

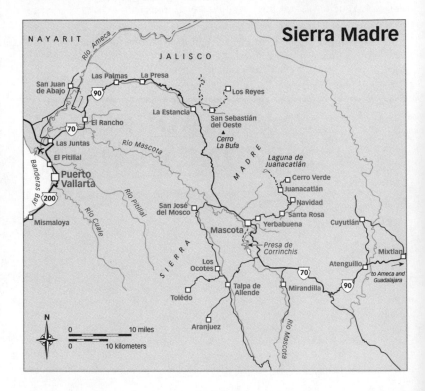

If the steep green mountains that border Puerto Vallarta on the east capture your imagination, rev up your rental car and tackle the newly paved mountain roads that climb as high as 7000 feet above sea level in the Sierra Madre Occidental. There you'll find small, hidden towns that have existed in almost total isolation until recently and still retain the feel of centuries past, when the hills were rich with gold and silver, breeding and training horses was the main occupation and rumors of miraculous visitations by the Virgin Mary spread far and wide. The towns of the Sierra have existed in blissful seclusion since the early 17th century. With their colonial Mexican ambiance and cool climate, they are so completely opposite from the scene along the coast that a visit to this area will add an entirely new dimension to any Puerto Vallarta trip.

The other-worldly quality of the high Sierra, with its volcanic peaks, pristine lakes, cool cloud forests, pastoral farm and ranch lands and colonial-era towns, makes for such a contrast to Puerto Vallarta that it's hard to believe how close they really are (as the crow flies, not by the circuitous, steep and winding roads you'll drive in your rental car). On an expedition into the Sierra you'll discover the scantly populated remains of a once-wealthy gold and silver mining city, the bustling market center of a broad green valley filled with farms and horse ranches, and one of the holiest sites in western Mexico.

Tourism is very new to the Sierra towns. Talpa de Allende, a major religious pilgrimage destination, could be reached from the city of Guadalajara on a 120-mile (200-kilometer) paved mountain highway, which continued as far as Mascota, the largest town in the area. The pavement ended there, making the drive on to San Sebastián del Oeste a harder trip than it was worth. From Puerto Vallarta, the only way to reach the towns of the Sierra—other than a tour operator's small plane excursions to San Sebastián—was on an unpaved four-wheel-drive road that climbed down and up the sides of a deep gorge and was impassable during the rainy months.

All that changed with the paving of the road from Puerto Vallarta to Mascota in 2005 and 2006 and the subsequent completion of the Progreso Bridge, spanning the gorge near San Sebastián, in 2007. Since then, Puerto Vallarta tour companies have started to offer bus excursions to San Sebastián. Mascota, however, remains far off the beaten tourist path, and Talpa remains the exclusive province of Mexican religious travelers, with few international visitors. Today, San Sebastián can be visited by rental car as a day-trip, while all the places covered in this short chapter can be explored in a three-day, two-night journey.

SAN SEBASTIÁN DEL OESTE

The road to San Sebastián del Oeste starts from Route 200. It's quite a climb, ascending more than 5000 feet in elevation in about 19 miles (32 kilometers). Be sure to start off with a full tank of gas. Coming from central Puerto Vallarta or the Hotel Zone, continue past the airport to the point where Route 70 splits off to Ixtapa and Las Palmas (signs also mark it as the way to the "Universidad"), just before the Río Ameca bridge. Stay on Route 70 for 15 miles (25 kilometers), passing Ixtapa—an agricultural town on the city's outskirts, not to be confused with the megaresort beach town of the same name in the state of Guerrero—and Las Palmas, another tourist-free Mexican town, perhaps named for the clusters of palm trees that shade its pretty central plaza. At the Las Palmas highway turnoff, keep going straight ahead as the road narrows and begins its climb into the highlands.

The road climbs for 19 miles, which may seem like 90, to the Puente El Progreso bridge, a concrete arc over the Barranca San Sebastián. Along the way, you'll experience a cross-section of the Sierra that includes ridgelines with panoramic views, claustrophobic canyons dripping with jungle vines and here and there an isolated homestead. The cuts where the new road was carved into the steep mountainsides are still recent enough so that rockslides are common, especially during the summer rains, and the road surface is pocked with dents left by falling rocks that have been hauled away. Soon after the bridge, a partially paved road under seemingly perpetual construction turns off to the left from the highway and goes about four miles (seven kilometers) through a tunnel of overhanging oak trees. The road becomes one-way as it enters the town, then meanders around before turning and heading back out the way you came. There's parking on the downhill side of the plaza.

San Sebastián del Oeste lies in a claustrophobically narrow valley at 4300 feet above sea level, at the base of an 8400-foot mountain known as La Bufa. Founded in 1605, San Sebastián was the center of one of the richest silver and gold mining districts in New Spain and grew to become a city of more than 30,000 people. In fact, the village that became modern-day Puerto Vallarta got its start as a supply port for San Sebastián, though having seen the route up here it's hard to imagine bringing shipments of goods in by mule train or ox cart. Mining was slowed by a workers' strike in 1888, which was never settled. It was further disrupted by the Mexican Revolution and ceased completely by 1921. Today, San Sebastián is virtually a ghost town, inhabited by about 600 residents who earn their livelihood growing corn, coffee and agave on the surrounding hillsides. Most of the palatial haciendas that dominated its hillsides have fallen into ruin, but whitewashed buildings with red-tiled roofs still line the town plaza. The town has recently been nominated as a UNESCO World Heritage Site; if approved, it will be one of 26 such sites in Mexico, along with ancient Indian cities such as Chichén Itzá, Palenque and Teotihuacan.

Guides can be contacted through any of the hotels in town to help you explore outlying areas and visit the remains of the old mines, including La Quitería, the largest in the district. It produced fortunes in gold and silver for more than 90 years before it became unprofitable and closed down during the 1930s, putting an end to San Sebastián's prosperity. Today only ruined buildings, rusted-out equipment and vast tailing heaps remain.

SIGHTS

PARADOR SAN SEBASTIÁN

⊠*Puente El Progreso* A short distance past the El Progreso bridge, near the turnoff to San Sebastián, this new tourist attraction demonstrates the traditional method of distilling raicilla, the wild-agave tequila moonshine favored by the people of the Sierra. It's a stop for tourist vans and buses on their way to San Sebastián del Oeste, but if you manage to arrive when no tour groups are there, you'll get a good look at how the hearts of agave plants are slow-roasted to soften them, then pounded to a pulp to squeeze out the syrupy sweet juice, which is fermented in large barrels. The final step is to distill it using a crude-looking wood, copper and bamboo still, from which crystal-clear raicilla drips slowly into a clay pot. Unless you're the designated driver, you can taste the raicilla and several varieties of flavored tequila made by another artisanal distillery under the same ownership. A hilltop *mirador* affords a dramatic view of the bridge and the gorge beneath it.

LA QUINTA

✉*At the entrance to San Sebastián* Run by the same family for five generations, this organic coffee plantation offers tours of the small processing plant where, amazingly enough, they dry and roast the beans from 25,000 coffee bushes. Their fresh-roasted coffee is for sale by the bag in their retail shop; it's also served in most of the town's restaurants and bed-and-breakfast inns.

PARQUE CENTRAL

✉*San Sebastián Centro* In the center of town, the main plaza contains an ornate gazebo-style bandstand and a fountain, and stone pathways run between colorful rose gardens. The building on the uphill side of the plaza, with the blue-domed clock tower, is the Presidencia Municipal, a government palace that still contains a handful of offices, including the tourist office, as well as the intact 19th-century dungeon and the town's only public restrooms. Flanking the plaza on one side, the **Hotel El Pabellón** used to be the city's main general store and still has some original furnishings, a secret passageway and fortified walls with guard turrets for times when silver was stored there awaiting shipment. On the opposite side of the plaza, under a shady, columned portal, is the town's only shopping area, a row of little stores that carry an eclectic mix of foodstuffs, liquors, hardware, handicrafts and curios.

CASA MUSEO
DE DOÑA CONCHITA

✉*San Sebastián Centro* Next to the Presidencia Municipal, this small museum is owned by a great-great-grandmother who, for a nominal fee, will show and tell you about the photos, documents, apparel and memorabilia of her ancestors, who have lived in the house, which is now the museum for more than 250 years. One of her daughters sells homemade candies at the museum.

PARROQUIA
DE SAN SEBASTIÁN

✉*San Sebastián Centro* San Sebastián's small but stately church stands not on the plaza but a block down the hill, facing away from the town center. The church, rebuilt from the ground up after an earthquake destroyed it in 1868, is a faithful reconstruc-

San Sebastián del Oeste

Las Palmas
HACIENDA JALISCO
CASA MUSEO DE DOÑA CONCHITA
PARADOR SAN SEBASTIÁN
EL FORTÍN
San Sebastián del Oeste
90

HACIENDA JALISCO

PAGE 207

Antique-furnished rooms and gourmet dining at a fully restored 1825 hacienda nestled in a pine forest

CASA MUSEO DE DOÑA CONCHITA

PAGE 205

Photos, apparel and other artifacts of a time gone by at a small family-run museum

PARADOR SAN SEBASTIÁN

PAGE 204

Tours and samples of raicilla, the local wild-agave tequila moonshine, at a hilltop distillery

EL FORTÍN

PAGE 208

Imaginative Mexican and international fusion cuisine—don't miss the sweet cornbread

tion of the original 17th-century church, with its squat, square bell tower. Cool blue hues predominate in the interior, along with stone columns, crystal chandeliers, statues of saints—some of them life-sized—and a mural depicting the martyrdom of Saint Sebastian. In front of the church, a statue of the Virgin Mary stands beside a mango tree, and a small building houses a museum of church artifacts.

LODGING

HOTEL REAL DE SAN SEBASTIÁN

$$ 6 ROOMS ✉Calle Zaragoza #41 ✆322-297-3223, 800-726-7322
✎www.sansebastiandeloeste.com, sansebastiandeloeste@hotmail.com

This colonial-style inn, perched on a hillside overlooking the town center, has smallish, L-shaped rooms with whitewashed plaster walls, dark rustic furniture and curtained alcoves with queen-sized beds. Guest rooms have no phones or TVs, though both are available in the living room area. Complimentary afternoon hot chocolate and coffee are served, and the room rate includes a full breakfast.

HACIDA JALISCO

$$ 3 UNITS   ✉ San Sebastián del Oeste   ✆ 322-222-9638
🖱 www.haciendajalisco.com, info@haciendajalisco.com

This hacienda was built in 1825 as the headquarters of the mining company and used to guard gold and silver awaiting shipment. Nestled in a pine forest, the fully restored hacienda has foot-thick walls, high ceilings, massive handmade doors and window shutters, and a wraparound second-story verandah. Rooms are furnished with antiques, and old documents and antique books are placed throughout the hacienda. On the ground floor, a two-room museum contains historical artifacts of the town's mining heyday. There is no electricity or telephone; oil lamps provide illumination after dark. Guest accommodations are suites, each with a large private bath and a fireplace. One suite, named after film director John Huston, who once stayed there, has a king-sized bed, while the others have a double bed and two twin beds. The room rate includes a hearty dinner and breakfast served family-style on the patio with a romantic, misty view of a bygone era. The four-course dinner, usually built around a pork or chicken entrée, is different every night and includes salad and side dishes from the hacienda's organic fruit and vegetable gardens. The meal is accompanied by Chilean wine and rich, dark coffee grown on the mountain slopes surrounding San Sebastián. No children under 12.

LA GALERITA DE SAN SEBASTIÁN

$$$ 3 UNITS   ✉ Camino a La Galerita #62   ✆ 322-297-3040
🖱 www.lagalerita.com.mx

Rustic luxury awaits guests at this modern stone, adobe and wood "eco-retreat" secluded in a lush natural forest setting uphill from the town. Bright, spacious suites have floor-to-ceiling windows filling one wall, as well as stone fireplaces for chilly evenings. The suites have minibars, satellite TV and wireless internet access.

HACIENDA ESPERANZA DE LA GALERA

$$-$$$ 3 UNITS   ✉ Calle Republica   ✆ 322-297-2952
🖱 www.haciendaesperanza.com

This colonial-style guesthouse surrounded by gardens has one suite on the main floor and two on the second floor, all individually decorated with handmade furnishings and accents. The upstairs suites have king-sized beds and fireplaces, while the lower-priced downstairs suite has a queen-sized bed and purple walls.

DINING

EL FORTÍN

$$ MEXICAN ✉*San Sebastián Centro* ✆*322-297-2856*
⌨*www.elfortin.com.mx*

Located right by the main plaza, this restaurant's imaginative Mexican and international fusion menu changes daily. Don't miss the sweet cornbread. The walls are hung with paintings by local artists, and a good wine list tempts some visitors to while away the whole afternoon there.

REAL Y MINAS

$ ITALIAN ✉*Pipila #11* ✆*322-297-2883*

Owned by an Italian expatriate and his wife, a San Sebastián native, this long-established local favorite serves outstanding pizzas as well as lasagna and other dishes with fresh handmade pasta.

NIGHTLIFE

The townspeople of San Sebastián linger in the town plaza in the late afternoon and early evening. There's not much else to do. Children play. Grown-ups gossip. There's usually someone playing a guitar and singing. Other than that, the only nightlife to be found is at **Cristy's**, around the corner from the basketball court. This restaurant-bar has pool tables and the town's only jukebox.

MASCOTA

After returning from San Sebastián to the main highway, if you want to continue exploring the sierra, turn left (south) and go another 27 miles (43 kilometers), over two mountain passes, and you'll descend into a broad ranching valley on the Río Mascota, surrounded by misty mountain slopes covered by forests of pine and live oak. In its center, at about the same elevation as San Sebastián—4300 feet—lies Mascota, the commercial center and largest town in the region, with a population of around 14,000.

The streets of Mascota are a haphazard maze that can be confusing to visiting motorists, but there are a few major thoroughfares, and the town is small enough so that as long as you keep going in the same direction and keep an eye out for the church spire, it's hard to stay lost for very long. As it enters Mascota, the highway from Puerto Vallarta and San Sebastián becomes Calle Hidalgo and leads directly to the town center, where just about everything of interest to visitors is located. To leave town, continue on the same street, which becomes Calle Morelos after passing the main plaza, for several blocks to a main street called Lerdo de Tejada, which changes names several times in about a mile. To continue on the main highway toward Talpa, turn left on this main street (which becomes Calle Juan Alvarez), go five blocks watching carefully for signs, and turn right on Calle Francisco I. Madero. If you stay on Calle Lerdo de Tejada/Juan Alvarez northbound, it becomes Calle Aldama and leads out of town toward Laguna de Juanacantan; take the same road southbound, and it becomes Porfirio Diaz and heads out toward Prensa Corrinches reservoir. There are Pemex stations on the highway at both ends of town.

In the 17th century, Mascota (the name has nothing to do with pets—*mascotas* in Spanish—but comes from the Nahuatl Indian word *maza-colta*, meaning "place of the deer and snakes") grew to become the second-largest community in Jalisco, after Guadalajara, and this in turn spurred the growth of the port settlement that would become Puerto Vallarta, as smugglers would land on the beaches of Banderas Bay, thus avoiding the steep tariffs assessed at the official seaport of San Blas on commercial goods bound for Mascota and other towns of the Sierra. Many of the oldest families in the Puerto Vallarta area have their roots in Mascota.

Mascota is best known for its horse ranches. People come here from all over Mexico to buy horses and to have their horses trained, and it's common to see men on horseback riding through the streets of the town, which is also renowned for its saddlemakers. Townspeople often sell ranch products, especially white ranch cheese, honey and sometimes authentic raicilla liquor, from the front rooms of their homes, marked by impromptu signs hand-lettered on sheets of paper and taped to the doors. Also watch for homemade fruit rolls, a Mascota specialty.

There is little in the way of tourist development, since neither the San Sebastián tour buses from Puerto Vallarta nor the religious pilgrims to Talpa from Guadalajara often make it this far, and that's what makes Mascota special. Strolling the cobblestone and dirt streets of the town, among low, colorful buildings with red tile roofs, you can almost feel as if you've stepped back in time to an earlier century, despite the cars and trucks. Traffic is never heavy, though driving is so casual on the narrow streets that traffic jams are common—some of them involving as many as five or six cars. Virtually nobody, including people who work in the few tourist-class hotels and restaurants, speaks any English at all. Easygoing local attitudes remind longtime travelers why they fell in love with Mexico in the first place.

SIGHTS

TEMPLO DE LA VIRGEN DE DOLORES

✉*Calles 5 de Mayo and Ponciano Arriaga* Adjacent to the central plaza, this church—with its impressive multilevel bell-and-clock tower—is by far the tallest thing in town. It was built over a pe-

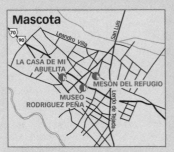

LA CASA DE MI ABUELITA

PAGE 213

A homey, family-run eatery featuring unique, regional Sierra recipes such as mushroom enchiladas

MESÓN DEL REFUGIO

PAGE 213

Bright guest rooms and handmade wood furnishings in a historic hotel, in operation since 1847

MUSEO RODRIGUEZ PEÑA

PAGE 211

Eight rooms of exhibits featuring local memorabilia in an original Colonial building

riod of almost a century, beginning in 1780, on the site of an earlier small church. An elaborate two-piece portal and altarpiece from the earlier church, sculpted from a marble-like stone called cantera that was quarried locally, are preserved inside. The long, narrow church interior gleams with gold-leaf columns and trim and a crystal chandelier.

On the north side of the church exterior stands a larger-than-life bronze statue of Father José María Robles Hurtado, a locally born priest who became an outlaw during the Cristiada holy war that shook much of Jalisco and other parts of Mexico in the 1920s. Following the Mexican Revolution, the new national constitution imposed severe restrictions on the Catholic Church and its clergy, and priests backed by their rural parishioners confronted the federal army in a series of incidents, sometimes leading to massacres. Father Robles erected a large cross in the mountains of Jalisco at what he believed to be the exact geographic center of Mexico and there, defying government prohibitions, preached sermons that drew crowds of as many as 40,000 people. Dubbed the "Madman of the Sacred Heart," he was arrested on June 25, 1927, and hanged the next day. Robles was canonized as a saint by Pope John Paul II in the year 2000, along with 24 other martyrs from the Cristiada. Today, the townspeople have rubbed the shoe of Father Robles's statue in prayer, polishing it until it gleams golden against the bronze patina. Behind the statue, dozens of handwritten plaques express thanks to the saint for prayers answered.

✉*Mascota Centro* Just north of the church, there's a classical colonial-style plaza filled with colorful rose gardens surrounding a gazebo bandstand. The only public Ladatel telephones in town are found here (few people in Mascota have land lines, since phone service began only recently and there is a long waiting list; most locals use cell phones instead). On the opposite side of the plaza from the church is the Presidencia Municipal, the town government offices, where you'll find public restrooms. On the west side of the plaza is the public market.

MUSEO RODRIGUEZ PEÑA ____

✉*Calle Morelos* One block west of the southwest corner of the main plaza, this private museum, organized by the schoolteacher whose name it bears in his ancestral family home, contains eight rooms of local memorabilia. There are exhibits about Father Robles, the martyred priest whose statue stands beside the main church, and posters, paintings and mementos of the late Mexican movie actress Esther Hernández, a local girl who came to be known as "the most beautiful woman of the golden age of Mexican cinema." She starred in more than 60 Spanish-language movies between 1933 and 1952 but retired after failed attempts to break into Hollywood and then turned her interest to painting. Also of interest is a gallery of remarkable paintings by renowned Mascota landscape artist Gilberto Guerra. Señor Rodriguez Peña himself escorts visitors through the rooms with a running patter of anecdotes in Spanish. On occasion he may even offer to sell antiques from the showcases to collectors who express interest.

CASA DE CULTURA ____

✉*Calle Morelos* Half a block east of the museum, this museum and exhibition space shows photographs of some of the thousands of pre-Columbian petroglyphs discovered around Mascota and Talpa by archaeologist Joseph Mountjoy, who still works in the area, sponsored by the U.S. National Geographic Society.

TEMPLO INCONCLUSO
DE LA PRECIOSA SANGRE ____

✉*Calle Rosa Dávalos, Colonia Preciosa Sangre* Away from the town center, visitors interested in churches will find the ruins of the neoclassical Church of the Precious Blood, a new church that was begun in the late 19th century. Construction was abandoned in the turmoil surrounding the Mexican Revolution. Its roof was never completed, and services were never held there, but its cantera stone archways and facade still stand as a monument to a failed dream. To get there, walk west from the plaza on Hidalgo for five blocks, angle north on Rosa Dávalos and go two more blocks.

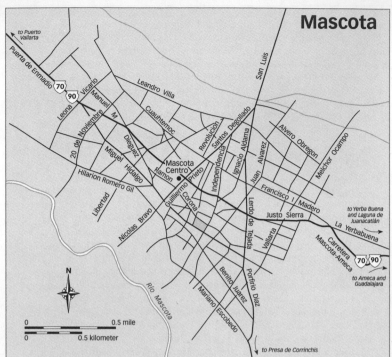

Mascota

LODGING

MESÓN DE SANTA ELENA

$$ 12 ROOMS ✉Hidalgo #155 ☎388-386-0313

✍www.mesondesantaelena.com, info@mesondesantaelena.com

Once the home of the family of José María Robles, the recently canonized saint whose statue stands beside the church, this hacienda has simply decorated guest rooms and suites with queen- or king-sized beds and dark wood-beam ceilings, surrounding a central courtyard festooned with copa de oro and other tropical flowers. There's a comfortable, antique-filled public living room with a fireplace to take off the chill on cool mountain evenings and a rooftop terrace with a view of the downtown area, the countryside and the distant mountains. A reasonably priced breakfast is served in the courtyard. There is free wireless internet access.

MESÓN DE SAN JOSÉ

$$ 16 ROOMS ✉Hidalgo #135 ☎388-386-1501 ✍www.mesonsanjose.com.mx, info@mesonsanjose.com.mx

A half-block closer to the plaza, this converted hacienda looks so much like the Mexón de Santa Elena that the two stately old structures could have been designed by the same builders. Fourteen of the rooms have king-sized beds, and all have modern bathrooms with tubs. There's a restaurant and bar on the premises, as well as a business center with internet access and a fax machine.

MESÓN DEL REFUGIO

$$ 11 ROOMS   ⊠*Independencia #187*   ✆*388-386-0767*
✐*mesondelrefugio@yahoo.com*

Located on a quiet side street a block from the town plaza, this hotel has been in continuous operation since 1847. It has 11 white-walled guest rooms brightened with modern paintings and furnished with queen-sized beds and heavy handmade wood tables and chairs. The wide, tiled second-floor verandah enjoys a view of the surrounding pine-clad mountains, and the hotel bar is one of the most popular hangouts in town. Off-street parking is available in the central courtyard. A continental breakfast is included in the room rate.

SIERRA LAGO
RESORT AND SPA

$$$ 23 UNITS   ⊠*Laguna de Juanacatlán*   ✆*388-101-2815, 800-823-4488*
✐*www.sierralago.com*

For a real getaway, consider this rustic luxury resort set on the shore of Laguna de Juanacatlán, 12 miles up into the mountains from Mascota at an elevation of 7000 feet. The resort's cabañas are warmly decorated in wood paneling and adobe with deep red accents and hardwood floors. Standard cabañas have king-sized beds and private bathrooms with old-fashioned tubs. Suite cabañas also have jacuzzis and electric fireplaces. Guests have the complimentary use of kayaks and mountain bikes, and you can rent gear for rock-climbing, fishing or sailing. Horse rentals are also available. The central spa area offers massages and steam baths. There are two restaurants on the premises—one for breakfast and dinner, another for lunch—and evening entertainment featuring folk dancers and precision-trained horses.

DINING

LA CASA DE MI ABUELITA

$$ MEXICAN   ⊠*Ramón Corona #102*   ✆*388-386-1306*

This very homey place two blocks from the plaza has been run by the same family for 30 years. Hotel managers say it is the best restaurant in town. Open for breakfast, lunch and dinner, it serves not only familiar Mexican fare but regional recipes of the Sierra. Try the mushroom enchiladas. You need to ask what some menu items are, since not only the cuisine but many Spanish words are unique to the local area (and, as everywhere in Mascota, no one here speaks English). The restaurant's name, which translates as "My Little Grandmother's House," says it all.

NAVIDAD

$ MEXICAN   ✉*Juan Diaz de Sandi #28*   ☎*388-386-0469*

Though it started out as a pizzeria and sports bar, this locally popular family restaurant just east of the plaza also serves seafood and a full range of Mexican favorites in a simple setting with exposed red brick columns and walls, a central fountain and garish magenta and green tablecloths.

EL COMEDOR
DE DOÑA ESTHER

$ MEXICAN   ✉*Above the public market*   ☎*388-386-1935*

Upstairs from the public market adjacent to the plaza, this casual eatery serves "comida autentico de rancho,"—authentic food of the ranches—from 6 a.m. to 6 p.m. Their specialty is *menudo* (tripe stew), a dish few gringos can stomach, but you can also try other local fare such as *costillita dorada* (baby back ribs), *birria* (goat stew) or *enchiladas de jocoque* (chicken enchiladas in a spicy sour cream sauce).

PARKS

PRESA DE CORRINCHIS

✉*Three miles west of Mascota on a well-maintained dirt road; from the main plaza, take Calle Juarez west to join Calle Porfirio Diaz, which becomes the road to the reservoir.*

 This manmade reservoir is a local favorite on weekends. Kayaks and canoes crowd the lake, and commercial concessionaires offer boat rides and sometimes parasailing. Foot trails wind through the cool pine and oak-covered foothills surrounding the reservoir. There are developed picnic grounds and several restaurants, including the government-run La Terraza, which on weekends serves fish caught in the lake to the accompaniment of mariachi music.

⛺ Wilderness camping is permitted all around the lakeshore. There is no charge.

LAGUNA DE JUANACATLÁN

✉*Twelve miles northeast of Mascota. Follow Calle Aldama out of town and stay on the main road.*

Sportsmen from Guadalajara come to this deep natural lake in the caldera of an ancient volcano on weekends to paddle canoes, sail catamarans and fish for mojarra, a fish similar to bass. Hiking and biking trails surround the lake. The drive out to Juanacatlán, on a cobblestone road through a pastoral valley and up over steep ridgelines, is a scenic adventure in itself.

TALPA DE ALLENDE

If you continue south on the main paved route through Mascota for four miles, after climbing over a mountain ridgeline with a spectacular scenic overlook, you'll reach a turnoff to your right (west). This good paved side road carries you for another eight miles to the colorful little town of Talpa de Allende, one of the holiest sites in western Mexico. It has been revered by the region's Catholics since 1644, when, according to legend, a diminutive figure of the Virgin Mary was discovered buried in the earth beneath a small chapel. The figure was taken to Mascota, site of the area's largest church at the time, but (so the story goes) it vanished from the church during the night and appeared the next morning back at Talpa. The "facts" that the distance from Mascota to Talpa is too far to walk in a night and that the wayward Virgin left a trail of tiny footprints even though the figurine had no feet are taken by the faithful as proof of the supernatural apparition. Ultimately, a basilica was built to house the figurine near the site where it was found. The Virgin of Talpa, along with similar figures at Zapopán and San Juan de Lago, are known as the *Tres Hermanas* and are said to protect Guadalajara. Like many sites where manifestations of Mary appeared to the Indians in early colonial times, Talpa had previously been a pre-Columbian sacred site dedicated to a female goddess—in this case Cihuacoatl, the "Feathered Snake Woman," who gave birth to the first man and woman according to Nahuatl mythology. Like the Virgin Mary, Cihuacoatl was often portrayed holding an infant.

Talpa draws religious pilgrims on all religious holidays but especially during a fiesta dedicated to the Virgin of Talpa, which runs from September 19 to October 7. In fact, each year the little town of 7000 receives four million visitors—more than total number of tourists who come to Puerto Vallarta in a year. Some, though not all, take the official 75-mile pilgrimage route, which starts in the village of Cofradía de la Luz near Guadalajara and climbs to shrines atop three of the highest mountains in the sierra before reaching Talpa, a wilderness journey that takes a week or more.

SIGHTS

ARCO MONUMENTAL

✉*Entrance to Talpa de Allende* Adorned with religious figures, the grand orange archway you drive through upon entering Talpa is emblazoned with words that translate into English as "The mother of the savior will guide your footsteps on the pilgrimage through life to the house of God the Father. He blesses and protects you, pilgrim."

216

Talpa de Allende

Los Ocotes
BASILICA DE NUESTRA SEÑORA DEL ROSARIO
EL CAMPANARIO
Talpa de Allende
Tolédo
MUSEO RELIGIOSO
MERCADO RELIGIOSO

EL CAMPANARIO

PAGE 217

Hearty, traditional Mexican and American fare—dine overlooking the central plaza

BASILICA DE NUESTRA SEÑORA DEL ROSARIO

PAGE 216

A historic, double-towered church with an elaborate cantera stone façade—dates to 1782

MUSEO RELIGIOSO

PAGE 216

Exhibits, displays and murals detailing the area's religious history and mythology

MERCADO RELIGIOSO

PAGE 217

Religious souvenirs and local crafts special to the region, such as walnut wine said to have healing powers

BASILICA DE NUESTRA SEÑORA DEL ROSARIO

✉ *Calle Hidalgo, Talpa Centro* The first place to visit in Talpa is the double-towered church with the bright yellow tile spires and elaborate cantera stone facade, built in 1782. It's located on the east side of the main plaza. Inside the basilica you'll find the original doll-like figure of the Virgin, dressed in finery and surrounded by images of worshipful angels. Notice that the only image of Christ in this thoroughly feminine church is a life-sized carving of Jesus lying apparently lifeless in his tomb, discreetly tucked away at the base of the north wall.

MUSEO RELIGIOSO

✉ *Behind the Basilica* The yellow two-story museum contains exhibits that tell the story (in Spanish) of the Virgin of Talpa, from her origin to recent apparitions and miracles attributed to her. Other displays explain the importance of the Virgin in Mexican Catholicism and examine the mythology surrounding the Tres Hermanas. There is also a mural detailing the pilgrimage trail to

Talpa and another that honors the martyrs of the 1926–29 Cristiada rebellion. Open only until 2:30 p.m., closed Monday.

LODGING

HOTEL LA MISIÓN

$ 49 ROOMS ✉ *Hidalgo #14* ☎ *388-385-0202*

This hotel, which fronts on the central plaza a short walk from the church, basilica and museum, is typical of most of the lodgings in Talpa, which are designed to serve religious pilgrims from the Guadalajara area. It is low-priced, simply furnished and decorated with Virgin images. It's easy to find budget-basic lodging without a reservation at this or any of the two dozen other hotels in town—except during pilgrimage times and religious holidays, when travelers are packed eight to a room. You'll enjoy more comfortable accommodations if you spend the night in Mascota and visit Talpa as a day trip.

DINING

EL CAMPANARIO

$ MEXICAN ✉ *Anahuac #2* ☎ *388-385-0000*

A prime location, hearty, traditional small-town Mexican food as well as shrimp and American-style hamburgers make this second-floor restaurant and bar looking out on the central plaza a good budget bet among the many modest eateries in Talpa.

SHOPPING

MERCADO RELIGIOSO

✉ *South side of the main plaza* This huge public market is filled with low-priced religious souvenirs—aisle after aisle of vendors selling *milagro* amulets, votive candles, and framed photos, paintings and statuettes of the Virgin of Talpa. Though many are factory-made (often in China), there is an interesting folk art tradition of shaping small, painted Virgin and saint figurines out of chicle, a rubberlike tree sap that is also used to make chewing gum. Another intriguing product sold here and throughout the town is a locally made, dark brown walnut wine that is said to have miraculous powers to cure just about anything that ails you.

OUTDOOR ADVENTURES

RIDING STABLES

Five- to seven-day pack trips from Puerto Vallarta to San Sebastián del Oeste and other settlements in the sierra are offered by **Rancho el Charro** (322-224-0114) and **Rancho Ojo de Agua** (322-224-0607). You'll also find entrepreneurs offering rental horses and guided horseback tours in both San Sebastián and Mascota.

HIKING

From San Sebastián del Oeste, the best mountain hike is to the summit of **Cerro La Bufa**, the mountain overlooking the town.

Mascota also has a local hiking trail to the cross high on the hillside of **Cerro de la Cruz**. There's good hiking along the shorelines and into the surrounding forested hills of both **Presa de Corrinches** reservoir and **Laguna de Juanacatlán**.

In the Talpa de Allende area, it is possible to hike into the **Bosque de Maple**, a rare cloud forest of sugar maples, fern trees and orchids that lies between the town and the nearby village of El Refugio. Discovered by botanists in 2000, it is one of only five known stands of maple tropical cloud forest on earth. It is undergoing regeneration under federal protection and should only be visited with a local guide. Visitors to Talpa can also make the gentle climb up **Cerro de Cristo Rey** to a lookout above town where a Christ monument stands beside two small chapels.

TRANSPORTATION

BUS

AUTOTRANSPORTES GUADALAJARA–TALPA–MASCOTA
✉*Lucerna #128, Puerto Vallarta* ✆*322-222-4816* ✆*388-386-0093 (In Mascota)* ✆*388-385-0015 (in Talpa)* This bus company serves the major communities of the western Sierra, operating four buses daily between Puerto Vallarta and Mascota, as well as connecting buses to Talpa and Guadalajara. Local buses run between the three communities, stopping at other small villages along the way.

VALLARTA ADVENTURES ✆*322-297-1212* ✑*www.vallarta-adventures.com, info@vallarta-adventures.com* Puerto Vallarta's largest tour company operates bus or van tours to San Sebastian.

AIR

AEROTAXIS DE LA BAHÍA ✆*322-222-2049* This small-craft airline operates daily small-plane flights from Puerto Vallarta to San Sebas-

tián, Mascota and Talpa. The cost is 500 pesos (under US$50) one-way, and the flying time is only about 20 minutes. Vallarta Adventures (see Buses above) also offers one-day guided tours to San Sebastián by small plane.

ADDRESSES & PHONE NUMBERS

TOURIST OFFICE ✉*San Sebastián, Calle López Mateos* 📞*322-297-2938*

TOURIST OFFICE ✉*Mascota, Presidencia* 📞*388-386-1179*

TOURIST OFFICE ✉*Talpa, Presidencia* 📞*388-385-0009*

MEDICAL CLINIC ✉*Centro de Salud de Mascota, Calle Rosa Dávalos #70* 📞*388-386-0174*

INDEX

INDEX

LODGING

HIDDEN GUIDES

Adventure travel or a relaxing vacation?—"Hidden" guidebooks are the only travel books in the business to provide detailed information on both. Aimed at environmentally aware travelers, our motto is "Where Vacations Meet Adventures." These books combine details on unique hotels, restaurants and sightseeing with information on camping, sports and hiking for the outdoor enthusiast.

PARADISE FAMILY GUIDES

Ideal for families traveling with kids of any age—toddlers to teenagers—Paradise Family Guides offer a blend of travel information unlike any other guides to the Hawaiian islands. With vacation ideas and tropical adventures that are sure to satisfy both action-hungry youngsters and relaxation-seeking parents, these guides meet the specific needs of each and every family member.

Ulysses Press books are available at bookstores everywhere. If any of the following titles are unavailable at your local bookstore, ask the bookseller to order them.

You can also order books directly from Ulysses Press
P.O. Box 3440, Berkeley, CA 94703
800-377-2542 or 510-601-8301
fax: 510-601-8307
www.ulyssespress.com
e-mail: ulysses@ulyssespress.com

HIDDEN GUIDEBOOKS

____ Hidden Arizona, $18.95
____ Hidden Baja, $14.95
____ Hidden Belize, $15.95
____ Hidden Big Island of Hawaii, $14.95
____ Hidden Boston & Cape Cod, $14.95
____ Hidden British Columbia, $18.95
____ Hidden Cancún & the Yucatán, $16.95
____ Hidden Carolinas, $17.95
____ Hidden Coast of California, $19.95
____ Hidden Colorado, $15.95
____ Hidden Florida, $19.95
____ Hidden Florida Keys & Everglades, $15.95
____ Hidden Georgia, $16.95
____ Hidden Hawaii, $19.95
____ Hidden Idaho, $14.95
____ Hidden Kauai, $14.95
____ Hidden Los Angeles, $14.95
____ Hidden Maui, $15.95
____ Hidden Montana, $15.95

____ Hidden New England, $19.95
____ Hidden New Mexico, $15.95
____ Hidden Oahu, $15.95
____ Hidden Oregon, $15.95
____ Hidden Pacific Northwest, $19.95
____ Hidden Philadelphia, $14.95
____ Hidden Puerto Vallarta, $16.95
____ Hidden Salt Lake City, $14.95
____ Hidden San Diego, $14.95
____ Hidden San Francisco & Northern California, $19.95
____ Hidden Seattle, $14.95
____ Hidden Southern California, $19.95
____ Hidden Southwest, $19.95
____ Hidden Tahiti, $19.95
____ Hidden Tennessee, $16.95
____ Hidden Walt Disney World, $13.95
____ Hidden Washington, $15.95
____ Hidden Wine Country, $14.95
____ Hidden Wyoming, $15.95

PARADISE FAMILY GUIDES

____ Paradise Family Guides: Kaua'i, $17.95
____ Paradise Family Guides: Maui, $17.95
____ Paradise Family Guides: Big Island of Hawai'i, $17.95

Mark the book(s) you're ordering and enter the total cost here ⇨ [   ]

California residents add 9.75% sales tax here ⇨ [   ]

Shipping, check box for your preferred method and enter cost here ⇨ [   ]

❑ BOOK RATE   **FREE! FREE! FREE!**

❑ PRIORITY MAIL/UPS GROUND   cost of postage

❑ UPS OVERNIGHT OR 2-DAY AIR   cost of postage ⇨

Billing, enter total amount due here and check method of payment ⇨ [   ]

❑ CHECK   ❑ MONEY ORDER

❑ VISA/MASTERCARD _____EXP. DATE_____

NAME_____PHONE _____

ADDRESS_____

CITY_____ STATE_____ ZIP _____

MONEY-BACK GUARANTEE ON DIRECT ORDERS PLACED THROUGH ULYSSES PRESS.

ABOUT THE AUTHOR

Richard Harris has written or co-written more than 20 other guidebooks including *Hidden Arizona, Hidden Cancún and the Yucatán, Hidden Colorado, Hidden Pacific Northwest* and *Hidden Southwest.* He has also served as contributing editor on guides for John Muir Publications, Fodor's, Birnbaum and Access guides and has written for numerous magazines including *Four Corners, Ritz-Carlton, Southwest Photographic* and *Southwest Profile.* He is past president of PEN New Mexico and an officer and director of the New Mexico Book Association.